ascension

ascension

john coltrane and his quest

eric nisenson

da capo press   *new york*

Library of Congress Cataloging in Publication Data

Nisenson, Eric.
   Ascension: John Coltrane and his quest / Eric Nisenson.—1st Da Capo
Press ed.
     p.   cm.
   Originally published: New York: St. Martin's Press, 1993.
   Discography: p.
   ISBN 0-306-80644-4 (alk. paper)
   1. Coltrane, John, 1926–1967. 2. Jazz musicians—United States—Biogra-
phy. I. Title.
ML419.C645N5   1995
788.7'165'092—dc20
[B]   95-16157
                                                CIP
                                               MN

First Da Capo Press edition 1995

This Da Capo Press paperback edition of *Ascension* is an unabridged
republication of the edition first published in New York in 1993.
It is reprinted by arrangement with St. Martin's Press.

Published by Da Capo Press, Inc.
A Subsidiary of Plenum Publishing Corporation
233 Spring Street, New York, N.Y. 10013

Manufactured in the United States of America

*For my father and Dr. John Falencki—to both of whom
I owe my life.*

contents

acknowledgments

Let the buyer beware, although the most important facts of Coltrane's life are contained within, this is not a formal biography of John Coltrane. This book is an attempt to understand the ideas and passions behind Coltrane's music, music that even his detractors concede was unique in its intensity and its effect both on listeners and fellow musicians. It is also an attempt, perhaps strained at times, to take Coltrane out of the cultural and intellectual ghetto in which jazz musicians are routinely placed, at least here in its native country, and to place his art and the thought that drove that art in the artistic, social, and intellectual context of the times in which he lived. Discussion of jazz used to be full of sound and fury, with fierce arguments a constant among its partisans. I hope that if my book does nothing else, and even if it is dead wrong, at least it may foment the kind of rancorous debate that once gave the jazz world life and heat.

There already exist three formal biographies of Coltrane—*Chasin' the Trane* by J. C. Thomas (Da Capo), *Coltrane* by C. O. Simpkins (Black Classic Press), and *John Coltrane* by Bill Cole (Schirmer). While none of these books is completely satisfactory, the Thomas book is the most thorough. But I am grateful to all three authors for certain facts and insights, and I refer the reader to these books if he desires more specific information about Coltrane's life.

I want to thank my editor, Jim Fitzgerald, for giving me the chance to write a book like this one. His courage and imagination (and patience) are rare commodities in any field of endeavor. And I want to make special mention of my agent, Phil Pochoda, for his encouragement and his contribution, well beyond the limits of duty.

The number of great jazz musicians who played or knew Coltrane is, tragically, thinning almost every week. Two of the greatest jazz musicians who were quite helpful to me deserve special mention—Dizzy Gillespie and Miles Davis. Also, posthumous thanks to the great jazz film archivist David Chertok, who sacrificed his own time in order to show me the few extant films of John Coltrane playing, bringing back memories and goosebumps.

Alice Schell read the manuscript as it was being written and provided invaluable advice and editorial direction, and to her I owe profoundly heartfelt thanks.

Also, thanks to Denny Norwood for his research, also invaluable. And special thanks to George Russell, who gave freely of his very valuable time and was of more help than he may have even realized. Special thanks, too, to Charles Mingus, Jr., and thanks to Art Taylor, Robert Palmer, Michael Cuscuna, Peter Occhiogrosso, Walter Booker, Jimmy Cobb, Cya Coleman, Maureen Barnes, and Sean Ducker (of course), and special thanks to Walter Nisenson (no relation), who graciously went out of his way to introduce me to Dizzy. And thanks to my brother Peter for introducing me to the music of John Coltrane so long ago, and to my sister-in-law Sally for the Coltrane interview tape— what a find!

Also, thanks to the folks at Fantasy Records, Columbia Records, Blue Note Records, and DRG for their discofile help. And special, lifelong appreciation to all the great jazz musicians I have either personally known or known through their music, for their constant provision of beauty and wisdom.

preface

I have often noticed the strangest reactions among those I have just met when I mention that I write about jazz. Jazz aficionados have a terrible reputation. We are thought of as musical snobs, which is often quite true; as fanatical purists, which also is often true; and as elitists who love having knowledge of obscure musicians and records known only to fellow members of the clique—again, too often true. Perhaps, then, it is partially our fault, ironically enough, that jazz has had such a rough time finding a large audience in its home country: Jazz—the most American art form—accounts for only 5 percent of all records sold in the United States, about the same as for classical albums; of course, most classical music is European. Even though jazz is having a surge of popularity now, it is still a minority music— just look at any *Billboard* chart of the best-selling albums.

There are certainly other factors responsible for jazz's poor showing. Among them are racism; the difficulty of the music itself; the insistence of most modern jazz musicians to be taken seriously as artists rather than treated as mere entertainers; the dominance of pop music; and Americans' general aversion to anything that resembles genuine art. But I can't help wondering if at least part of the blame does lie with us, those who listen to and love the music.

We jazz listeners have not really communicated effectively what it is about this music that is so vital to our lives, though I think the best jazz writers have done so at times. Martin Williams once wrote a wonderful book called *Where's the Melody?* for novice listeners. His title, of course, is a standard complaint among those first encountering this music. For many outside it, the jazz world appears coldly exclusive. The most famous comment about jazz, usually ascribed to Louis Armstrong, is probably "If you have to ask what it is, there ain't no way I can tell you." The problem is that many who first hear this music *do* have to ask what it is, and they often feel put off by the condescension of those of us in the know.

Among great jazz musicians, no one has simultaneously deeply moved so many as he has turned others off than John Coltrane. Coltrane's ability to polarize his audience, far more than Charlie Parker, may have something to do with the decade that he dominated as a jazz influence, the 1960s. Many of us in that decade used Coltrane's music as a kind of litmus test, a way of determining who was truly "hip." In Ken Kesey's novel *Sometimes a Great Notion* is an episode that perfectly dramatizes this phenomenon. The protaganist, Lee, plays jazz albums for his redneck brother, Hank, mostly white West Coast jazz. When Hank demands something with balls, Lee has no trouble deciding what to play: "And I put on what? Of course, John Coltrane, *Africa Brass*. I recall no malice aforethought in this choice, but who can say? Does one ever play Coltrane for the uninitiated without subconsciously hoping for the worst? Anyway, if such was my wish my subconscious must have been greatly pleased, for after a few minutes of that tenor sax ripping away at the privates, Henry reacted according to schedule. 'What kind of *crap* is that?' (Anger, frustration, gritting of teeth; all the classic responses.) 'What kind of godawful manure pile is that?' "

That's exactly what this book is all about: explaining to the many Hanks of this world why I find Coltrane's music not only beautiful but also genuinely uplifting to the spirit. I hope to convey here, not the minutiae of interest only to fellow aficionados, but the reasons for giving one's serious attention to Coltrane's often difficult music.

Coltrane's quest, I realize, sounds like the type of convenient linchpin usually found in literary criticism and term papers. But his quest was very real for him; it was the center of his life and his art. Coltrane did not intend to produce obscure art—he wanted to reach all of us at the deepest center of our beings, to uplift us and even change us. For this he might be called pretentious. But in this jaded postmodern world, I have found my renewing involvement with Coltrane and his quest truly refreshing. His themes were big ones, not very fashionable these days, but they were profoundly thought-provoking and universally relevant.

Much of his music was extraordinarily beautiful, although some of it forces us to redefine the very meaning of beauty. He was a constantly changing and innovative musician, always trying to find what he called the "essence" of music. Naturally, for such an experimenter, many times he faltered, but just as many times he produced music of such unmistakable radiance that it could enthrall even novices to jazz.

Coltrane and his music should not be the property only of a small clique. He and his courageous quest and the wonderful sounds that came out of his saxophone belong to all the world.

introduction

apocalypse at the half note

The Half Note was the kind of jazz club that deserved the epithet "joint," so unpretentious a place that one could easily have mistaken it for just another neighborhood bar. It was located in a lonely part of lower Manhattan, on Hudson Street, not far from the downtown docks. With its painted windows and hearty but plain Italian food, it was not the sort of place you would even begin to associate with a life-changing event, except as the perfect place for an alcoholic's last drink as his first step toward sobriety. It was here that I first saw John Coltrane play with his great quartet, and I will remember it as well as the room in which I lost my virginity.

It happened to be Coltrane's favorite club, for quite obvious reasons, since he was a man who constantly eschewed pretentiousness or glitz. When I walked into the club I spotted him immediately at a corner table, smoking a pipe and looking at the cover of one of his albums that was about to be released. The album was music recorded years previously by Coltrane's former record company. Later I would read that he hated the cover, a rather abstract portrait of the saxophonist by some poor man's Picasso, which explained why he remained staring at it with so little joy that night. He seemed perfectly at ease among the patrons, where he sat undisturbed by fans or autograph seekers, sipping a glass of orange juice. He was shy, and I doubted if he could have remained so undisturbed if he did this at one of the uptown clubs or even the Village Vanguard, but the atmosphere at the Half Note had an earthy simplicity that made both patrons and musicians feel completely at ease.

When Coltrane and his quartet (it was his classic quartet with McCoy Tyner on piano, Jimmy Garrison on bass, and the mighty Elvin Jones on drums) finally mounted the bandstand, it was with such casual movement that most of the patrons at first didn't even take notice. The bandstand at the Half Note was unusual, a triangle that jutted into the center of the club. The band was surrounded on three sides by listeners, giving the music added immediacy. The music wasn't far from any one table, creating a special bond between the performers and listeners.

The first notes out of Coltrane's horn, as the band was tuning up, caught me completely by surprise. Rather than the famous tone that has been called "hard as iron," Coltrane played notes as round and fluffy as those of Stan Getz, whose tenor usually sounded as different from Trane's as a clarinet did from a trumpet. Coltrane's career had been marked by constant and consistent change, but certainly the very sound of his horn couldn't have altered that much.

I was right. As soon as the band launched into the first tune, a modal piece I did not recognize (but with the same basic structure of the famous "Impressions," which itself was based on Miles Davis's classic "So What"), that dark hard sound, which was often described in terms of various types of metals, but which I thought to be quite beautiful, filled the club with far more power and strength than one would have expected from listening to Coltrane's records. Of course, he had to play with volume and force simply to be heard over Elvin Jones's drums, which from the start were incredibly loud but even more amazingly complex, playing dense polyrhythms as if he were a one-man corps of West African drummers playing along with Max Roach or Roy Haynes at their most prodigious. Coltrane took a lengthy solo full of snakelike melodies at once exotic and bedrock as the Delta blues. McCoy Tyner followed with a solo that seemed to want to emulate Coltrane's snaky lyricism, and maybe succeeded if I could only have heard him clearly over Jones's drumming. I don't remember much about the second "tune" except that it was at the same medium-fast tempo as the first, and the long tenor solo impressed me far more than those of even my favorite Coltrane albums.

Then it was time for the apocalypse. Much gaseous prose has been written about Coltrane and his music, but at least some of the hyperbole is understandable to anyone who saw him on a great night like this one. The third piece, a fast blues, started out like the others. After Coltrane had soloed for a long while, Tyner and Garrison left the stand, leaving the saxophonist in a furious duet with Jones. Coltrane, facing Jones's flailing drums, played roiling arpeggios alternating with ribbons of intense lyricism often accentuated by saxophone cries and wails. Playing at this level for even a few minutes would have exhausted most musicians, in terms of both imagination and sheer physical taxation. But Coltrane kept up at this level for what seemed hours. It was probably no more than a single hour, but time seemed to stop or at least become irrelevant; I could sense that the rest of the audience, too, was in the grip of this astonishing performance. Coltrane eventually was almost completely bent over forward, his face flushed, and at one point saliva poured out of the side of his mouth. He seemed to be not in this world, and I, as well as most of the audience, I am certain, felt that we had long left it far behind, too. At this point I looked at my companion with concern; if this man didn't stop, I thought, surely his heart would give out. Here was a performance where one could no longer objectively judge aesthetics; the feelings it engendered were closer to the awe one felt for a volcano or a mind-boggling religious revelation. My body felt exhilaration, transport, even as much as my mind and spirit. Finally it ended, and when it was over, Coltrane left the stand as calmly as he had walked on it, as if this were just another night in the world of jazz.

Well, maybe for him it was (and maybe that was one of the reasons he died a few months before his forty-first birthday). As for me, I felt that my mind and senses were overloaded to the breaking point. As much as I wanted to stay, just to see if he would reach this height again, I couldn't. I needed air and a chance to come down from the ionosphere (incidentally, I had taken no artificial stimulants that night, not even alcohol). I instantly knew that this was one of those nights that would, so intoxicating to the soul and imagination, stay clear in my memory to my dying day. My companion, I discovered, had an entirely different reaction. "It was like a total assault on all my senses, like being raped by music," she said. But eventually she would be drawn back to Coltrane in "performance" (that word falls so far short of describing the experience) again.

If the word "apocalyptic" sounds a bit bombastic for a musical experience, it is nevertheless a word I have heard other first-time Coltrane listeners use. The power of his music moved people in special ways unlike even the greatest of his jazz colleagues. The sort of awe in which he was held by his admirers was more intense than even that for, say, Charlie Parker. It wasn't that he was a greater musician than Armstrong, Young, Ellington, Parker, Davis, Rollins, et al.; but the emotions he evoked were of a unique intensity, and such feelings were directly connected to the great quest that was the center of his life. A man who studied all religions as well as Einstein's theory of relativity, Coltrane dared to try to discover through music a way toward what Stephen Hawking has called "the mind of God" for modern man. That quest was not just pretence on his part. Anyone with ears and heart and soul could hear and feel it.

This book is about the way that Coltrane both reflected and changed the world around him. By the late 1950s he was a musician with an agenda; he pursued the musical ends that he did as a way of finding his place in the universe, as he seemed to do that night at the Half Note (nights like that, I would find out, were not all that unusual), when he acted like a musician with the hubris to grasp the rims of heaven and bring it hurtling to earth, to enrapture us all with a very real and visceral grace. In the Sixties, "when the music mattered" (to quote the name of a book about the rock music of that era), his music reflected and influenced culture and society at least as much as did that of Dylan, the Beatles, the Stones, and the Doors. His music did not receive nearly as much flak as theirs, of course, but the ripples in the cultural waters created by Coltrane are still creating waves. Although his music and the swift evolution of his style and musical approach reflected the furious tempo of those times, his best music, like all great art, has a value that I believe is eternal. In the two and a half decades since Coltrane's death, there has not appeared on the horizon an innovator of nearly his stature. There have appeared in the history of jazz, beginning in the early years of this century with Buddy Bolden, a series of innovators who either consolidated the various strands of the music around him and moved forward or, like musical Hucks and Jims, simply lit out for new musical territory. Some talented musicians have come along, and every year seems to produce at least a few fine new players. Most of them have looked backward rather than forward, though, often playing music that was au courant before they were born. Others have delved in interesting experimental music that has had little effect on the mainstream of jazz. Was there something about Coltrane's music that for all practical purposes ended jazz history (if by "history" we mean here the ongoing progress of a medium)? Or was he so successful in fulfilling his great ambition that there was simply nothing left to say?

Coltrane's shadow looms over more than just the jazz world. He had a profound effect both on contemporary so-called classical music (a regrettable term, but I refuse to use "serious music"—no one ever made more serious music than John Coltrane, or than Armstrong and Ellington, for that matter) and even rock, though few of its hordes of fans have probably ever heard him. Many of the architects of modern rock did.

Who was this man who casts such a long shadow over modern culture a generation after his death? John Coltrane was a soft-spoken, gentle man who did not begin to discover the greatness within until an age well past that at which most jazz musicians find their mature styles. That process of discovery would continue until virtually the day he died. Since his discoveries helped so many of us find beauty, hope, and meaning in this chaotic and desperate modern age, his quest is our quest, his journey our own.

part one
resolution

1 traneing in

John Coltrane's life was based on a series of discoveries, most of them a result of both hard work and the deepest introspection. His greatest discovery was that of finding out who he really was. Coltrane was no prodigy and not until he was well into his twenties did he come to realize how truly extraordinary his talent was. The surface of his life offers few clues as to the brilliant fate toward which, at times haltingly, he strode. Unlike many great men, for Coltrane no obvious path led toward inevitable triumph. And because this fate was at first hidden from him, he was able eventually to discover the vast hidden continent of his genius, the exploration of which led ineluctably to his great innovations and triumphs.

John Coltrane was plagued throughout his life with dental problems, an extremely painful difficulty for a saxophone player. His alcoholism and drug addiction were forms of self-medication to ease that pain, some have speculated. One of the main reasons for his bad teeth was his lifelong addiction to sweets. And his favorite of all sugary goodies was sweet potato pie, a legacy of his southern origins.

Coltrane's southern heritage affected more than his teeth. His earthy, unaffected manner, his fascination with religion, the gentility of his manner, and the bedrock blues at the heart of his music were all, to at least some extent, the result of his early years growing up in the South.

John William Coltrane was born in Hamlet, North Carolina, on September 23, 1926. Later, there would be those who read significance into the name of his hometown, but Hamlet was just a nondescript small southern town when Coltrane was born, the closest city being High Point. His mother was the daughter of the Reverend Walter Blair, the pastor of St. Stephen's African Methodist Episcopal Zion Church. His father, John Robert Coltrane, was a tailor who loved to play violin and ukelele for fun. When John was three, the family moved in with the reverend at his house in High Point.

John Coltrane lived the life of a typical young black boy in the South, dutifully attending his grandfather's church services on Sunday and later sharing huge feasts of hominy grits, rice, oatmeal, fried chicken, corn bread, collard greens, and the inevitable sweet potato pie. He was a quiet boy who enjoyed playing baseball and looking at new car models, movies, and comic books. In J. C. Thomas's book (*Chasin' the Trane: The Music and Mystique of John Coltrane*), we are told that he had a special fascination for a comic book character called Doc Savage, an early prototype for Indiana Jones, who constantly found himself involved in bizarre and dangerous adventures in exotic lands. John was a good student in grade school, but that changed in high school after he discovered music, which increasingly took the place of his studies.

His first instrument was the clarinet, which he played in his high school band, though his interest in music at first was minimal. The leader of the community band in which he participated was a minister, so even at this early time Coltrane had at least a limited awareness of the connection between music and religion. The clarinet is a difficult instrument, but Coltrane became proficient enough to become first clarinetist of the community band, although he was no more involved in music than he was in baseball or comic books or any other of his youthful pursuits. At one point he even became a Boy Scout. When John was twelve years old, his father, a lovable and outgoing man, suddenly died. His mother got a job soon after her husband's death, and under the continuing providence of his grandfather, Coltrane never really knew dire poverty, unlike so many of his colleagues in the jazz world.

During his senior year in high school, his interest in music greatly accelerated when he heard the great alto saxophonist Johnny Hodges playing with the Duke Ellington band on the radio. The beauty of Hodges's playing immediately appealed to Coltrane, and he decided he had to play the alto saxophone instead of the clarinet. (It is no coincidence that the major influence on Johnny Hodges was the magnificent New Orleans soprano saxophonist Sidney Bechet. Hodges actually doubled on soprano, and when he did the Bechet influence was even more obvious. Thirty years later, when Coltrane himself took up soprano saxophone, at that time an instrument virtually never used in modern jazz [with the exception of Steve Lacy], he would go back and study the music of Sidney Bechet for inspiration, even writing a lovely blues in honor of the older musician.) Since he could not afford to buy a saxophone, Coltrane borrowed one from a friend. He became so proficient on the instrument that he won the place of first saxophone in the community band and came to be even something of a local celebrity, at least among his fellow students. By this time he had a new idol: Lester Young, the great tenor saxophonist he had heard on the radio playing with the classic Count Basie band of the late Thirties. Young was the most avant-garde player of his time, his style a precursor to the modern jazz that was in its embryonic state in the early Forties. Young would prove to be a seminal influence on Coltrane, as well as every important musician finding his way at that time.

In 1943, after graduating from high school, Coltrane moved to Philadelphia along with a couple of friends in order to find work and be closer to his mother, who had a job in Atlantic City. He had become a handsome man, like his father, and fairly tall, at about five-eleven. His most striking feature was his luminous eyes, which always seemed lit from within and often fixated on the farthest edge of the horizon. By this time he was becoming increasingly obsessed with music, and living in Philadelphia gave him the opportunity to hear all kinds, especially the rhythm and blues styles, which were becoming more prevalent. He was accepted at the Ornstein School of Music, but his studies were soon interrupted when he was inducted into the Navy in 1945 and sent to Hawaii, where he was made a member of the Navy band. He played clarinet exclusively with the band, although his fascination remained with the alto saxophone.

Upon being discharged in the spring of 1946 he returned to Philadelphia, now totally committed to becoming a professional musician. Most of the music he heard in Philadelphia was rhythm and blues, but he became aware of the great changes that had occurred in jazz since the end of the year. This was the era of the bop revolution, and almost every young musician was excited about the new music being made by Charlie Parker and Dizzy Gillespie, who brought to jazz a new level of complexity on every level, harmonically, rhythmically, and melodically. Bebop seemed to be making a social statement as well as a musical one. Now that young black men were returning from a war against white supremacy at its most insane, there was a genuine hope, as well as a demand, for social change.

John Coltrane was immediately taken with the bop movement, especially since its prime mover, Charlie Parker, also played alto saxophone. There is an amazing photograph in C. O. Simpkins's book *Coltrane* of the young Coltrane, cigarette in hand, watching Parker play, utterly transfixed. Eventually the cigarette actually burned his fingers; he was so hypnotized by Parker that he was unaware even of heat and pain. The idea of music as trance would arise significantly during the height of Coltrane's own career.

At this point, although he was continuing his studies at the Ornstein School, he was able to support himself by playing music, though not the modern jazz that was increasingly fascinating him. He was able to work regularly in the many rhythm and blues bands in Philadelphia. Coltrane appreciated the erotically primitive power of rhythm and blues, and its ability to reach its audience with such basic musical techniques, but he was bored by the music. His experiences in these bands would leave their mark, however. Many rhythm and blues saxophonists would routinely honk and shriek on their horn, overblowing and using tonal distortion to create extreme, and sometimes almost ludicrous effects, intensely bending and twisting their bodies as if in thrall to demons. Some of these effects, in a different context and with different meanings, would be used with equal intensity in the avant-garde movement, to which Coltrane devoted himself in the last few years of his life.

He met a pianist named Red Garland who supposedly had formerly been a pro boxer, and the two of them played together in Eddie "Cleanhead" Vinson's band. Garland would eventually play a key role in Coltrane's career and become a close associate. Vinson could play excellent straightahead jazz as well as rhythm and blues, and was himself a superb alto saxophonist. He was also the actual composer of two famous tunes appropriated by Miles Davis, "Four" and "Tune Up." Vinson insisted that Coltrane switch to the tenor saxophone. Coltrane was at first reluctant to change after all the strides he had been making on the alto horn, but eventually he began to find his voice on the larger horn. Later he would say, "When I went with Eddie Vinson on tenor, a wider area of listening opened up for me. On alto, Bird had been my whole influence, but on tenor I found there was no one man whose ideas were so dominant as Charlie's on alto. Therefore, I drew from all the men I heard during this period on tenor, especially Lester Young and his melodic phrasing."

He listened intently to Coleman Hawkins, buying Hawkins's record of "Body and Soul," which was something of a hit and known, even memorized, by every jazz musician, especially saxophonists. Hawkins is considered the first truly great jazz saxophonist, his career having begun in the Twenties, when he played a gimmicky slap tenor style with an early Fletcher Henderson band. By the early Thirties his style had matured, and he developed into a prodigious improvisor and a tremendously influential stylist. His large, earthy tone, harmonically oriented lines, and often heavy-footed rhythm were a sharp contrast to the light, airy, vibratoless tone, brightly melodic style, and subtle, smooth rhythm of Young. Most saxophonists in the Thirties were influenced by Hawkins, but that would change radically with the coming of the modern era, when every other tenor saxophonist on 52nd Street seemed to exhibit the influence of Young. Coltrane's mature style would eventually reflect both Hawkins's harmonic ideas and Young's melodic and rhythmic sensibility.

While with Vinson, Coltrane became known among his fellow musicians as a man unusually devoted to his art, constantly practicing, even when the others were relaxing or partying. The world of show business was a strange one for a man like John Coltrane, who was unusually shy and withdrawn, an inner-directed man in a world that was all surface and show.

After leaving Vinson's band, he got gigs when he was able, the most substantial being in a band lead by the saxophonist Jimmy Heath, brother of the bassist Percy Heath (later a charter member of the Modern Jazz Quartet) and the drummer Al "Tootie" Heath. Like many modern jazz groups, the band struggled for work, until the trumpeter Howard McGhee took over as leader. That helped a bit, but the group eventually fell apart simply because there weren't enough gigs available. Coltrane continued his studies. For the first time he began to listen seriously to European classical music, especially the harmonies, and concentrated on applying that knowledge to improvising on the saxophone. Dizzy Gillespie and Charlie Parker used to refer to attending classical concerts as "going to church."

Coltrane continued to struggle to find work. It was probably around this time, and quite inevitably, that he got involved with heroin. The involvement of jazz musicians with narcotics is so complex that sorting it out could easily fill a volume or two on its own. From the vantage point of our own times, it is easy to see only the destruction in terms of lives destroyed, careers wrecked or at least greatly damaged, time wasted, and so on. However, drugs created among the musicians a unique, if bizarre, feeling of fraternity. It alienated the clique of modern jazz even further from mainstream, "straight" society, creating a bond difficult to comprehend from the outside. As Dexter Gordon said, "Dope was simply part of the young musician's social scene at the time."

Much of the drug use stemmed from the example of Charlie Parker. Although he insisted that drugs or alcohol had nothing to do with his musical prowess, most of his acolytes followed his example rather than his word. In addition, organized crime targeted the black community as its main market for heroin sales, and places like Harlem were flooded with dope by the late Forties. There are those who would romanticize this period, but most musicians look back at their years of addiction as time sorely wasted, time that they could have devoted to their music. Musicians continued to fall into the world of dope well into the Fifties. Eventually, Coltrane more than any other musician would vociferously oppose the use of drugs or alcohol by his fellow musicians, serving as a key example to impressionable young musicians and auguring an age where most serious musicians avoided the use of dope. By the early Fifties, though, he was just another young musician hooked on junk.

He was given the unique opportunity to join Dizzy Gillespie's big band in the fall of 1949. (Gillespie was one of the few bop musicians to avoid dope, thanks to a remarkably strong and understanding wife.) This particular band was Gillespie's final attempt to keep a large band together in the years immediately following the big band era, a time that was so economically discouraging for the few remaining big bands that even Count Basie eventually had to cut his great band down to an octet. Of course, Gillespie's band attracted some of the best of the young modern jazz musicians, since they had to play the difficult, harmonically complex charts and be able to play bop solos that could share the stage with the brilliance of Dizzy's improvisations. Coltrane was still something of a southern bumpkin, often even going barefoot on the stand, and his sophisticated colleagues nicknamed him "Country John"—how far he was still from the master shaman and father figure that he would become in the Sixties!

Being on the road and being a junkie was difficult. Trying to find places to buy dope in strange cities while avoiding the police was itself a major problem. Fortunately or unfortunately, depending on your point of view, there were a number of other fellow junkies in the band, including Coltrane's new pal Jimmy Heath, and somehow he managed to get what he needed. Among the pieces the band played was a long one called "Cubana Be, Cubana Bop," composed and arranged by George Russell, that featured a fairly lengthy introduction based on modes rather than chords, probably the first use of modes in jazz history (as well as the first major fusion of jazz and Latin music). Years later, Russell's modes would be an enormous influence on Coltrane's mature music.

There is a wonderful photograph from this time of Charlie Parker and Dizzy posing in front of the band. Peering at them from behind in his seat in the band is the obviously admiring face of John Coltrane. Coltrane's appearance in the photograph was a coincidence, but a serendipitous one in framing the three greatest innovators of modern jazz.

Gillespie finally had to forgo the big band, but he put together out of it a small group that included Coltrane on tenor sax, as well as such other young comers as Milt Jackson on vibes and piano and the superb Detroit guitarist Kenny Burrell. Talking to Gillespie shortly before his death, I found that he had only faint memories of Coltrane's time in his employ. He did remember that, like most young saxophonists, Coltrane's alto playing seemed to be like that of the horde of Parker acolytes so ubiquitous at the time.

The group made some recordings for Gillespie's own Dee Gee label, and on one tune, "We Love to Boogie," Coltrane recorded his first solo (on tenor saxophone). The influence of Dexter Gordon is obvious here, with a bit of Sonny Stitt. Stitt had become Coltrane's latest idol on the tenor. Stitt, like Coltrane, had started out on alto and had developed a style very similar to Charlie Parker's—*before,* so he insisted, ever having heard Bird. In order to avoid the inevitable comparisons with Parker, he switched to tenor. On a good night, Stitt could be a brilliantly exciting player, though lacking the genius of Charlie Parker. Years later, Coltrane said about him, "Sonny's playing sounded like something I would like to do. He sounded like something between Dexter Gordon and Wardell [Gray], an outgrowth of both of them. All the time I thought I had been looking for something and then I heard Sonny and said, 'Damn! There it is! That's it!' " In this statement we can hear in its early stages that quest for a sound that always seemed to lie just out of reach for Coltrane. In Stitt's style he found the rhythmic complexity he had been searching for combined with the warmth and melodic invention of Gordon and Wardell Gray. As would prove so typical of Coltrane's career and musical quest, it was only a temporary solution.

Dizzy eventually had to let Coltrane go, mainly because of his drug addiction and the attendant problems it created—lateness to gigs, nodding on the stand, and so on. It is important to dwell on what didn't happen to Coltrane's career now as much as what did. Generally, playing with a figure as popular with the public and as respected by musicians as Dizzy Gillespie was the ticket to an important career in jazz. Coltrane was about twenty-five years old when he left Gillespie, the age by which many, if not most, jazz musicians have found their own voice. Although he was recognized as a fine player by certain insiders such as Dizzy, his style was still an amalgam of the leading bop players. Unlike, say, Sonny Rollins, whose early records revealed a clearly unique voice, one that would grow and develop, with a sound unlike anybody else's. The young John Coltrane still had to wait at least a few more years for his voice to come. But when it emerged, it would sound so original that it seemed to come out of nowhere.

Coltrane now had to find work in a variety of rhythm and blues bands. The best R & B band at the time was lead by Earl Bostic, a technically masterful alto saxophonist. Bostic's band provided employment and a chance for Coltrane to learn more about his horn from a master saxophonist, despite the bedrock simplicity of its rhythm and blues. The Bostic band was also, according to one former member, "a drinking man's band." Coltrane had started drinking when he moved to Philadelphia but now, like many junkies, he drank heavily, either as a substitute for junk or even in addition to it, in order to get blindingly high. He was surely discovering what has been called the "left-handed way" to God, finding the Absolute through excess rather than asceticism. Coltrane was first learning about alternative routes to spiritual knowledge—alternative, that is, to the Christianity that he still accepted as his faith. One friend, the saxophonist Bill Barron, gave him a book on yoga, which he read with fascination, and through a number of other friends he began to learn something about Islam. Several musicians in the Forties, especially those who had been turned around by the message of bebop, were attracted to Islam (of which Elijah Muhammad's Black Muslims were only one sect among many).

This was a time of profound spiritual upheaval for Coltrane, who was deeply aware of the contradiction between his growing use of heroin and alcohol and his Christian fundamentalist religious faith. He was a man who even at this early period had visions and prophetic dreams. In one dream Charlie Parker, whom he had met, told him to forgo the alto saxophone for the tenor. Coltrane was also seriously playing chess now—like many musicians, fascinated with the logic and mathematics of the game. He was beginning to perceive that his lessons in music theory, his growing knowledge of his instrument, his increasing involvement in spiritual advancement, and the purity of mathematics and physics were all interrelated, but too many things were tearing at him for him to be able to put it all together at that time.

In 1953 Coltrane joined the band of Johnny Hodges. "Rabbit" (Hodge's nickname), the star saxophonist with Duke Ellington's band for years, was trying in the early Fifties to develop a band of his own. Most of the charts were either of Ellington (or Strayhorn) tunes, however, or charts as close as possible to the Ellington spirit. Once again, Coltrane learned from proximity to such a great musician. Years later, Coltrane would talk about developing a "sound," and if there was anybody in jazz who had his own sound, identifiable after only a few bars, it was Johnny Hodges. Coltrane's words about his experience in Hodges's band are surprising to one who knows only the ultramodernist Coltrane: "We played honest music. It was my education to the older generation. I really enjoyed that job. . . . Nothing was superficial. It all had meaning and it all swung. The confidence with which Rabbit plays! I wish I could play with the confidence he does. Besides enjoying my stay with Johnny musically, I also enjoyed it because I was getting firsthand information about things that happened way before my time." Coltrane's profound understanding of the jazz tradition, and his return to it when in need of fresh inspiration, set him apart from many of his generation who believed that jazz was born with bebop.

Around the time that he joined Hodges's band, Coltrane met Juanita Grubb. A lovely, intelligent, and sensitive woman who loved jazz, Juanita, who was called by her Muslim name, Naima, was about a year younger than Coltrane. The two hit it off and, despite John's continuing addiction to both heroin and alcohol, they eventually married, finally giving Coltrane a bit of stability in his life.

Unfortunately, Coltrane's dope habit had reached the point where it was obvious even on the bandstand, where he would often nod off. The fastidious Hodges liked Coltrane as a man and a musician, but he ran out of patience after giving Trane several warnings and reluctantly had to fire the young saxophonist in the fall of 1954. At this point, Coltrane's career reached its lowest, most degrading point. After returning to Philadelphia, he was forced to play with all sorts of rhythm and blues bands, any job that would put food on his table and, more important, dope in his arm. One of his worst jobs was described years later by a colleague, the pianist Bill Evans: "Coltrane once told me about a band he worked with called Daisy Mae and the Hepcats. This was the kind of band you'd find in Las Vegas lounges ten years later. Daisy Mae would shimmy out front in a sparkling dress while her husband the guitar player was boogieing behind her. John said the guitarist had discovered the lost chord, because it sounded as if he'd found the one chord that fitted everything—a chromatic crunch."

The jobs he hated most, though, were those in which he was forced to "walk the bar." In the midst of one his wild R & B solos he actually climbed up on the bar and walked its length, honking and wailing. This kind of display was anathema to the shy and introverted Coltrane, who was nevertheless forced to endure the ordeal in order to keep his job. There is one story of a fellow musician and friend who came into a club where Coltrane was walking the bar. When Coltrane saw the musician, the tenor saxophonist and composer Benny Golson, he felt so embarrassed that he immediately jumped off the bar and walked out the door, never looking back.

One of his better jobs at this time was with the organist Jimmy Smith, who would go on to be the leading organist of the Fifties and Sixties, the first to genuinely adapt modern jazz to that somewhat cumbersome instrument. But hearing the roar of those organ chords almost drove Coltrane to distraction. "Wow," he said later, "I'd wake up in the middle of the night and hear that organ! Those chords screaming at me."

Fortunately, Coltrane's career was about to have a major breakthrough. The cause of that breakthrough would be Miles Davis. For several years thereafter the careers of the trumpeter and Coltrane would be, except for some key periods apart, inextricably linked. Here, briefly, is a summary of Miles's career up until 1955 (for further details on Miles, consult either my own book *Round About Midnight,* or better yet, Miles's autobiography *Miles,* or best, Jack Chambers's superb *Milestones Volumes I and II,* one of the best biographies ever written about a jazz musician). Born the same year as Coltrane (May 25, 1926), he grew up in East St. Louis, Illinois, in a fairly well-to-do black family (his father was a dentist and hog farmer), then moved to New York in the mid-Forties to be near his idol, Charlie Parker. He wound up playing in and recording with Parker's group. Miles would say later, "I quit every night. I said [to Parker] 'What do you need me for?' " Miles could not play in the upper range like his idol Dizzy Gillespie, so he developed a style based on his strengths, his harmonic intelligence, and, especially, his melodic invention.

After leaving Parker's group in the late Forties, he led a nonet that, although it played only a handful of gigs and recorded only a dozen sides, changed jazz history. It would be known as the "Birth of the Cool" band, and it launched the cool jazz movement, which flourished in the early Fifties, predominantly on the West Coast. Around that time, Miles developed an addiction to heroin that lasted several years.

In the early Fifties, despite the fame Miles had won playing with Bird, his career went into eclipse, another victim of the heroin plague. Then in 1954, Miles kicked dope on his own, and his career began to turn around. In 1955 he appeared at the Newport Jazz Festival, and although Miles said about the performance, "I just played the way I always do," he was the hit of the festival with both fans and critics. After years of recording for Prestige, often referred to as "the junkie's label" for its practice of paying great junkie jazz musicians small amounts in cash to record (thus enabling them to immediately score dope), he was signed to Columbia Records, then as now the largest record company.

Miles then decided to put together a regular group, instead of playing with whatever musicians had been available, as he had been doing during the early Fifties. First he formed a Chicago group involving the saxophonist John Gilmore and the pianist Andrew Hill, both of whom would go on to become important members of the avant-garde movement of the Sixties. Many believe that Coltrane was directly influenced by Gilmore, and he certainly did admire the tenorist, who gained famed playing with the Sun Ra Arkestra. For whatever reasons, that band failed to gel, so in New York Miles put together a band with the up-and-coming, hard-driving drummer Philly Joe Jones, the pianist Red Garland, and the teenaged bassist Paul Chambers. Originally Miles intended to use Sonny Rollins, at the time considered by musicians as the most important young tenor man on the scene. But Rollins was undergoing his own difficulties—kicking a heroin habit by removing himself from the jazz scene and working as a laborer—so Miles had to look elsewhere. Both Philly Joe and Red Garland immediately voted for Coltrane.

Miles had played with Coltrane a few years previously in a short-lived band (it probably lasted for only one gig at the Audobon Ballroom) in which Sonny Rollins had also played tenor. According to Miles, Rollins at the time was such a superior player to Coltrane that "Sonny had just blown him away . . . that night Sonny set his ass on fire." Other than that, he had not made much of an impression. He went along with Jones and Garland, though, and invited Coltrane into the group. Coltrane immediately agreed, knowing that Miles was one of the great torchbearers of modern jazz, that torch handed directly from Coltrane's idol, the greatest single figure in the bop revolution, Charlie Parker. Miles had already indicated his continuing dedication to innovation, and it would be difficult for any creative musician to turn down an opportunity to play with him, even after the years of obscurity Miles had suffered during his addiction to drugs in the early Fifties. This decision would make John Coltrane a jazz star and, more importantly, force him to dig deeper into his mind and soul and face the genius within.

Playing with Miles Davis's quintet put Coltrane in a group that was at the fulcrum of a pivotal moment in jazz and its evolution. It was with Miles that Coltrane first began to discover the true nature of his talent, as well as the means to develop it. For Miles was more than a great musician—he was, in his taciturn, Zen-like way, a great philosopher and teacher of the music. For Coltrane, his philosophy and teachings would be especially relevant.

2 in the tradition

When John Coltrane joined Miles Davis's quintet in 1955, he could not have had any idea of how significant a moment this would be in jazz history. To him it meant work, playing the music he loved with a boss he respected, but probably not much more. One wonders if he even had many hopes about the longevity of the group, since jazz bands of all sizes come and go in the always-variable American cultural climate. Miles, although a fairly well known member of the jazz scene since the mid-Forties, was not yet a superstar, and the rest of the group was a motley collection of unknowns. Yet this quintet came to preside over an era of jazz history that a number of critics have described as a golden age of jazz classicism, and as the bridge between the bop revolution of the Forties and the Free Jazz movement of the Sixties. And John Coltrane became the central figure around which much of this evolution took place. Until the very end of the Fifties he was considered at best a talented and perhaps promising saxophonist, but certainly not the great innovator and leading influence he would become in the Sixties. Coltrane would not have been able to reach the particular musical conclusions he eventually did, however, if it weren't for his immersion in the music of the Fifties, a time of quietism and timidity in American society and of fervent creativity in jazz.

The Fifties, for jazz, was an era of exploration and constant artistic movement and change, although it was more along the lines of rapid evolution than the bop revolution of the Forties. Many eras have been hailed as "the Golden Age of Jazz"—the early Twenties, the middle and late Thirties, and even, amazingly enough, the present (based on what, I am not sure—the emergence of a bunch of young musicians parroting bop licks that originated long before they were born?)—but that title perhaps applies best to the Fifties. Although it would never again have the mass popularity it gained during the Swing Era of the Thirties and early Forties, jazz nevertheless seemed to have found a fresh young audience, on college campuses (the type of collegiate music fan who now listens to "alternative rock") and in such successful events as the Newport Jazz Festival. Modern, postbop jazz in particular began to gain a hard-won acceptance as the new mainstream of jazz.

The vast popularity of such "cool jazz" musicians as Dave Brubeck and Paul Desmond, Gerry Mulligan and Chet Baker, and Shorty Rogers (all white men, incidentally) had a lot to do with the popular acceptance of modern jazz, albeit a watered-down version of revolutionary bebop. Although cool jazz was also known as West Coast jazz and usually associated with California, the cool era for all practical purposes began in New York with the nonet founded by Miles Davis with the aid of Gil Evans, John Lewis, and Gerry Mulligan. Both the band (it only played a total of about three gigs) and its records for Capitol hardly made an impression with the public, but they greatly influenced a growing number of musicians. The other great influence on the cool jazz movement was Lennie Tristano, who in the Forties developed his own approach to modern jazz, which seemed to be based on a cerebral distillation of the bop line. Tristano and his adherents produced a slippery, icy music, emotions held well in check, with little blues feeling but with a cold and strangely moving beauty.

Cool jazz was bop with pastel sonorities and an emphasis on subtle lyricism. It reflected the Charlie Parker of "Yardbird Suite" and "Embraceable You" rather than the fury of "KoKo." Lester Young was actually more of an influence on the West Coast musicians than Bird. Rhythmically, cool jazz was quite basic. From Tristano most coolsters had gotten the notion that the drummer should simply keep the time on the cymbals like a metronome, not interact with the soloist or play complex rhythms. Although most West Coast jazz had low dynamics, perhaps the most popular West Coast act of all was the bombastic big band of Stan Kenton, the Wagner of jazz, and his blaring brass, which he dubbed "progressive jazz."

For a while in the early Fifties California seemed to be the new center for jazz. Increasingly, white men on the West Coast, playing adulterated bop, dominated the jazz polls and the clubs. Some wonderful music was made by the best of the coolsters, particularly the alto saxophonist Art Pepper (whose fiery playing could scarcely be labeled "cool"); Gerry Mulligan, who formed the first pianoless quartet (a device later explored with devastating results in the Sixties by Ornette Coleman); and Paul Desmond, whose devotion to long melodic lines expressed the keenest understanding of the first true "harmolodicist"—to use Ornette Coleman's theoretical term—Lester Young, while sounding absolutely individualistic. Desmond, interestingly enough, would be a major influence on such avant-gardists as John Tchacai and, especially, Anthony Braxton, just as his boss, Dave Brubeck, would be one of the early major influences on Cecil Taylor. And, of course, there was the great tenor man Stan Getz, although by the late Fifties his style had developed a strength and drive that transcended any narrow classification such as "cool" (he would also be listed by Coltrane in the Fifties as one of his four favorite tenor saxophonists).

By the mid-Fifties many musicians, particularly black modern jazz musicians, felt that the cool movement had lost sight of many of the basic elements of jazz, particularly the blues. West Coast jazz reflected a white middle-class outlook in its mild timbres and mellow rhythms. Once again it seemed as if white men had appropriated a black innovation, in this case bop, commercialized and weakened its impact and message, and cashed in. The reaction to that co-optation produced a further step in the evolution of jazz.

This new movement, which would be labeled "hard bop," was announced in two separate recording sessions in 1954. One was by Miles Davis, acting as an *agent provocateur* once again, in a sextet recording that included the bop trombonist J. J. Johnson, the perenially underrated tenor man Lucky Thompson, and the funky pianist and composer Horace Silver, a key figure in the hard bop movement. The other session was the first by the Jazz Messengers, a collective group at this time including, once again, Silver, the hard-driving drummer Art Blakey, the trumpeter Kenny Dorham, and the tenor man Hank Mobley, another musician to whose name seems forever attached the word "underrated." Hard bop was basically a bluesier, funkier form of bebop, usually played in medium or medium fast tempos rather than with the zip of bop, with perhaps a greater emphasis on composition and arrangements than most free-flying bop performances (not counting those of such bebop composers as Tadd Dameron or Thelonious Monk). In some ways it was a return to earlier jazz principles—in the words of many musicians at the time, a return to "roots."

The third event that established hard bop was the emergence of the magnificent Max Roach/Clifford Brown Quintet. Until his untimely death in a car crash in 1956, Brown, with a style heavily influenced by Fats Navarro, was the *enfant terrible* of the trumpet, a thrilling player with a golden sound who, if he had lived, would have been one of the dominant musicians in jazz. Along with Miles, Brown was the most influential trumpet player of the postbop era, and he continues to exert an inordinate amount of influence on young trumpet players.

By the mid-Fifties one record company, Blue Note, which over a twenty-year history had recorded both traditional jazz and some important bop (most importantly the first records made under Thelonious Monk's leadership, including some of his most brilliant and difficult compositions), began to record hard bop almost exclusively, beginning with the first Jazz Messengers record. By the early Sixties the company's owner, Alfred Lion, together with the great recording engineer Rudy Van Gelder, had established what was known as the "Blue Note sound," usually with groups with the same personnel as the Messengers—trumpet, tenor sax, occasionally trombone, and rhythm—and that sound was emblematic of the whole hard bop movement.

As far as John Coltrane was concerned, the most important

aspect of the hard bop movement was its great emphasis on the tenor saxophone. The tenor sax emerged as the leading instrument of the Fifties, and there were many fine players around. Mobley was hailed as the middleweight champ for his "round" sound, as he described his own tone, and his lyrical ideas. Rhythmically, Mobley's playing was perhaps the most bop-oriented of all the tenor men who emerged in the Fifties, although his conception owed quite a bit to Lester Young. Tenor men like Benny Golson and Lucky Thompson were chiefly influenced by Coleman Hawkins and Ben Webster, who had flourished in the late Thirties, when the tenor also reigned. But undoubtedly the most important tenor player of the Fifties until the emergence of John Coltrane was Sonny Rollins.

A silly controversy of the late Fifties and early Sixties pitted these two friends against each other. Unlike Coltrane, Rollins was something of a prodigy, gaining a reputation as a promising musician and recording with such key modernists as Fats Navarro, Bud Powell, Thelonious Monk, and Miles Davis while still in his teens and early twenties. His large, powerful sound, much like Coleman Hawkins's but with far less vibrato, his wealth of ideas, his innovative "thematic improvising," and the influence of Monk on his playing were all factors that made him by the mid-Fifties the dominant tenor man of the time, despite his youth. He is, quite simply, one of the greatest saxophonists in all of jazz and inarguably one of the most prodigiously inventive improvisers in the history of music.

The difficulty is that he was constantly compared with Coltrane, and in the late Fifties jazz fans and critics loved to argue over which one was "better," as if there were some way of objectively determining the relative quality of two men who were clearly both great artists and virtuosos of their instrument. Both men were musical geniuses with very different but equally valid artistic agendas. Here is an aspect of the jazz scene that I truly find regrettable, this spirit of competitiveness engendered by the jazz polls and by too many fans and critics. This most American music could not help adopting certain less fortunate traits of its native land, such as that extreme competitiveness so endemic to the American way of life. In art, competition, though perhaps unavoidable, is basically irrelevant. Both Coltrane and Rollins were ultimate masters of their instruments and the art of improvisation, and the style of each man was so deeply personal that comparisons are fruitless. Nevertheless, the competition, engendered by the jazz press and continued in every bar or hangout where jazz fans gathered, became intense enough to force Sonny Rollins into a retirement that lasted about two years. What was worse, it put a crimp in the friendship between the two men.

The difference in quality between the two men's work was primarily in their recorded performances, since Rollins never felt comfortable recording; for such a great genius, too many of his records fell short of representing his playing at its best. Rollins did have his share of masterpieces, beginning with *Saxophone Colossus, Freedom Suite,* and the bizarre but wonderful *Way Out West*—Sonny poses as a gunslinger on the cover with a sax in place of a revolver, and among the tunes played are "Wagon Wheels" and that traditional jazz favorite "I'm an Old Cowhand." Coltrane, while preferring live performance to the studio, nevertheless regularly produced brilliant albums. In addition, because Rollins, unlike Coltrane, never kept a group together very long, he was not known for leading a great group as well as his ability as a player.

A number of other excellent tenor men emerged in the Fifties. To name just a few: the little-known but deeply soulful Tina Brooks; the frequent Mingus sideman Booker Ervin (who had a tough, hard sound often compared to Coltrane's); J. R. Montrose; Clifford Jordan; Zoot Sims and Al Cohn, forever linked together in lyrical swing; Harold Land; Johnny Griffin (known as the fastest tenor man in jazz until Coltrane developed his mature style); and George Coleman. All of these men played with individuality, power, and beauty, and they all helped in the development of the tenor sax as the single most important instrument in jazz. Jazz is an art of the individual, celebrating originality and imagination, and simultaneously a group art, an art of the collective consciousness. If Coltrane's mature style seems to have sprung out of nowhere except the recesses of his mind, it must be remembered that even the most personal styles in jazz do not develop in a vacuum, but are formed within the incubator of the "jazz brotherhood," as the drummer Art Taylor put it.

Talking to jazz musicians, one discovers that the jazz world is a brotherhood (yes, one that includes women), a family of musicians, some famous, many not, all of whom have worked together to advance their art form. Too often, jazz history is presented as a series of great men, each of whom singlehandedly brought about change in the music. But the truth is more complex. Art Taylor told me that when he went to a recording session with Coltrane, he was always prepared for Coltrane's latest innovations even if he hadn't played with him in a while, because all of the musicians present had been evolving as part of this brotherhood. Since jazz has not until recently been taught academically, the only way to learn the secrets of jazz was to be part of the jazz scene, to "pay your dues." One can learn technique and harmony and theory, but finding your own voice, creating your own musical world, can be gained only through experience.

While hard bop provided the meat-and-potatoes jazz of the Fifties, at the same time there was a swift undercurrent of often feverish experimentation. Although Monk had made his classic series of records in the Forties and early Fifties, he was "rediscovered" in the mid-Fifties. Never really a bopper (though dubbed the "High Priest of Bop"), Monk reworked harmony and form, producing an idiosyncratic, eerily displaced music filtered through a twisted and cracked prism, comparable to the great works of cubism. Listening to him play was like hearing simultaneously the very early stride pianists and the playing of an avant-garde so futuristic it seemed from a decade not yet born. Monk was a living and breathing jazz paradox, and nobody made funnier or more sublime music. When he hired John Coltrane in 1957, his difficult yet childlike music gave the saxophonist the final shove into his mature style.

Another musician that Coltrane admired was the bassist Charles Mingus, another febrile experimenter. Mingus was a great innovator on his instrument; by playing strong melodic lines behind the soloist and by taking solos every bit as complex as those on a horn, he made the bass an aggressive part of the jazz ensemble rather than a mere accompanist. Mingus's greatest contributions, however, were those as a composer, arranger, and group leader, roles to which he brought one of the most brilliant and innovative minds jazz has ever known. He once stated that his prime influences were Duke Ellington, Charlie Parker, the legendary pianist Art Tatum, and the church, and all of those influences can be heard in his most compelling work. In the early Fifties Mingus experimented with music similar to that of the Third Stream movement, which attempted to marry jazz and modern "classical" music, but his work became increasingly freer, using forms similar to the modes that would be so central to Coltrane's music in the Sixties and even dabbling with atonality. Mingus's pieces often used constantly changing tempos and meters, using dazzlingly rich tonal colors that made one think of Ellington on LSD. He also experimented with program music, often with spoken sections protesting racism or the plight of the artist in no uncertain terms (one record label refused to allow him to declaim the lyrics on one incendiary piece about the racist governor of Arkansas). As hard and furious as Mingus's music could be, he also produced some of the most achingly lyrical music of the Fifties. Mingus, like Miles, believed that innovation was a tool to drive his musicians into fresh areas of improvisations, making them eschew the licks and clichés that often become crutches for many jazz players.

Although the work of John Lewis and the Modern Jazz Quartet was seemingly as different from that of Mingus as that of Erik Satie, both Lewis and Mingus were in fact working toward similar goals. Lewis, like Mingus, tried to integrate true improvisation with composition mostly in the confines of the group for which he was musical director, the MJQ. Mingus used to complain that he was bored with the simple instrumentation of that group: Lewis's piano, vibes (played by Milt Jackson, usually considered the greatest vibraharp player in jazz), bass (Percy Heath, brother of Coltrane's friend Jimmy), and drums (originally the first true bop drummer, Kenny Clarke, later replaced by Connie Kay). But Lewis's ability to constantly find fresh musical options for this limited instrumentation is to his credit. Lewis, like Mingus and Monk and Ellington earlier, was attempting to use the tools and tradition of jazz to expand its possibilities and to resolve the seeming imbroglio between composition and improvisation.

Still another player on the field, though one far less lionized, unfortunately, than Mingus, Monk, and Lewis (and let me include in this list Horace Silver, the great auteur of hard bop), was the composer/arranger/jazz theorist George Russell. Russell began his career by co-composing and arranging the first true marriage of jazz and Afro-Latin music for Dizzy Gillespie's big band, "Cubana-Be, Cubana-Bop." In addition, the opening section of that piece probably marked the first use of modes in the history of jazz. Coltrane's first introduction to modes was when he was in the Gillespie band and played this piece, though like most other musicians he probably did not take much notice of it at the time. In the early Fifties Russell designed a theory for jazz composition and improvisation, *The Lydian Chromatic Concept of Total Organization,* which was the blueprint for the evolution of modal jazz. He only infrequently was given the opportunity to record his compositions and arrangements, but he made the most out of them, recording two masterpieces in the mid-Fifties: the long piece for orchestra "All About Rosie," and an album of compositions for a sextet featuring Art Farmer and one of the earliest on-record appearances of Bill Evans, who plays brilliantly. A couple of years later he recorded an album called *New York, New York,* on which Coltrane played.

These men are just some of the prime movers and shakers of the Fifties, men who restlessly pushed the envelope just a little further with each new creation. The decade also produced a bumper crop of superb postbop players, all of whom advanced the art form to one degree or another. So many names come to mind—from the trumpeters Lee Morgan and Booker Little to the vibraharpist Milt Jackson, to the organist Jimmy Smith, to the early Cecil Taylor and early Bill Evans—that it would require an entire volume to discuss even briefly all the fine new talent that came to the fore in the Fifties. In addition, of course, many of the great figures of bop—Charlie Parker until his death in 1955, Dizzy Gillespie, Thelonious Monk, Bud Powell (when he wasn't in psychiatric hospitals), the pianist Elmo Hope, the composer/arranger Tadd Dameron—were still around and still making wonderful, if no longer revolutionary, music.

Moreover, most of the first great geniuses of the music were alive and playing, giving young musicians a chance to rub against a very much living tradition. Duke Ellington produced some magnificent work in the Fifties. Louis Armstrong was still playing with his customary warmth and beauty—if not with the total creative abandon of the Hot Five and Seven days, then with a burnished maturity and wisdom that can only come with age. Sidney Bechet was alive in the early Fifties, even if living in distant France. Basie was still giving lessons in swing. Lester Young and Billie Holiday were still making beautiful music, albeit different in feeling (naturally) from their youthful work. So were Coleman Hawkins, Roy Eldridge, Benny Goodman, Johnny Hodges, and many others. John Coltrane reported that among the greatest music he ever heard was listening to Art Tatum at an after-hours joint jam with his young acolyte Oscar Peterson. Being able to hear and associate with jazz innovators from earlier eras was most instructive to the new generation of jazz musicians. Sometimes they even played or recorded together, and in John Coltrane's case that opportunity produced striking results.

Jazz in the Fifties was also creating the most profound effect on the culture at large since the Twenties. Although the Eisenhower era seemed to be one of calm and conformity, beneath the surface was a vortex of anger and discontent. The most obvious symbols of this new surge of nonconformity were the beats. To most of the beats, the jazz musician was the new shaman, a holy man that they nearly worshiped. To those grounded in Freud, improvisation seemed to be a way of hooking the creative hand directly to the id and avoiding the superego's dictates of socialization. Jack Kerouac typed *On the Road* on a continuous roll of paper so he could write in one uninterrupted improvisation, putting down whatever flux of words came to mind. Painters such as Jackson Pollack, not all of them beats but sharing aspects of their philosophy of art, were also heavily influenced by modern jazz, improvising on the canvas.

Many beat poets began to recite their jazzlike poetry to the accompaniment of a real jazz band, producing, I suppose, a precursor to rap. Beats wrote novels about jazz (John Clellon Holmes's *The Horn*) or poems honoring great jazz musicians—there was a cottage industry of poetry about Charlie Parker after Bird's death in 1955. No one deified jazz musicians more than Kerouac, although he often chose strange jazz musicians to worship, such as, in *On the Road,* George Shearing (to give Jack at least some benefit of the doubt, it was the *early* Shearing, before he formed his famous freezingly cool quintet). Norman Mailer, in his famous essay on the hipster "The White Negro," called jazz the music of orgasm, the sound of orgy roiling beneath the outward calm of American society in the Fifties.

The attitude of many beats—that jazz musicians were "noble savages" whose ability to blow jazz endlessly through the night was simply part of their animal nature—makes it obvious that the beats didn't really understand the process of improvisation. They underestimated the process of thought and hard work that goes into developing the various methods and techniques of the jazz musician which is called his conception. Many of them did view jazz as a deeply spiritual music and helped create a new level of respect for the music among intellectuals and hip college students. For better or worse, they helped shape the general public's attitude toward modern jazz as the music of eccentrics and rebels with and without causes. The lingo of jazz and the supposed whacked-out attitudes of jazz musicians became the stuff of comedian's routines, both the new hip (or as they were called at the time, "sick") comedians like Lenny Bruce and Mort Sahl and such middle-brow favorites as Bob Hope and Jack Benny. Most jazz musicians resented being represented as stoned weirdos, but such notoriety actually created an interest in jazz among the curious and the would-be hip, especially those who read magazines like *Playboy,* which extolled jazz as the perfect music for the "with it" guy about town.

Jazz was still not popular music in the Fifties, far from it. The music I remember best from that decade is that of the Four Aces, Frankie Laine, Rosemary Clooney, Johnny Ray, et al. Of course, in the last few years of the decade the so-called Rock Era began, with the appearance of records by Chuck Berry, Little Richard, and Elvis and his clones, music that seemed even further from jazz. However, jazz seemed to have a niche in the music business, fortunately, with both jazz clubs and records abounding, and a young jazz musician like John Coltrane could feel confident about maintaining a career playing the music that he loved.

The Fifties were a ripe time for an aspiring young jazz musician. Excitement and change was in the wind, and members of the jazz community believed that the music in its maturity could go anywhere, that its vistas were limitless. Playing jazz has always been a risky vocation, but the Fifties, apart from the rarity of once-ubiquitous big bands (and therefore of available jobs in them), was on the whole a good time to pursue a career in this most American river of sound. And the best place to pursue that career was in the group led by Miles Davis, Charlie Parker's protégé and the prince of modern jazz.

3 workin'

John Coltrane could not have known that joining the new quintet of Miles Davis would change his life. Until then, he had been a journeyman bopper, better than most, but scarcely an original voice. In 1955, when Miles formed the band, Coltrane would turn twenty-nine, an age by which, as in sports, most players have long established their greatness and the direction of their careers. Charlie Parker was only twenty-five when he recorded such masterpieces as "KoKo" and "Now's the Time," and some would even argue that by the time he was twenty-nine, most of Bird's great work was already behind him. (Much of his work for Norman Granz in the Fifties exhibited a new, even more expressive, evolution of his style, however.) Miles was the same age as Coltrane, and in 1955 had been playing with a completely original style for almost a decade, although his style did not really coalesce until about the time he stopped using heroin, in 1954. Coltrane at twenty-nine still sounded like an amalgam of other players, mostly Dexter Gordon and Sonny Stitt, as did many other tenor men at the time.

Playing with Miles almost immediately affected Coltrane's style, and that change had much to do with Miles's approach to group leadership: on the surface, no leadership at all. Miles virtually never rehearsed the group, he never told anyone what to play, and he even left the bandstand while other members of the group were soloing. "What for?" was his answer when asked why he didn't stay on the bandstand after his own solo. His groups invariably reflected his musical conception and played with a sense of group coherence envied throughout the jazz world. Part of it was his genius in selecting the members of his group. Miles never felt too insecure to hire men who had the potential to be leaders themselves. Most often in any of his groups, at least until the mid-Seventies, this meant using musicians with strong, individual conceptions, rather than players who just complemented Miles.

For this first quintet Red Garland was the pianist, Paul Chambers, just barely out of his teens, the bassist, and Philly Joe Jones the drummer. Miles's favorite pianist at the time was Ahmad Jamal, and he chose Garland for his similarly light touch and his ability at times to sound like Jamal. In Chambers he recognized a burgeoning talent. Philly Joe was easy: he played with the fire and explosiveness that Miles wanted. As for the other horn, he realized he needed a contrast to the airy lyricism of his own style. His original choice was Sonny Rollins, but Coltrane functioned in that role even better since at the time he had, in Whitney Balliett's words, "a dry, unplaned tone that sets Davis off like a rough mounting for a fine stone."

Things did not go smoothly at first for Coltrane. Miles, his heart still set on Rollins, did not initially appreciate Coltrane's playing. Coltrane continually annoyed the usually taciturn Davis because, in Miles's words, "Trane liked to ask all these motherfucking questions back then about what he should or shouldn't play. Man, fuck that shit; to me he was a professional musician and I have always wanted whoever played with me to find their own place in the music. So my silence and evil looks probably turned him off." In the very early days of the quintet, Coltrane, insecure about his playing and unsure of his musical direction, could not expect any direct help from Miles. Only by playing night after night and following his own instincts could he finally find himself musically.

Despite never having played together before, the five men quickly cohered into a tightly knit group. Part of this was social; the group almost immediately got the appellation "the D and D" band—"Drunk and Dope." Everyone in the band was an addict except Miles, who had kicked dope the year before and, much to his credit, was strong enough to withstand any temptation. Addiction had a way of bonding the members of the group almost as much as their work together. For the quintet soon began to make important musical discoveries—all on the bandstand, since Miles never rehearsed—that would greatly influence all jazz combos. The music had constant contrast, shadow and light, through the varied styles of the primary soloists: Miles's airy lyricism, Coltrane's dark, hard, charging tenor, Garland's skipping wit. The group seemed to change kaleidoscopically as each man soloed; in the words of the writer Joe Goldberg in *Jazz Masters of the Fifties:* "At least part of the unique quality of the quintet performances lay in a particular principle which Davis grasped, a principle so simple that it apparently eluded everyone else. To put it in terms of this particular group, a quintet is not always a quintet. It could also be a quartet featuring Miles, and at different times on the same tune, it could be a quartet featuring Coltrane, or a trio featuring Garland or Chambers. The Davis rhythm section, Jones in particular, was well aware of this, and gave each of the three principal soloists his own best backing. Behind Davis, the rhythm was full of space, with few chords; behind Coltrane, it was compulsive; and with Garland, it lapsed into an easy, Jamal-like feeling."

Coltrane loved this rhythm section. Garland always seemed to accompany him with the perfect chord, letting him roam harmonically without fear of clashing with the pianist; and the boiling drumming of Philly Joe spurred him on, driving him, like a great drummer should, to creative heights; Chambers became his favorite bassist in all jazz, and the man he used most often on his own record dates throughout the Fifties.

In the beginning, there were complaints from some critics about the group, most of them centering on Philly Joe and Coltrane. Philly Joe, they grumbled, was too loud, too busy, he overwhelmed the dynamics of the group. But to that Miles replied, "I wouldn't care if he came up on the bandstand in his B.V.D.'s and with one arm, just so long as he was there. He's got the fire I want. There's nothing more terrible than playing with a dull rhythm section. Jazz has got to have *that thing.*"

Jones upped the ante for the role of the drummer in a group. His playing was closer to full-fledged dialogue with the soloist than mere accompaniment, and this innovation profoundly affected Coltrane, who upped the ante even further when he formed his own great quartet with the even more dynamic Elvin Jones playing drums.

As for Coltrane, much of the initial dissatisfaction, from fans as well as critics, came simply from the fact that he wasn't Sonny Rollins, the man Miles had been recording with frequently and at the time the most important and exciting young tenor player in jazz. Coltrane's hard sound turned many of them off, but probably much of the criticism was justified to an extent. In the very early days of the group, he seemed to fumble among the chord changes, to squirt out a crazy quilt of ideas, many of them seemingly unconnected. The only time that he sounded truly comfortable, understandably after all his R & B gigs, was when he played the blues. Miles was frequently asked to fire Coltrane, but the more he heard the saxophonist play, the more he could detect his burgeoning talent. In his autobiography, Miles writes (referring to Balliett's metaphor), "After a while [Coltrane] was a diamond himself and I knew it, and everybody else who heard him knew it, too." Well, not everybody. Actually, far from everybody, especially critics.

Coltrane's private life was improving, too. Shortly after joining the quintet he married his longtime girlfriend, Naima Grubb, in a ceremony where the entire band stood as "best men," an indication of how close these men were becoming off the bandstand as well as on. Despite his continued addiction to heroin and liquor, Coltrane lived a quiet, sedate life, a lifestyle that matched his personality. I think it was Flaubert who said that his own life was orderly and bourgeois so that his art could be wild and adventurous. The same was definitely true of Coltrane.

Shortly after the official formation of the band in September 1955, the goup made its first recordings. Miles was signed to Prestige Records but had decided to move to Columbia, for obvious reasons: Prestige had never paid musicians much, and Columbia was offering Miles a lucrative deal. Miles secretly recorded two tunes for Columbia, though they were not immediately released, and in October the group recorded the first entire album of the quintet under his existing contract for Prestige. While recording these sides, Coltrane got his first taste of Miles's recording philosophy: one take per tune only, unless some really dreadful mistake occurred. This approach kept musicians fresh and, more important, reflected Miles's feeling that the more spontaneous the music was, the truer it was to the genuine spirit of jazz. He firmly believed that jazz records should be released with all their mistakes, instead of having them edited out (which was, and still is, the common practice), because the gofs were as much a part of the creative process as any other aspect of the music. In the studio, as well as on the bandstand, Miles was a true musical Zen master. (Miles was not the only great jazz musician with such a philosophy toward jazz recording. Duke Ellington, for one, had a similar attitude. Interestingly, Coltrane did not.)

On this first record, called simply *Miles*, the group is obviously feeling its way, and the music certainly lacks the coherence of its later recordings. Coltrane has evolved considerably since his days with Gillespie, and while his style is not yet formed nor as startlingly original as it would sound even a year later, important elements of his mature approach are already in place. That is obvious in retrospect, but to those hearing him at the time, his nascent originality was far less apparent. Most aspects of the group's methods were also in place here, including Miles's extensive use of the Harmon mute, through which he produced a delicately nuanced tight pit of sound; the study in contrast between the soloists; the surprising choice of tunes ("S'posin'," "How Am I to Know?"); the use of a delicious medium swing for some tunes, which this rhythm section carried off with a panache and subtle drive that seemed to elude most other groups; and the tender ballads ("There Is No Greater Love"), on which Miles invariably used the Harmon mute and on which, except for a single instance, Coltrane invariably laid out. These ballads, perhaps more than any other aspect of the band, brought it and Miles a large audience, including many who would otherwise find little interest in jazz. Did Miles feel that Coltrane would spoil the mood? Perhaps he was right in the early days of the quintet, when Coltrane's playing was unsteady and often even clumsy. But Trane (as he was called by most musicians around the time he joined Miles's band) was to become one of the great balladeers in his own right.

Many in the jazz community continued to feel that Coltrane was a deficit to an otherwise brilliant jazz group. After praising the other members of the quintet, *Down Beat*'s reviewer of their first record wrote, "Coltrane, as Ira Gitler notes . . . is a mixture of Dexter Gordon, Sonny Rollins, and Sonny Stitt. But so far there's very little Coltrane. His general lack of individuality lowers the rating" (of the album, which got four stars, rather than the maximum of five). It is amazing to realize that within two or three years of this review Coltrane would be chastised for developing a style that seemed to some critics too abrasive in its originality! Incidentally, this review was written by Nat Hentoff, who eventually became one of Coltrane's most enthusiastic supporters.

From this time on, Coltrane would record almost continuously until his death. Sonny Rollins once described his own frequent recording activities in the Fifties as "promiscuous." But if Rollins was promiscuous, Coltrane had an advanced case of recording satyriasis. He recorded in a profusion of settings, most of them blowing sessions (one of them with Johnny Griffin was even called just that, "A Blowing Session"). Partially this hyperactivity was due, at least until mid-1957, to his addictions and his constant need for cash, but much of it was simply because of his love of playing. When he wasn't on the bandstand or in the recording studio, he was practicing. If he wasn't practicing, he was at the piano, working out intricate harmonies and chord substitutions. Because he recorded so frequently, we have an extraordinary opportunity to follow the evolution of his style, even in its smallest shifts forward, sometimes as it changed from one month to the next.

For example, one month after the recording of *Miles* Coltrane recorded under the nominal leadership of Paul Chambers (most of this recording session has only been recently released). Even here, Coltrane seems to have made advances, his style coalescing into a far more personal sound than that on the first Davis quintet album. It is clear that he is still grappling with the music, however, particularly in terms of chord changes and melodic continuity. Listening to these early records, one can understand why critics at the time were unable to detect Coltrane's potential, despite all the time and energy he was putting into his music. Dope also took up much of his time, of course; just scoring it could be difficult when traveling with the group. Miles's attitude toward the addictions of his sidemen was simple: If you have a habit, that's your own business. But keep it under control and don't embarrass me on the bandstand.

Things worked out fine, for a while. During the first tour to Detroit, according to Miles, "we were having a lot of fun together, hanging out, eating together, walking around Detroit." Many listeners were giving Coltrane a second chance. As throughout his career, his latest record never reflected the advances he had already made since his last recording session. Many who saw Coltrane play with the group within a few months after the record's release were amazed at how much stronger and more individualistic he was now in person. One such listener, Columbia Records executive George Avakian, remembers watching the group and with each tune becoming more impressed with Coltrane. According to Avakian, "Coltrane seemed to grow taller in height and larger in size with each note that he played."

In early 1956 Miles had an operation to remove nodes on his vocal chords. Because Miles, contrary to his doctor's instructions, had a screaming match with an agent shortly after leaving the hospital, his voice was permanently damaged, resulting in the famous whispered growl that became part of the Davis legend. While he was recovering, he disbanded his quintet. Coltrane returned to Philadelphia, his future uncertain. He must have been especially worried when, upon full recovery, Miles formed a new quintet, with Sonny Rollins in the tenor chair, and even recorded it (though only half an album) for Prestige.

Much to Coltrane's relief, in May 1956 Miles reorganized the original quintet and immediately brought the band into the recording studio. He had worked out a deal with Prestige: if he gave them four more albums, he would be free to move to

Columbia. Miles's solution was simple and typical of his approach to recording. He brought the band into the recording studio for two massive recording sessions during which he made enough sides for four albums, which were to be released over a period of years. He simply acted as if he were at a nightclub playing typical sets of the band's repertoire, with absolutely no retakes (at the end of one tune Coltrane can be heard asking for the beer opener). What is most remarkable is how durable the albums assembled from these sessions, *Cookin,' Workin', Relaxin',* and *Steamin',* have turned out to be. Miles's playing by this point is simply exquisite; his placement of notes, his use of space, his ability to create mood (especially on the ballads), all make it clear that he has become one of the great masters of improvisation. The rhythm section, too, has grown considerably since its debut and now is inarguably the best in jazz. Garland's playing is slick and happy, although many labeled him a "cocktail pianist." That didn't bother Miles much, since they said the same thing about his idol, Ahmad Jamal.

If the band had any problem, it was Coltrane. On the blues and the bop tunes with some of the more familiar harmonic structure, Trane is forceful and clearly coming into his own. Miles was also playing several tunes, many from Ahmad Jamal's repertoire, with unfamiliar chord changes, and it is on some of those ("Surrey with the Fringe on Top," "Diane") that Coltrane sounds lost. Bits of strong melodic ideas come plummeting out of his horn, but his solos often lack a sense of continuity and at times even lapse into obvious fumbling. Yet the roughness of his style prevents the group from becoming too smooth, maybe even gutless. Again, Coltrane does not play on the ballads, with one exception: Miles's classic version of "Round Midnight," arranged by Gil Evans. After Miles states the theme, playing with the Harmon mute and creating a funereal atmosphere, the horns play a brief fanfare and, with the rhythm section playing double time, Coltrane takes a solo. There are two versions of this piece, one on Prestige and the other on Columbia. On both (though especially the Columbia), Coltrane takes his first great solo on record, a lyrical *tour de force* that for the first time

announces a genuinely new voice in jazz, and quite obviously
an important one.

In addition to the large amount of music he was recording
with Miles, Coltrane was also recording in numerous other
settings; most of them were routine jam sessions, but a few of
them were unusual, even bizarre. For example, one Prestige session was a typical jam except that all four horns were tenor
saxophones. Hank Mobley was one of the tenor men—no
surprise there, since both he and Coltrane were considered part
of the "hard bop" movement. But the other two were Zoot Sims
and Al Cohn, two wonderful players, both heavily influenced
by Lester Young ("All those white tenor players sound alike,"
Miles Davis said once) and usually thought of as on a totally
different stylistic axis from Coltrane and Mobley. This·session
proves, if nothing else, the incredible versatility of the tenor sax.
To the untrained ear, Sims and Cohn are playing a totally different instrument from Coltrane's. But even in a session like this,
Coltrane would try to reach for the extraordinary. The best track
on the session is Irving Berlin's ballad "How Deep Is the
Ocean?," where Coltrane demonstrates his ability as the superior
balladeer he was becoming. Possibly the single most difficult
kind of improvisation is that on a slow ballad, especially if the
player does not resort to double time; Coltrane's playing here
is lovely and indicative of things to come.

Coltrane was rarely satisfied with the first take when he recorded, unlike his boss Miles. When Davis was not part of a
session, Coltrane would insist on re-recording tunes until he was
satisfied that his solo was as close to perfection as possible.
According to the pianist Mal Waldron, with whom Coltrane
recorded frequently in the Fifties, Coltrane "would have a ten-
dency to say, 'I don't sound too good at that bar there, so let's
do it over.' But we would talk him out of it. We'd say, 'Hey,
John, what do you mean, that was fantastic, baby.' "

Between the two long sessions for Prestige, Miles recorded
most of the material for his first Columbia album, *Round About
Midnight*. The album is similar to the Prestiges in its mix of
surprising pop tunes ("Bye, Bye, Blackbird") and bop classics

(Charlie Parker's "Au-Leu-Cha"). Although it was recorded at around the same time as the Prestige albums, Coltrane's playing seems far more prominent, and forceful, on the Columbia LP. One reason is his superb solo on the title tune (well, kind of title tune; the actual title of Monk's tune is "Round Midnight" with no "About").

At the time of these sessions, Coltrane and his wife had moved to New York, the headquarters of the quintet and the city where most jazz recording took place. The move didn't do much to help stem his addiction, since New York also had better dope. Nor was he helped by his bandmates, particularly Philly Joe. Jones was very open about his drug addiction, often acting like the Dean Martin of heroin, as if it were a matter of hilarity (one of his best friends was Lenny Bruce, incidentally, who had a similar attitude). Coltrane, in this atmosphere, found himself sinking deeper and deeper into self-destruction.

The band was beginning to really make it now, financially as well as artistically. Miles was becoming one of the most famous, and in some ways notorious, of all jazz musicians. His fame had as much to do with his clothes, his white Ferrari, and his women as it did with his music. Miles became the apotheosis of "cool," even in his treatment of his audience. He never talked to the audience, even to announce tunes or introduce the members of the band, and he frequently even turned his back to the audience ("to hear the drummer better," was his excuse). Instead of turning off the public, such demeanor added to his notoriety, causing many to attend his performances just to observe his behavior. Although some argued that Miles showed contempt toward his audience, actually he was doing just the opposite. He was playing the most subtle, intense, innovative music of his time, and to those who could listen the rest was irrelevant. He believed that anything else was pandering to the audience. Such was his philosophy up until the last few years of his life, when he did go out of his way to acknowledge the audience, even to ham it up a bit onstage. By then he realized he no longer was making music of nearly such exquisite quality.

As successful as the quintet was, both musically and financially, by late 1956 Miles was losing patience with his band, especially Philly Joe and Coltrane. Although all the members of the group were junkies, Philly's and Trane's habits were getting out of control. Miles didn't care what they did in their private lives, but he would not tolerate them making their addiction so obvious on the bandstand. Philly Joe would loudly joke about drugs and Coltrane, according to Miles, "was getting to be pathetic. He'd be playing in clothes that looked like he had slept in them for days, all wrinkled up and dirty and shit. Then he'd be standing up there when he wasn't nodding—picking his nose." Worse, Coltrane often showed up for gigs late and occasionally not at all. Their constant demand for cash advances tried Miles's patience. One night Miles was so exasperated with his saxophonist that he slapped him and punched him in the stomach. Coltrane, a mild man under any circumstances, was so passive from dope that he didn't react at all. But Thelonious Monk happened to observe the scene and told Coltrane, "Man, as much as you play on saxophone, you don't have to take nothing like that; you can come and play with me anytime." Even in this sad state, Coltrane was able to stick Monk's offer in the corner of his mind.

In November 1956, a month after the second long session for Prestige that completed Miles's obligation to the label, Coltrane participated in a recording session with the composer, arranger, and pianist Tadd Dameron on which he played his finest solos of this period. Coltrane always seemed to respond with interesting playing when recording with idiosyncratic composers and arrangers such as Dameron, Monk, and Ellington, and here his improvisations have a power and confidence not heard even on the second Davis Prestige session. Increasingly we can hear a unique musical personality being born. What once may have sounded like clumsiness or roughness of sound is slowly and painfully being brought into sonic light and shape and becoming alive.

His playing was gaining strength. His private life wasn't. When Coltrane's condition had become even more obvious on the bandstand, Miles finally had enough, and he fired both him and Philly Joe. Thus began the darkest period of Coltrane's life. Those who saw him then, looking like a hobo in ratty clothes, unshaven and unwashed, staggering around the Village or Midtown, his eyes glazed over, assumed that he would shortly join that tragic list of musicians destroyed by their immersion in the self-destructive aspects of the jazz life: Bix Beiderbeicke, Charlie Christian, Bunny Berigan, Fats Navarro, Charlie Parker, Billie Holiday, and many others, famous and otherwise.

Being fired by Miles, apparently for good, put Coltrane into a deep depression. For the first time he even thought about permanently giving up music. After all, he had been given the chance of a lifetime, playing with the best jazz group in the world, and had blown it. He was still very far from playing the music he heard in his head, and at this point he thought it beyond his grasp. Confused, deeply depressed, and badly strung out and broke, he returned to his mother's house in Philadelphia. He did not record at all for several months after the Dameron session, too depressed to play or record.

In the early spring of 1957 something happened to John Coltrane, something that would alter his life forever and set him on the great quest that would be at the center of his life from here on. For he had, so he stated, a momentous religious experience.

It happened when he finally decided to free himself from his addictions. He lay down in a room in his mother's house and instructed his wife to bring him only water. By this time, alcohol was more of a problem than heroin, and his withdrawal was at first painful and dark. His wife and mother didn't think he would make it; he became sick and agitated, both physically and psychologically. Early on during this period, he said, he was somehow touched by God, with whom he made a deal of sorts: get him through this torment and he would devote his talent to God, he would make music that would bring people to experience the same kind of revelations he was witnessing. Believe or doubt him, but after this experience he was able to calm down and wait out his cure. He lay quietly in bed, eating nothing, drinking only water, exorcising the demons that had plagued him for years. According to the legend, in less than two weeks he was able to get out of bed a healthy man, completely free of his addictions for the first time in years (with one exception—he was unable to stop smoking). As with any legend—and Coltrane became a genuine jazz legend—the truth was more complicated than the myth. There is no doubt, however, that from this experience Coltrane had a new sense of purpose in his life and even more dedication to his work than he had previously. He was playing for God now. And he was at least on the road to renouncing the demons that had dominated his life for so long.

There will be much more about Coltrane's view of God, but I think it is important to dwell a bit on his religious revelation of 1957, to him the most significant moment in his life. Most of us "sophisticates" who make up the bulk of the jazz audience tend to blanche these days upon reading of somebody's religious experience. Jimmy Swaggart, Jim Jones, Jerry Falwell, Jim and Tammy Faye Baker, and assorted gurus and cults have assaulted us over the years and made many of us deeply suspicious of anything crawling around under the cloak of religion. Worse, the hypocrisy of opportunistic politicians who cut off funds to the poor with one hand and hail Jesus with the other, like the example of criminals, former politicians or not, who use religion as an angle for early probation, has undermined for many of us any legitimate quest toward God. Coltrane's quest was undoubtedly legitimate, though, for it touched all the areas of his life.

Many people who are put off by Coltrane's religious obsessions see them as pretentiousness and an overly developed sense of self-importance. Jazz is usually thought of as a secular music, although its roots are deep in the black church. Coltrane's sense of religion was never dogmatic, however. He never said in what form he perceived God; although he was raised a Christian, he didn't see a vision of Jesus or the Virgin Mary or any form identified with any particular religion. Although his wife was Islamic, his vision was not of Allah. Rather, he saw in his vision of God a unity of all people and all things. All paths that led to the Absolute, ultimate reality, were equally valid. His religion was not doctrinaire but ultimately one of profound simplicity, a desire to be part of the "force that is truly good," in his own words. He believed that his humanity, his music, the material world, and God were all one, and that feeling of unity governed his life. He believed that discovering this unity was man's best hope.

It is because of his pursuit of God—his great quest—that Coltrane's music has the ineffable charisma that continues to fascinate so many. If one is still put off by Coltrane's religion, dwell on this: certainly Handel's *Messiah* or Bach's *St. Matthew Passion* would not have been nearly as powerful or as soaringly beautiful if Handel or Bach had not deeply believed in the religious doctrines on which their musical works were based. Even an atheist cannot help being moved by this glorious music or, for that matter, the music of John Coltrane.

To Coltrane, God was a gateway to infinite possibilities, supreme encouragement to explore unblinkingly the unknown. Coltrane would spend the rest of his life pursuing the truth he believed inherent not only in all religions, both through music and otherwise (since, as we shall see, he came to the conclusion that his music was inextricable from his life), but in any cosmic conception of the Absolute, such as that of Einstein. And he must have had the realization that God was part of him and he was part of God, for that is the idea he would try to express from this point on, often producing music that seemed superhuman. All of this was part of the quest that would dominate his life. Later he would say, "My goal is to live the truly religious life, and express it through my music. If you live it, when you play there's no problem because the music is part of the whole thing. To be a musician is really something. It goes very very deep. My music is the spiritual expression of what I am, my faith, my knowledge, my being."

4 sheets of sound

Coltrane had always loved the music of Thelonious Monk and had learned many of the pianist's intricate compositions. He had, in a sense, even auditioned for Monk by playing "Monk's Mood" for the pianist at the apartment of the jazz patroness Baroness Pannonica de Koenigswarter, of the Rothschild dynasty. Monk was impressed, and Coltrane, shortly after returning to the New York scene, participated in the making of one of Monk's greatest records, *Monk's Music*. Also on the date was the man known as the first true jazz tenor saxophonist, Coleman Hawkins, whose career had begun in the Twenties as part of Fletcher Henderson's big band. On this remarkable album one can thus hear the two men who are the alpha and omega of jazz tenor saxophone styles. This was a notorious session as far as Coltrane was concerned, however: after Monk's solo on "Well, You Needn't," Coltrane was due to solo. Unfortunately, he had nodded off, and Monk can be heard calling out, "Coltrane, Coltrane." The saxophonist finally delivers his solo, understandably unfocused at first, but as it continues it becomes a strong indicator of Coltrane's empathy with Monk's music. This, of course, raises a problem: according to the Coltrane legend, he had completely freed himself of his addictions a couple of months earlier. But with such a long-standing habit as Coltrane's nothing is that simple. Although he had brought his habit under control, he apparently had not yet obliterated it. The same thing happened with Miles Davis—after going through a self-induced cold turkey withdrawal in 1954, he continued to use dope off and on for months afterward before he had it completely out of his system. The same was true for Coltrane. By all indications, by the end of 1957 he had totally ceased using heroin and alcohol altogether.

Because of his constant recording, Coltrane's career is as sharp a demonstration of the power of sobriety as is imaginable. Listen to his solos before he kicked, or at least controlled, his addictions, and then listen to them just a few months after. There were other factors besides his sobriety, but his increased capability to conceptualize his music so much more clearly is obvious even if you know nothing about jazz. By the last few months of 1957, and from there on, his solos sound much more focused, his ideas more fluid, and his sound clearly more powerful. "Live right," he would tell young musicians who aspired to play at his level of inspiration. No one knew why better than he.

Upon moving back to New York with his wife, Coltrane began to record feverishly, making up for lost time. One can follow his growth now almost week to week, certainly month to month in 1957. Many of these sessions are less than illustrious, and Coltrane often does not sound inspired, but on almost every one of these records there is at least one track where he is fired up and plays brilliantly. On some of these sessions, particularly in the later months of 1957 and 1958, Coltrane's playing is so advanced that he makes the other soloists sound hopelessly out of date.

This phenomenon was not unique to Coltrane. When Louis Armstrong played with Fletcher Henderson's band in the Twenties, his rhythmic conception was so adventurous and flowing that he made the other players (including the young Coleman Hawkins) sound as if they were back in New Orleans at the turn of the century. Lester Young's playing in the Basie band, even when listened to now, seems as if he had traveled back in time from the next decade. When Charlie Parker played at Norman Granz's "Jazz at the Philharmonic" concert, he made the other players, including Lester Young, in the words of John Lewis, "sound like old men." Now Coltrane's playing was having the same effect in the late Fifties, even on those players, almost all influenced by Charlie Parker, who had at one time believed themselves to be the last word in modernism.

Coltrane signed a contract to record under his own name for Prestige. The first record he made under his own leadership, simply called *Coltrane,* summarizes all his gains since the last record he had made before leaving New York in 1956, the session with Tadd Dameron. He seems far more secure, and his solos have a cohesion they previously lacked. His inherent lyricism is now more apparent, even radiant, on a lovely slow tune, his own "While My Lady Sleeps."

Around this same time, the spring of 1957, Coltrane's career and musical quest took a huge leap forward. He became the saxophonist in the Thelonious Monk Quartet, a group many would name as one of the greatest in the history of jazz. Unfortunately, that acclaim is based on memory and legend, since the group in its greatest formation, with Wilbur Ware on bass and Coltrane's former bandmate Philly Joe Jones on drums, never recorded. The quartet was given a superb chance to develop by being booked into the East Village club the Five Spot from the spring of 1957 through that fall. Playing with Monk night after night was one of the most significant musical experiences of John Coltrane's career. Monk's tunes were full of surprising melodic and harmonic twists and turns, and his eccentric accompaniment (which Miles disliked so much that he refused to let Monk comp under his solos during a famous recording session in 1954) often used dissonant chords, weird melodic phrases, and forceful reminders of the melody—Monk never wanted his soloists to merely play on the chords and totally ignore the original melody in their improvisations. Coltrane would say later, "I always had to be alert with Monk, because if you didn't keep aware all the time of what was going on you'd suddenly feel as if you'd stepped into an empty elevator shaft." Playing with Monk was more than worth the effort. He would later say about the experience, "Working with Monk brought me close to a musical architect of the highest order. I felt I learned from him in every way— through the senses, theoretically, technically. I would talk to Monk about musical problems, and he would sit at the piano and show me the answers just by playing them. I could watch him play and find out the things I wanted to know. Also, I could see a lot of things that I didn't know about at all.

"Monk was one of the first to show me how to make two or three notes at one time on the tenor. . . . Monk just looked at my horn and 'felt' the mechanics.

"I think Monk is one of the true greats of all time. He's a real musical thinker. I feel myself fortunate to have had the opportunity to work with him. If a guy needs a little spark, a boost, he can just be around Monk, and Monk will give it to him."

Monk encouraged Coltrane to play long solos, accompanying the saxophonist for the first few choruses, giving direction, and then laying out, maybe even leaving the piano altogether to do his eccentric little dance, while Coltrane wailed on. As word got around the jazz community about the increasing strength of the group, and particularly of Coltrane, the club began to fill every night with musicians, fans, critics, and many of the local artists drawn to modern jazz. J. J. Johnson, the great bop trombonist, said about the quartet's Five Spot engagement, "The most electrifying sound I've heard since Bird and Diz."

It was during this gig that Coltrane metamorphosed from a promising tenor man into one of the important voices in jazz. The discipline required to play Monk's music, as well as the opportunity to play at length night after night (his solos were becoming increasingly long), together with his new sobriety and the wealth of time he could now devote to music, all combined to create a dramatic change.

Until very recently, it was believed that the only recordings of this important group were three tunes recorded for the Jazzland label, a division of Orrin Keepnews's Riverside company. Unfortunately, Keepnews did not record the date of this recording, and he is still not sure if they were made while the group was playing the Five Spot or whether it was reconstituted later in order to get at least some chronicle of this group's short but brilliant existence. The date of the recording is of greater significance than simply being the sort of information that only dyed-in-the-wool jazz aficionados find relevant. Coltrane's playing was undergoing one of its most radical spurts of evolution while he was with Monk, and it would have been helpful to know at what point in that evolution these three pieces were recorded.

Those three numbers are among the great treasures of jazz. Coltrane's improvisations, cerebral yet urgent, have an unearthly beauty quite different from anything else in his body of work. He seems to explore every nook and cranny of Monk's tunes, particularly the trickily complex "Trinkle Tinkle" (Monk was a master at titling his work). And his tone, no longer "unplaned," has a cellolike resonance that makes it one of the most original and beautiful among all saxophonists.

Recently, Blue Note Records issued an album of the Monk/Coltrane quartet that was recorded live at the Five Spot by Coltrane's wife Naima. The sound is poor—she used her own home tape recorder and only one microphone. But the music is magnificent and for the first time gives us an actual glimpse of Coltrane at work "woodshedding" at this key gig and developing the "sheets of sound" approach which would dominate his playing for at least the next couple of years. One of the numbers is once again "Trinkle Tinkle," and comparing this version with the one made in the studio, the Five Spot version is rough and tumble, less worked out, more spontaneous. The studio version is a coherent work of music and one of the great jazz solos on record.

It is interesting to hear Coltrane's playing on "In Walked Bud" on the Five Spot version, because it is almost purely horizontal, rather traditional melodic playing. Clearly, Coltrane was still not totally convinced that the purely vertical approach he was increasingly exploring was the only way to go. Or so it seems until one hears the mind-numbing "I Mean You" on the Five Spot album. For other saxophonists, hearing Coltrane play these lightning streak arpeggios, played all over his horn, and work them into a kaleidoscope of rhythmic patterns must have been as disheartening as pianists of an earlier generation felt listening to Art Tatum's harmonic and pianistic fireworks. Coltrane's playing is simply astonishing here, a great leap forward for both saxophone technique and jazz improvisation.

In September 1957, while continuing to play with Monk at

the Five Spot, Coltrane recorded his first truly great record under his own name. Significantly, it wasn't for Prestige but for Blue Note, where musicians were treated with far more respect and their music handled with more care. Blue Note even paid to have the musicians rehearse their music for a couple of days before the recording session, an idea foreign to Prestige, where jazz records were knocked out like cars on an assembly line—the quicker the better. Along with Blue Note's owner, Alfred Lion, Coltrane assembled a band consisting of some of the most exciting new talent on the modern jazz scene: the trombonist Curtis Fuller, the brilliant teenaged trumpet phenom Lee Morgan, the pianist Kenny Drew, and Coltrane's favorite rhythm section, Paul Chambers and Philly Joe. The record, *Blue Train,* became an instant classic, owing mainly to its haunting title track, an eerie blues with a lengthy, magnificent solo by Coltrane, the kind of solo that some compared to a "backwoods country guitar playing the blues." It is clear on this record where his style is going: his lines are increasingly arpeggiated, his solos more harmonic, more vertical, than melodic or horizontal. Rhythmically, his solos tend more to stampede the rhythm section with the sheer weight of their inner rhyme than to correspond in a more direct way to the section's rhythmic thrust. He was playing neither behind nor on the beat, but rather flying over it.

As he continued to play with Monk night after night at the Five Spot, this harmonically oriented approach was increasingly dominating Coltrane's playing. He had, of course, long been obsessed with chords and harmony, ever since his days studying with Dennis Sandole at the Granoff School in Philadelphia. By the end of 1957, chords had become an obsession. He began to perceive music in a different light; when he heard a piece of music he heard it as a series of chords rather than as a melody, the way most of us hear a tune. Coleman Hawkins, the first important jazz tenor man, was also a vertical, basically harmonic player, whose lines were played in terms of sweeping, often dramatic arpeggios. Coltrane began to take this approach even further. He would play three chords in place of one, and play the entire scale of each chord; he had to play these chords very fast in order to fit them into the line, which was often impossible.

As he said, he "had to put notes in uneven groups like fives and sevens in order to get them all in. . . . I thought in groups of notes, not of one note at a time." He was, so he said, "trying for a sweeping sound."

Here was music as pure harmony. It was almost as if he were trying to exhaust the possibilities of European harmony by so thoroughly exploring it. Ira Gitler aptly termed Coltrane's style at this time as "sheets of sound," a perfect metaphor for the way his playing actually reached the ear. Coltrane gave up a lot to play this way—he could be, when he wanted, one of the most unceasingly inventive melodic players in jazz. It is fascinating to follow Coltrane's metamorphosis from a fine but not particularly unusual postbop tenor man to the avant-gardist he became—for that's certainly what his "sheets of sound" made him in the eyes of many critics and listeners, an appellation that would continue to be associated with his name throughout his career. John Coltrane left no diary, no cache of letters that could explain to us his development as a musical thinker—or any other aspect of his obviously complex inner life, for that matter. His vast body of recorded work, created on a regular basis from 1955 until his death, gives us a clear reflection of his consistently changing moods as a man and musician, especially since he was such a nakedly expressive artist.

The year 1957 was, in terms of recording, the most prolific of his career. He played on about twenty records, only a few under his own name, and if you follow them chronologically, the thrust of change in his style is apparent. For example, he recorded a quartet date called *Traneing In* in August 1957, in the middle of his gig with Monk. One can clearly hear the "sheets of sound," those sweeping arpeggios, but his solos (particularly his long one on the title track, a themeless blues) are still basically melodic.

A little over five months later he recorded one of his best Prestige records, *Soultrane*. His growth as a player is immediately obvious, even to those who know little about jazz, and he plays with tremendous confidence and strength. Trane takes a particularly joyous, lyrical solo on Tadd Dameron's "Good Bait," the kind of surging solo that gives powerful meaning to his nick-

name. Just as Charlie Parker's soaring improvisations remind
one so perfectly of a bird in flight (though, as with Coltrane,
that was not the original reason Bird got his moniker), the solos
of John Coltrane seem to move forward with a thundering ceaseless forward thrust, instantly bringing to the mind's eye the image
of a locomotive roaring down the tracks.

Although the "Good Bait" solo is constructed vertically, it
still has melodic logic. As 1958 wore on, however, despite his
great lyrical powers, Coltrane would increasingly eschew melodicism for what one can only call pure harmonic thinking. Was
Coltrane merely obsessed with harmony, and therefore basically
practicing on the stand or in the recording studio? I don't think
so. I think he was attempting to open up whole new avenues
for the improviser.

Jazz moves forward through the attempts of musicians to expand the expressive possibilities of their music, an often taxing
and fearful process, since the art form is still so new and really
without precedent. A jazz saxophonist, no matter how brilliant
his musicality, is limited by the very nature of his medium. His
music cannot have the harmonic depth, the texture, that a composer can get through any musical organization, from a full-
scale orchestra to a string quartet. Coltrane's "sheets of sound"
produced a thick, deep, richly harmonic texture that heretofore
had seemed possible only with a group of musicians, and it was
this texture that was as important as the complex harmonies
that produced it. When a jazz composer attempted to create such
a sound, he arranged for a big band or large group. An improvising soloist who, like Coltrane, was interested only in playing,
not in arranging (although he did compose tunes to blow on),
could only despair at the limitations of his medium. Coltrane
would later attempt to solve this problem with harmonics and,
shortly before his death, an electronic saxophone that could
create parallel lines an octave apart, creating the illusion of two
saxophones playing simultaneously.

Coltrane, from here on in, would attempt to bring new textures to the most basic form of jazz, the heartbeat of jazz, the
improvised solo. By the time he recorded the album *Black Pearls*
in late May 1958, his solos were virtually amelodic, consisting

of nothing but these massive "sheets of sound," arpeggios played so quickly that it is quite impossible to distinguish one note from another, resulting in the illusion of glissandos, shooting stars of sound plunging in the night sky. *Black Pearls* is so Byzantine in its harmonic intricacy that the music would sound utterly abstract if it weren't for Coltrane's blistering delivery. On a themeless blues, Coltrane connects streams of arpeggios with very brief blues phrases. Only those occasional phrases let the listener know that this is indeed a blues. Coltrane, whose playing was always steeped in the blues, has now moved beyond even this basic element of his music. His playing is still so impassioned that the hairs on one's neck rise; even if the listener is not sure exactly what Coltrane is doing musically, he can still *feel* it on a visceral level.

From this point on, Coltrane seemed to seesaw between playing fiercely adventurous, difficult music and stepping back in order to make that music, in his own term, "more presentable" and more palatable to a wider audience. Not that he ever "sold out"—his music was always challenging and personal—but there were times when he was caught up in an obsession and had to see it through, and other times when he was more concerned with how he was communicating to his audience. He once said, later in his career when he was in his "free" period, a time when many found his work unintelligible, if not hideously unpleasant, "Sometimes I wish I could walk up to my music as if for the first time, as if I had never heard it before. Being so inescapably a part of it, I'll never know what the listener gets, what the listener feels, and that's too bad."

With *Black Pearls,* and in some of the other work of this period, Coltrane had stretched his harmonic explorations about as far he could go. Despite Coltrane's passion, this is surprisingly austere music, and many listeners, critics, and fans just did not get it. Coltrane was so fascinated by the trees that he lost sight of the forest. He had broken down tunes to their molecular structure, but while admiring the musical atoms he had forgotten the purpose of that structure and the tune as a melodic and harmonic whole.

Coltrane was now a man even more totally devoted to music.

He would practice between playing sets at a club and then go home and practice some more. According to his friend the great saxophonist James Moody, when friends would visit, Coltrane would often point out the kitchen and the bathroom and then go back to practicing. There are other stories of those who witnessed him literally falling asleep at night with the horn still in his mouth. To some degree he was undoubtedly making up for lost time. Maybe he had some prescience about his early death. No doubt, in music he saw a path to the profoundest wisdom, and the only way to persevere down that path was through hard work. This almost pathological obsession also meant he sometimes didn't comprehend the effect of his music on its listeners, however. This basic problem of Coltrane's— growing too close to the music and losing awareness of its effect on his audience—would occur again, years later, with far more devastating results.

There were reasons for his obsessions, profound obsessions, other than musical one-upmanship. Coltrane frequently stated that his idol was Einstein, who, believing that "God doesn't throw the dice with the universe," spent the last several decades of his life trying to discover the universal force or principal that ultimately lay behind the motor of the universe. Similarly, Coltrane's goal was to discover the music that was most "essential" (in his term), pure sound without those extrinsic aspects that tie it to one time or culture; universal music, the song of God. With such a lofty goal, it should be no surprise that Coltrane's musical thinking got lost in the ether.

One person who spent a considerable amount of time at the Five Spot listening to the Monk quartet was Miles Davis. He was, needless to say, happy to see Coltrane clean and alert, and genuinely moved by the new surge of power in his playing. As Miles recalled, "Man, he was playing great, playing good with Monk. . . . Trane could fill up all that space with all of them chords and sounds he was playing then. I was proud of him." Miles understood, probably better than anyone else, what Coltrane was trying to do. "I . . . don't understand this talk of Coltrane being difficult," he told Nat Hentoff. "What he does, for example, is to play five notes of a chord and then keep changing it around, trying to see how many different ways it can sound. It's like explaining something five different ways. And that sound of his is connected with what he's doing with the chords at any given time." Miles, like Coltrane, thought of music in terms of pure sound.

That personal sound produced by great jazz musicians is a product of their musical *conception,* a term that in jazz is used to describe the whole of a musician's working methods, everything from the timbre of his horn to his harmonic approach. Any good jazz musician has developed, from hard work and hard thought, a personal conception. When he improvises successfully on the stand or in the recording studio, it is only after much thought, practice, and theory have gone into that conception, and it is that conception which makes him different from other jazz musicians. Once he knows what he is doing, in other words, he can let himself go and find areas of music through improvisation he didn't know existed. Jazz improvisation, therefore, is based on a paradox—that a musician comes to a bandstand so well prepared that he can fly free through instinct and soul and sheer musical bravery into the musical unknown. It is a marriage of both sides of the brain, so that this music has coherence as well as, in Whitney Balliet's well-worn but wonderful phrase, "the sound of surprise."

You cannot understand John Coltrane's music unless you comprehend that the ideas he worked out came from his knowledge, memory, and musical curiosity as well as from the spontaneity of improvisation. Coltrane practiced constantly, working out on his horn and on the piano ideas that he would turn into music when playing before an audience or if he was recording. Picture a jazz musician walking on the stand, knowing exactly what he is after musically, but having no idea what he will play until the notes come out of his instrument, and you can perceive the paradox that is at the heart of jazz. In addition, he will be interacting with the other members of his group, who will also be improvising, and they will force him to alter his musical conception in order to create an apposite group sound. Is jazz the music of the individual or that of the group consciousness? Once again, it is both, simultaneously.

Miles had replaced Coltrane with Sonny Rollins in his group and Philly Joe with Art Taylor, one of the best and most ubiquitous drummers of the Fifties. But he missed his old bandmates. Coltrane refused to leave Monk's group, however, at least until he had fulfilled all his commitments to the group's engagements. Without dope or booze, he was a real straight arrow. Miles eventually hired the heavyweight (in more ways than one) alto saxophonist Cannonball Adderley, but he was still not satisfied. Then in late 1957 Monk, a true eccentric, for some reason disbanded his greatest group, and in December Coltrane rejoined his former boss. Finally Miles could put together the band that he had been hearing in his head: the great rhythm section of Garland, Chambers, and Jones, and two saxophonists, Adderley and a rejuvenated John Coltrane.

Upon returning to Miles's fold, Coltrane was surprised to learn that the trumpeter had undergone his own musical transformation. "On returning [to Miles's group]," Coltrane said later, "I found Miles in the midst of another stage of musical development. There was one time in his past that he devoted to multichorded structures. He was interested in chords for their own sake. It now seemed that he was moving in the opposite direction to the use of fewer and fewer chord changes in songs. He used tunes with free-flowing lines and chordal direction. This approach allowed the soloist the choice of playing chordally [vertically] or melodically [horizontally].

"In fact, due to the direct and free-flowing lines in his music, I found it easy to apply the harmonic ideas that I had. I could stack up chords. . . . That way I could play three chords on one. But on the other hand, if I wanted to, I could play melodically. Miles's music gave me plenty of freedom."

Miles had always given his musicians plenty of leeway, but he sensed that jazz was coming to a crossroads, a new era of rapid change. Since Coltrane's style was developing with such rapidity at this point, it was crucial that he be given an opportunity to explore his music in whatever direction his muse pointed. As Coltrane said later about this period, "Miles's music gave me an opportunity to see both sides of the question. . . . I had mixed emotions about it. Sometimes I'd follow Miles's lead and 'play lyrically'; other times I'd say, 'That's the end of it' and play the other way." In other words, he was free to play with a new melodic freedom, or, in the same piece, continue harmonic explorations, the "sheets of sound" approach.

The only record the sextet made with the old quintet rhythm section is a true jazz classic, *Milestones*. Its making reflected the chaos the group was going through at the time, in April 1958. While the "front line" of the group, Miles, Trane, and Cannonball, were clean (Cannonball never was an addict), the rhythm section was made up of junkies. The ones with the worst habits were Philly Joe, no surprise, and Red Garland. Ironically, the far more lucrative financial deal Miles had with Columbia caused him great problems with the junkies in the group. When they recorded for Prestige, they were paid in cash the day of recording, so the junkies could score their dope. Columbia, while paying much more, paid by check, which usually took ten days or two weeks to arrive—an eternity for Jones and Garland, who were constantly desperate for cash.

Because of that problem and other dope-connected complications and irritants, the sextet was in disarray by the time it made its first record. Miles brought in another drummer, Jimmy Cobb, to play on some tracks and had no pianist other than himself on one cut. Nevertheless, the music is magnificent. The title track, Miles's own "Milestones" (or "Miles," the title it was later given so as not to confuse it with an earlier Miles composition), is Davis's first attempt at using modes rather than chords as the basis for a composition. Modes were nothing new in Western music—they were used as far back as Gregorian chant—and they had been used for centuries in African, Indian, and other non-Western musics. Nor were they totally unheard-of in jazz: George Russell had experimented with modes in "Cubana Be, Cubana Bop" as far back as the Forties. It was directly from Russell that Miles first got his notions about modes. Russell laid out his theory to Miles one evening in 1957, and Davis was immediately intrigued. "George," Miles told Russell that night, "if Bird were alive, this would kill him." That night would prove to have momentous implications for Coltrane, since it would result in opening a direction that would shape his most important work of the Sixties. And because of Coltrane's influence, modes would strongly affect most jazz musicians who came of age from the Sixties on.

As was so typical of Miles's genius, with "Milestones" he took Russell's theory and developed a logical, and on its surface uncomplicated, setup for improvisation: starkly simple scales on which each player based his solo. His own solo, a masterpiece itself, clearly shows that Miles was ready for the new technique. Even Cannonball jumps right in, playing with confidence and fire. It is, ironically, Coltrane who seems a bit uncertain. His solo has some wonderful moments, but it is clear that he does not feel altogether comfortable playing modally. That is understandable—he was still deeply involved in his labyrinthine explorations of chordal structures, his "sheets of sound," and modes demanded the opposite, a horizontal, melodic approach to improvisation.

No such hesitancy affects his playing on the rest of the record, however. On one particular cut, Monk's "Straight, No Chaser," his solo is so stuffed with ideas, both melodic and harmonic, that it sometimes seems to stagger under the weight. Here, unlike his solos with the old quintet, he has all the elements, technical, musical, and emotional, under control, and he delivers as great a tenor solo as had ever been heard up until that time. On the slow blues "Sid's Ahead" he plays with that raw power and fiercely gripping, raw-nerved emotion that, as with so much of his best work, has such a visceral effect on one's nervous system.

Milestones announced to the world what most jazz insiders already knew: that John Coltrane had emerged at the relatively late age (for jazz, that is) of thirty-two as the most exciting and original saxophonist since Sonny Rollins first made an impact. Not everyone agreed, though. Many critics continued to routinely attack Coltrane's style, as they would throughout his career, now because of its unrelentingly propulsive drive. When the Davis sextet played at Newport, a critic wrote: "The group did not perform effectively. Although Miles continues to play with delicacy and infinite grace, his group's solidarity is hampered by the angry tenor of Coltrane. Backing himself into rhythmic corners on flurries of notes, Coltrane sounded like the personification of motion-without-progress in jazz. What is equally important, Coltrane's playing apparently has influenced Adderley. The latter's playing indicated less concern for melodic structure than he has illustrated in the past . . . With the exception of Miles's vital contribution, then, the group proved more confusing to listeners than educational."

Coltrane's album *Black Pearls* was recorded about a month after *Milestones* and it gives us an indication of the effect that playing with Miles was having on him. Whereas on *Black Pearls* his playing is almost totally harmonically oriented, playing with Miles forced him to basically eschew the "sheets of sound" and play more melodically. But there always seemed to be more than one Coltrane. His playing at the studio during the day would often be stylistically months behind the music he felt free to play at a club the same night.

The phrase "angry tenor," which was routinely used to describe his work, would plague and puzzle Coltrane, the gentlest of men. By the mid-Sixties some critics went even further, calling his playing "hate music." One thing about the above review that was correct, however, was the influence Coltrane was having on Adderley, and vice versa. Miles would actively encourage the men to compete on a friendly level, using all kinds of techniques to fire up his men; for instance, whispering in the ear of one while the other was playing in order to stir up curiosity and maybe even some envy. The two saxophonists became very close, and certainly Adderley, who in his later career as a band leader was popular but not particularly musically ambitious or innovative (except for his early use of electric piano), never played better than he did when he was with this group. (Of course, some said the same about Coltrane.)

Both the new use of modes and the sly whispers were part of Miles's strategy to get the most out of his musicians. An amateur boxer, Miles viewed the creation of jazz as something akin to a prizefight. As Miles put it in his autobiography, "See, if you put a musician in a place where he has to do something different from what he does all the time, then he can do that—but he's got to think differently in order to do it. He has to use his imagination, be more creative, more innovative; he's got to take more risks. He's got to play above what he knows—far above it—and what that might lead to might take him above the place where he's been playing all along, to the new place where he finds himself right now—and to the next place he's going and even above that! So then he'll be freer, will expect things differently, will anticipate and know something different is coming down. I've always told the musicians in my band to play what they know and then play above that. Anything can happen then, and that's where great art and music happens."

It is mostly from Miles that Coltrane developed his insatiable musical curiosity and his drive to constantly innovate, for which he was both derided and admired. Some people have questioned the notion that constant innovation is as much a key part of the jazz tradition as, say, improvisation or the concept of swing. But unceasing innovation is a vital part of jazz for several reasons, not all of them strictly musical. Since its inception, jazz has been a statement by its principally black players of their lives and social situation in this country. It is descended from the coded field songs of the slaves, which acted as catharsis for their pain and indignity. When Louis Armstrong became the first great jazz soloist, his music spoke for all those blacks who, like Louis, had moved north with fresh hopes as well as new disappointment. Ellington, Billie Holiday, and Lester Young announced a changing, more prideful attitude among blacks of the Thirties. Likewise, the music of the great jazz musicians of the bop revolution, Charlie Parker, Dizzy Gillespie, and Bud Powell, spoke for the new militance of those young blacks who had fought in World War II and expected America to be a new country after defeating the forces of bigotry and fascism.

It is dangerous, of course, to draw too exact a parallel here. These men and women were all great artists, after all, and the content of their music certainly transcended their particular social situation, which is why it is so universally loved. It is easy to understand why jazz musicians would, every night they played, wish to make further progress, constantly looking toward the future and forever moving away from a painful and ugly past. Miles Davis once said to me, "The reason I've won all those awards is because I can't remember anything worth a damn."

By innovating, the jazz musician can redefine himself, as well as his music, in his own terms, rather than those of a society that holds him in so little regard. Constant improvising, saying something new every night, going beyond what one has played before to fresh ground, means that innovation is inevitable and essential if the music is to be healthy.

In *Jazz: A People's Music,* one of the best books ever written about the music, especially for its time, 1948, Sidney Finkelstein says this about innovation as a constant in jazz: "Jazz can be defined, but only in terms of a flexible, growing art which changes as the conditions under which it is performed change, and because thinking individuals arise who, responding to fresh needs, add something new to something old. The 'something new' is to be judged . . . by whether it is a genuine addition to the music, to its human content, technique and expressive breadth. When it is, the result is 'real jazz' precisely because it is different, and because experiment and change are the essence of jazz."

5 giant steps

After the chaos of the *Milestones* recording session, Miles made Jimmy Cobb the permanent replacement for Philly Joe Jones. Cobb, a much-underrated drummer, was not as innovative as his predecessor but was nevertheless a fiery and steady player. To replace Garland, Miles hired a twenty-nine-year-old pianist named Bill Evans. Before playing with Miles, Evans had played with the clarinetist Tony Scott and, more importantly, George Russell, who first introduced him to modal improvisation, undoubtedly one of the main reasons Miles hired him. (After Evans left the band, Miles told an interviewer, "I sure learned a lot from Bill Evans.") He had gradually developed perhaps the most lyrical piano style in all of jazz, and he would influence a whole generation of pianists—one of the very few white jazz musicians to be of such influence.

Like Coltrane's, Evans's mature style was just coming into focus when he joined Miles's group. Of course, Miles's style hadn't really coalesced until 1954, when he was twenty-eight, so like Evans and Coltrane, he was hardly a prodigy, although he did record and play in Charlie Parker's quintet while still a teenager. Evans saw great relevance in this and said later, in words that apply equally to Coltrane, "[Miles is] an example of somebody I think was a late arriver, even though he was recorded when he first came on the scene. You can hear how consciously he was soloing and how his knowledge was a very aware thing.

He just constantly kept working and contributing his own craft. . . . And then at one point it all came together and he emerged with maturity, and he became a total artist and influence, making a kind of beauty that had never been heard before or since. . . . I always like people who have developed long and hard, especially through introspection and a lot of dedication. I think what they arrive at is usually . . . deeper and more beautiful . . . than the person who seems to have that ability and fluidity from the beginning. . . . And, yes, ultimately it turned out that these people weren't able to carry their thing very far. I found myself being more attracted to artists who have developed through the years to become better and deeper musicians." In these latter remarks Evans might well have been thinking directly about the sextet (he once said about it, "I felt the group to be composed of superhumans"), because Adderley was an excellent example of a musician who from the start had "that ability and fluidity" but mainly repeated himself for the rest of his career, while Evans, Coltrane, and Davis continued to grow and innovate.

Actually, Evans had many qualities in common with Coltrane other than being, along with Ornette Coleman, the most influencial musicians of the Sixties. Too often they are portrayed as being polar opposites, Evans the gentle, introspective impressionist, Coltrane the overtly expressive raging terrorist of the saxophone. Both Coltrane and Evans, a Zen Buddhist, were supremely introspective men, dedicated to distilling the emotional and spiritual essence of music. Coltrane could play some of the most tender and subtly moving ballads ever heard, and Evans could, when he wanted, be a muscular, driving soloist.

Both men were attacked for the same reason: their unconventional rhythmic attack. I once heard a famous critic expound for minutes on end (years after Evans's death) about what a "punk" Bill Evans was because he couldn't swing like Red Garland or the man who replaced him in the sextet, Wynton Kelly. Of course, Evans had a different, very personal and original rhythmic drive to his playing, just as did Coltrane, who was also criticized for not swinging in the conventional way. Anyway, musicians knew better. Miles told an interviewer that Evans was one of those pianists who "when they play a chord, play a sound more than a chord." As for his rhythmic attack, Miles wrote in his autobiography, "Bill played underneath the rhythm and I liked that, the way he played scales with the band. Red's playing had carried the band, but Bill underplayed it and for what I was doing with the modal thing I liked what Bill was doing better. . . . The sound he got was like crystal notes or sparkling water cascading down some clear waterfall."

With this formation, the three horn men and the rhythm section of Evans, Chambers, and Cobb, the Davis sextet became the greatest small group of the Fifties and, for many listeners and critics, of all time. Like any great group, from Armstrong's Hot Five to the Beatles, the whole is greater than the sum of the parts. And what parts! The thing that gave the group such power was the different philosophical attitudes evinced by the four main soloists. Miles was the cool, world-weary existentialist, the Melancholy Dane of jazz. Cannonball was the joyous celebrant, a funky Dionysus. Bill Evans was the deeply introspective romantic, whose view on life was aesthetic and ultimately tragic. And Coltrane was the obsessed spiritual visionary, a man strenuously propelling himself toward some kind of apocalyptic end. As different as each man may seem, especially from the vantage point of their subsequent solo careers, together they formed a band of singular brilliance and produced at least one unchallengeable masterpiece.

Not everyone agreed on the merits of the Davis sextet, at least during its existence. In one review of a concert at New York's Town Hall, Whitney Balliett wrote, "Davis's group, which includes John Coltrane and Julian Adderley, followed, and, in the space of just three selections, unraveled steadily (Coltrane's grapeshot runs, Davis's attempts to squeeze into the upper register, Adderley's flooding ruminations) until . . . everything fell apart."

Coltrane, more than any other member of the group, continued to receive the lion's share of disapproval. The trumpeter Maynard Ferguson often played opposite Miles's group in clubs, and as he recalled, "In baseball, the more of a power hitter you are, the more often you miss, because you swing so hard. I worked opposite Miles Davis when he had Cannonball and Coltrane, who admired each other very much. But Cannonball had the better average in the baseball sense. Because Coltrane was the experimenter. Maybe he had a minimal cult then, a tiny number of people starting to really love his music. And some that would resist it and then suddenly hear something in it. And it was a great education for me not to make judgments on people in the first ten hearings. Whereas some people make judgments on their first hearing."

Coltrane did have a few supporters in the critical fraternity, however. Dom Ceruli, writing for *Down Beat,* recognized his importance and continuously wrote positive reviews of Coltrane's playing. In reviewing *Soultrane,* Ceruli wrote, "In this very, very good LP, John Coltrane gives a picture of himself which is true in several dimensions. This set, first of all, is one I consider representative of what Coltrane is doing today with the Miles Davis group. That I consider him one of the most exciting tenor-playing individuals in jazz today has no bearing on the rating, but I do use the word 'individuals' in its fullest connotations. Coltrane has been, and is here, playing in a highly personal manner. What he is doing has been described variously as sheets of sound or ribbons of sound or by some less interested ears, as a haphazard running of as many notes as possible. I find a logic in his playing. And although he does sometimes fail to get his flow underway, the times that it does happen are among the most tingling in modern jazz. What I do admire in him is that he is always going for something beyond him, and that he never falls back on easy or accepted ways of doing what he wants to do." Few critics at this time, even those who liked Coltrane, evinced such a deep understanding of his intentions, or that of most other musicians, for that matter.

But Ceruli's review was not enough for Coltrane. He felt he had to speak out in defense of his musical path, and he did just that in an interview with the critic who had been his earliest supporter, Ira Gitler. Asked by Gitler about the "angry tenor" moniker applied to his playing, Coltrane replied, "It is interpreted as angry. It is taken wrong. The only one I'm angry at is myself when I don't make what I'm trying to play." No one was more aware of the strengths and weaknesses of his music than Coltrane. For instance, as for the "sheets of sound," Gitler writes, "This approach, basic to Coltrane's playing today, is not the result of a conscious effort to produce something 'new.' He has noted that it has developed spontaneously. 'Now it is not a thing of beauty and the only way it would be justified is if it becomes that,' he said. "If I can't work it through, I will drop it. . . . I have more work to do on my tone and articulation. . . . I must study more general technique and smooth out some harmonic kinks. Sometimes while playing, I discover two ideas and I work on two simultaneously and lose the continuity.' " Here, at the end of 1958, Coltrane had a code for his life, which he outlined for Gitler: "Keep listening. Never become so self-important that you can't listen to other players. Live cleanly. . . . Do right. . . . You can improve as a player by improving as a person. It's a duty we owe to ourselves. . . . Music is the means of expression with strong emotional content. Jazz used to be happy and joyous. I'd like to play happy and joyous." There is no direct mention here of his religious revelation in 1957, but he is obviously a changed man, a radically changed man, from the irresponsible junkie and alcoholic he had been until that experience.

Coltrane continued to record frequently throughout 1958, under his own leadership as well as that of others. In September he participated in a big band session for Decca led by George Russell. The resulting album, *New York, New York,* was Russell's aural portrait of the Big Apple, consisting of both standard tunes and some Russell originals. The band was a stellar one, consisting of some of the finest modern jazz musicians on the scene, including Art Farmer, Phil Woods, Bob Brookmeyer, and Coltrane's bandmate Bill Evans. Russell specifically sought out Coltrane to play on the date, but Trane was able to play on only one tune, Richard Rogers's "Manhattan."

As Russell recalled the session decades later, "When we got to the part where Coltrane was to solo, things got hectic. Coltrane called a halt and went into a corner of the studio, where he stayed for close to an hour. One of the musicians grumbled to me, 'He's not so great. He can't even read the chord changes.'

It took me years to figure out what Coltrane was doing, but I finally did. He was reharmonizing the arrangement, working in his own substitutions for his solo. Now, I had already reharmonized the stock arrangement of the tune, so Coltrane was reharmonizing my reharmonization! It wasn't that he couldn't read the changes at all. I think he just felt confined by my chords in that solo. After about an hour, we had to make Coltrane stop what he was doing and go back to recording, because time in the studio with those high-paid players was just too expensive to let one musician hold things up for so long. He ended up mad at me. But I came to realize that he had a highly developed theoretical system, and he was just trying to work it into this arrangement for the purposes of his solo." Coltrane's solo was another one of those brilliant bursts of energy that seems so alive and new. Once again it makes the playing of these other star jazz musicians sound hopelessly out of date. One has to be amazed at Coltrane's dedication at this session, his working so hard at reharmonizing the piece, since most musicians approach a brief appearance like this as just another gig, something to be done and gotten through as painlessly as possible.

Certainly one of Trane's most provocative sessions, both in its own terms as well as in regard to the music he would be making several years hence, was a recording under the leadership of the iconoclastic pianist and composer Cecil Taylor. Taylor, a conservatory-trained musician, at the age of twenty-four had already begun to make waves for bringing jazz together with the tonal and atonal advances of such twentieth-century composers as Stravinsky, Bartók, and Schoenberg. If Monk's accompaniment could be spiky, Taylor's could be rough indeed, especially to jazz musicians unfamiliar with atonal composition. The trumpeter on the date, Kenny Dorham, virtually raised a mutiny, but Coltrane (playing under the pseudonym of "Blue Train" due to his contract with Prestige) was intrigued by Taylor's musical methods. Taylor specifically asked for Coltrane, who, he said at the time, was his favorite saxophonist. About him Taylor said, "He has great insight, a feeling for the hysteria of the times and a conception that goes beyond that of his own horn."

The record was an attempt to bring Taylor into the musical mainstream by pairing him with such well-known musicians and using a conventional modern rhythm section. Like Miles, Taylor was trying to simplify the harmonic framework for improvisation, using only a very few chords (although Miles despised Taylor's playing). Listening to these elements trying to blend is like eating lumpy gravy, especially when Dorham solos while obviously trying to ignore Taylor's comping. Coltrane, however, is fascinating. Although he was still deeply involved in his "sheets of sound," his playing here is his most melodic since early 1957. Clearly, all these musical experiences, even a recording session that lasted one chaotic afternoon, were more fuel for his creative fire.

At the end of 1958 Coltrane finally left Prestige and signed a two-year deal with Atlantic Records, agreeing to an advance of seven thousand dollars a year for the length of the contract; seven thousand dollars may seem minuscule now, but at the time any advance for a jazz musician was considered extraordinarily generous, particularly after being exploited by a "junkie's label" like Prestige, which was often called "the Plantation" by musicians.

Fantasy Records, which owns the Prestige catalog, has released Coltrane's complete Prestige recordings on a sixteen-CD set (with the exception of his work with Miles, which is available on Fantasy's *Complete Prestige Miles* set). Originally, Coltrane's recordings were released over a period of years, with many of his records assembled from different sessions from various periods. As we have seen, Coltrane's evolution was so extraordinary that even a period of a few weeks often brought about sharp changes in his music. Therefore, hearing that evolution during the two-year period covered by the set is reminiscent of time-lapse photography where, say, the growth and flowering of a plant, an event which may take weeks, seems to occur in a matter of minutes right before one's eyes. Listening to all this music, one session after the other, concentrated on these CDs, Coltrane's development from talented journeyman bopster to jazz master blossoms right before the awed listener. Especially amazing is the evolution of his harmonic sense, from early fumbler over difficult chord changes to probably the greatest harmonist in all of jazz.

After signing Coltrane, Nesuhi Ertegun, the president of Atlantic Records, immediately brought him into the studio to co-lead a session with one of Atlantic's biggest jazz stars, Milt Jackson. Without doubt, this was an attempt to make Coltrane palatable to a wider audience, since Jackson's bluesy style, albeit quite subtle, was accessible to even the most unsophisticated listener. For Trane and Jackson the session was something of a reunion, since they had both been part of Dizzy Gillespie's group in the early Fifties. It was with that group that Coltrane had recorded his first solo, and the growth of his playing since then could only be measured in light years. That is especially true for the most exciting track, a version of Dizzy's classic tune "Be-Bop." Coltrane's solo is a disquisition on the rhythmic and harmonic approaches of bop, early modern jazz, and the further advances he was now making. Here the arpeggios are more like Coleman Hawkins, containing more melodic material than the "sheets of sound" at their most extreme. But on the visceral level this roiling solo is just plain thrilling; the ears ride it like an aural roller coaster. For a number of reasons—playing in the sextet, Miles's increasingly melodic musical philosophy, the new company, the new year, perhaps simply discouragement with the "sheets of sound" approach, and just because his muse was always going forward—Coltrane's music was obviously going through some major changes.

Meanwhile, there was also a change in the Davis sextet. Bill Evans had quit the group, apparently from exhaustion, but also because of the hostility he encountered from some black members of the jazz community who resented a white man's holding the most prestigious piano chair in all of modern jazz. None of this hostility came from the members of the group (except facetiously—Miles had a notoriously warped sense of humor). This was a time of growing black awareness, which in jazz occasionally manifested itself in what was called at the time "Crow Jim": the freezing out of white musicians. Even such giants as Miles and Charles Mingus, who vociferously attacked white racism while hiring the best white musicians, were often attacked by lesser musicians. This sort of thing particularly infuriated Miles, who said once, "I remember when I hired [the white saxophonist] Lee Konitz, some colored cats bitched a lot about me hiring an ofay in my band when Negroes didn't have work. I said if a cat could play like Lee, I would hire him. I didn't give a damn if he was green and had red breath." But to a deeply sensitive man like Bill Evans, the muttering and carping hurt. These issues wouldn't disappear, but were to become more intense. Coltrane would eventually find himself at the center of them.

Evans was replaced with Wynton Kelly, a wonderfully swinging, blues-oriented pianist who was one of the best accompanists in jazz. This rhythm section became extraordinarily tight, really giving the soloist a lift. Coltrane must have enjoyed it, because his solos became longer and longer, sometimes lasting as long as twenty minutes or so. When Miles asked him why, Coltrane replied, "In order to get it all in." Indeed, his ideas, now as much melodic as harmonic, never seemed to run out, but to become actually more inventive as his solo drove on. In probably the most famous story about the length of Coltrane's solos of the time, Miles asked Wynton Kelly to inquire of Coltrane why he played so long. Coltrane replied, "I don't know how to stop." When Miles heard this, he said, "Tell him to take the horn out of his mouth." Another night, while Coltrane was soloing a drumstick accidentally slid out of Jimmy Cobb's sweaty hand and flew right past Trane's head, narrowly missing. When the set was over, Coltrane laughingly said to Cobb, "You almost got me that time." Actually, Cobb didn't mind playing behind Coltrane at all. "He knew that I loved his playing," recalls Cobb.

That is an example of Coltrane's sly, soft-spoken sense of humor, although humor is rarely heard in his music (unlike the other tenor titan of the time, Sonny Rollins, the Vladimir Nabokov of jazz). But Coltrane's gentle, almost doelike personality got him out of at least one major scrape. As Jimmy Cobb remembers it, the sextet was playing a club in Philadelphia, and during an intermission a vice cop routed the drummer and Coltrane into the men's room, telling them, "Don't make a scene, I'm a narcotics officer." Claiming that a woman told him that the musicians were on drugs, he had the two men remove their shirts. There was no problem with Jimmy since he had never been involved with drugs of any sort. But Coltrane, although clean at the time, still had visible tracks on both arms. When the cop asked, "What are those marks?" Coltrane looked shy and sheepish and said, "Those are birthmarks. I've had them as long as I can remember." He looked so "boyishly innocent that the narcotics cop believed him and he ended up letting both of us go."

Miles Davis continued to explore his freer approach to improvisation. When he and the arranger and composer Gil Evans recorded their magnificent version of *Porgy and Bess,* Miles had Evans create passages that were based on as little as one chord. In an interview with Nat Hentoff, Miles explained in detail his new ideas: "I think a movement in jazz is beginning away from the conventional string of chords, and a return to emphasis on melodic rather than harmonic variation. There will be fewer chords but infinite possibilities as to what to do with them. Classical composers—some of them—have been writing this way for years, but jazz musicians seldom have. . . . I've been listening to Khachaturian carefully for six months now and the thing that intrigues me are all those different scales he uses. Bill Evans knows too what can be done with scales. All chords, after all, are relative to a scale and a line. . . . The music has gotten thick. Guys give me tunes and they're full of chords. I can't play them." This statement is Miles's expression of his revolt against many of the tendencies that had grown in jazz since the advent of bop. Modern jazz musicians were caught, at least in Miles's view, in a labyrinth of chords, stifling melodic invention. (Incidentally, years later Miles told me that he introduced Coltrane to the music of Khachaturian and that the Armenian composer was tremendously influential on the music Trane would make in the Sixties.)

The culmination of Miles's new theories were two recording sessions of the Davis sextet in March and April 1959. The resulting album was *Kind of Blue,* one of the few records for which one can fearlessly claim that overused term "masterpiece." The group that created this magnificent work was the sextet with both Evans and Wynton Kelly. Evans had left the band months before, but Miles believed that Bill had a deeper understanding of modal forms than Kelly, who played on only one tune, the blues "Freddie Freeloader" (named after a rather obnoxious character on the jazz scene). Besides playing piano, Evans also collaborated with Miles on one piece, the lovely, crystalline "Blue in Green." As Bill Evans writes in his superb liner notes, "Miles conceived these settings only hours before the recording dates and arrived with sketches which indicated to the group what was to be played. Therefore you will hear something close to pure spontaneity in these performances. The group had never played these pieces prior to the recordings and I think without exception the first complete performance of each was a 'take.' . . . Although it is not uncommon for a jazz musician to be expected to improvise on new material at a recording session, the character of these pieces represents a particular challenge."

These sessions are superb examples of Miles making his musicians "play above what they know." Except for "Milestones," on the album of the same name, the band members (with the exception of Bill Evans, who had played with George Russell) had never improvised on modal settings before. The pieces on *Kind of Blue* have a deceptive simplicity. For instance, as Evans describes it in his notes, the first piece, "So What" (a favorite expression of Miles's), "is a simple figure based on 16 measures of one scale, 8 of another and 8 more of the first." But such a piece calls for an approach entirely different from that of the chordal tunes jazz musicians had routinely been playing until this time. The improvisor must rely totally on his melodic abilities, for there are no chord changes to follow.

The formality of these haunting pieces (none is faster than medium tempo) alone makes this session historic. But you do not have to know anything about modes or scales to respond to the music on *Kind of Blue*. The music, particularly the solos of Miles and Coltrane, is so powerful, so ripely beautiful, that the heart understands it immediately even if the mind doesn't. If *Kind of Blue* has a dark melancholy sound overall, it is because Miles was trying to capture a particular feeling. As he put it in his *Autobiography,* "I added some other kind of sound I remembered from being back in Arkansas, when we were walking home from church and they were playing these bad gospels . . . That feeling is what I was trying to get close to . . . that feeling I had when I was six years old, walking with my cousin along that dark Arkansas road." Miles succeeded beyond his greatest expectations, for the feeling conveyed by *Kind of Blue* has indelibly affected countless listeners, even those who could not care less about the difference betwen a mode and a chord. I first heard *Kind of Blue* as a teenager, and more than any other record it gave me a lifelong fascination with jazz. I have listened to it at least a thousand times since, and every single time it engulfs me in its indigo moods.

Miles's solos on *Kind of Blue* are some of the greatest jazz trumpet statements since Louis Armstrong's work of the Twenties and early Thirties. But it is Coltrane whose playing is the most powerful, producing the greatest solos of his career until that time. Completely gone is the hesitation that affected his playing on "Milestones"—especially surprising, considering that he did not even see these new modal pieces of Miles's until the day of recording. The pieces on *Kind of Blue* virtually forced him to play melodically, and not to be hung up on his harmonic obsessions. George Russell had explained to Coltrane that with "modes you don't have to think about all those chords. With modes you have a far broader based tonical association and you can play any chords you want." Coltrane's solos on every tune sound as if he had been playing these pieces for months. There is a parallel here between the problems Coltrane seemed to have with some harmonically complex tunes in the first records he made with Miles, and the ultimate harmonic master he became in his "sheets of sound" period. Remember how Miles prevented him from playing on ballads during the quintet period? Coltrane's solos on the two slow pieces here, "Flamenco Sketches" and "Blue in Green," are among the great lyric statements in jazz. Particularly striking is the latter solo; only a few bars long, it is a perfect improvised statement, as profound and complete and touchingly fragile in its brevity as haiku. On "All Blues," a model tune in $\frac{6}{8}$ time played over a hypnotic pedal point, his

solo is so intense, so bursting at the seams with ideas and vehemence, that one can't help being reminded of a black Baptist
preacher crying out his love of God and fear of hell.

Coltrane's sound is complete here, utterly original. His melodic ideas are unlike anything ever heard in jazz or anything
else, steeped in blues tradition but also with a patina of Arabic
and East Indian flavors. The John Coltrane of 1959, both as
musician and man, had gone through a sea change; through
hard work and deep introspection he had discovered who he
really was.

Shortly after the *Kind of Blue* session in 1959, Coltrane made
his first record for Atlantic under his sole leadership. That record,
Giant Steps, is almost on a par with *Kind of Blue.* In *Giant
Steps,* a quartet session, Coltrane seems to be summing up all
the work he had been doing in his mastery of harmony and the
"sheets of sound," as well as indicating the new directions he
was moving in. All the compositions are his. He had rarely
recorded his own compositions when he was with Prestige, and
Miles never played them, so it was rather a surprise to the jazz
community to hear an entire album of superb Coltrane pieces.
The title tune has such difficult chord changes that ever since
the record's release it has been used by musicians as a kind of
ultimate harmonic challenge, an etude for aspiring improvisors.
Coltrane soars over the changes, hurtling like a rafter in white
water. Instead of a string of arpeggios, however, his solo has a
melodic thrust and continuity as well as great harmonic complexity, almost like bebop brought to its logical conclusion. On
"Cousin Mary," one of Coltrane's favorite forms, a minor blues,
he plays with the power and force that was heard in "All Blues"
and "Freddie Freeloader." While other tunes also have complex
chord changes, some tunes show a new direction for Coltrane,
a direction formed out of the influence of Miles's latest ideas.
Tunes such as "Syeeda's Flute Song," harmonically simple, encourage melodic thinking rather than harmonic, improvising.
Another tune in this category is "Naima," a gorgeous ballad
named for Coltrane's wife. This would become probably Coltrane's most famous composition, and one he would continue

to play until his death, although some of the later versions would have quite a different mood from this rapturous one. Coltrane actually recorded the entire album with a different rhythm section (except for the stalwart Paul Chambers, who plays on both sessions) a few days before the final session. He was so dissatisfied that he brought in a different rhythm section and re-recorded each tune, working unceasingly on each one until he was certain it was as near perfect as was possible. The two versions of "Naima" offer an excellent example of Coltrane's creative thinking. In the first version he improvises on the beautiful melody, but on the final version (actually recorded at still another recording session a few months later), he elegantly states the theme and only the pianist, Wynton Kelly, improvises a solo; Coltrane plays the theme again and ends the piece with a lovely rising coda. The sound of his horn conveyed so much feeling that he didn't have to improvise to make a valid emotional and artistic statement, and he was now a mature enough artist to realize that. He was also beginning to comprehend the value, at times, of pure simplicity.

Giant Steps is, in a sense, a manifesto. Modern jazz had hit a dead end, the music becoming too often formulaic and cliché-ridden. But with the title tune, the bop technique of playing melodically over complex harmonic structures, which had been the basis for most of modern jazz since the mid-Forties, was taken to its final extreme. In the freer pieces, like "Syeeda's Flute Song" and "Naima," as in his work on *Kind of Blue,* one can almost hear Coltrane's spoken voice: "This is the end of one era and the beginning of another. It is time to move forward." At the time when *Giant Steps* was released, jazz was a brotherhood that clearly understood the signals and portents of its leaders, just as the counterculture of the late Sixties would study the lyrics of the Beatles or Dylan to try to decipher the future of its movement. But the jazz subculture didn't need words. Coltrane's music spoke loud and clear.

Coltrane's stature could no longer be ignored, and a number of critics began to take him very seriously. One of the best pieces ever written about him was published in 1959 in the toney *Jazz*

Review by conservatory-trained Zita Carno, a young pianist/ composer who had successfully performed with Leonard Bernstein and the New York Philarmonic. "Coltrane's style is multi-faceted," she wrote. "There are many things to watch for in his playing, and the fact that he is constantly experimenting, always working out something new—on and off the stand—leads to the conclusion that no matter how well you may think you know what he's doing, he will always surprise you. . . . His command of the instrument is unbelievable. Tempos don't faze him in the least; his control enables him to handle a very slow ballad without having to resort to the double-timing so common among hard blowers, and for him there is no such thing as too fast a tempo. His playing is very clean and he almost never misses a note. . . . His range is something to marvel at: a full three octaves upward from the lowest note attainable on the horn. . . . What sets Coltrane apart from the rest of them is the equality of strength in all registers which he has been able to attain through long, hard practice. That tone of his . . . is an incredibly powerful, resonant and sharply penetrating sound with a spine-chilling quality. Those listeners who say he plays out of tune have been deceived by that sharp edge in his sound. . . . Coltrane seems to have the power to pull listeners right out of their chairs. I have noticed his terrific impact on rhythm sections he has played with; he pulls them along with him and makes them cook, too. . . . Coltrane's harmonic conception is perhaps the most puzzling aspect of his style, inasmuch as it is so advanced. For one thing, he really knows what to do with the changes of the tunes he plays. . . . He's very subtle, often deceptive—but he's always right there. . . . Coltrane's sense of form is another source of wonderment. He has few equals at building up a solo, especially on a blues—and building on a blues is not easy."

Certainly Coltrane could not hope for anything more in terms of a true understanding of both his achievements and goals. Not every critic was so sympathetic, however; far from it. Probably the most famous jazz critic, Leonard Feather, in the course of writing notes for the classic *Ben Webster and Associates*, went out of his way to eviscerate Coltrane. Although he does not name him, it was obvious to anyone who was to any degree knowledgeable about jazz whom he was referring to: "After listening to this album I made a mental note to send a copy, as soon as it is released, to a young tenor player whom I heard at Birdland the other evening. He was making up to 32 notes per measure with a stove pipe tone, absolutely no relationship to the harmonic structure of the pieces on which he blew and a complete rejection of emotion coupled with an evident desire to implant out-and-out ugliness as the mood of the moment. He is an idol of many jazz fans and has been praised by supposedly reputable critics. If he were willing to learn, he could gain more out of a study of eight measures of Ben, or Bean [Coleman Hawkins], or Budd [Johnson] than I gained from eight minutes of listening to *his* tortured mind at work."

As the Fifties ended and the Sixties began, Feather's opinion, though shared by a number of critics and jazz fans, was increasingly a minority viewpoint. The Sixties, the most traumatic and vibrant decade in our "American Century," would be remembered, with both joy and tears, for many things. But in jazz, the Sixties was the Decade of Coltrane.

6 equinox

Writing objectively about the Sixties is virtually impossible, particularly if you, like me, were part of the Baby Boom that came to maturity in that decade. It was a decade that defied you *not* to participate in it. John Coltrane was as inextricably a part of that decade as any of the other major cultural manifestations, including the Beatles, Dylan, Warhol, McLuhan, Malcolm X, and the Haight-Ashbury. Coltrane reflected in so many ways the contradictions of those times: its feeling of constant apocalypse and the seeking of inner peace, the riots as well as the love-ins, the great creativity and the equally great self-indulgence.

The decade began with a feeling of hopefulness. A young man with fresh ideas, declaring this an era of a "New Frontier," was elected and replaced the gray administration that dominated the Fifties. Martin Luther King, Jr., seemed to be making real breakthroughs, perhaps even beginning a true healing of the racial cancer that ate away at the heart of America. We were heading toward outer space, perhaps the greatest adventure of the century. It was a thrilling time to be alive, a perfect time for an innovative musician, especially one such as John Coltrane, who viewed music from a global perspective, to make his move.

Coltrane was feeling pressure, from both internal and external forces, to leave Miles Davis's group, form his own group, and set his latest ideas into motion. He could no longer contain his restlessness. As much as he continued to admire the trumpeter who had meant so much to his career and musical thinking, he simply had to leave Miles and forge his own way.

Undoubtedly Coltrane's restlessness had something to do with the shocking and exciting new currents in the jazz world. The chief progenitor of these currents was the Texan alto saxophonist Ornette Coleman, whose several-month gig at the Five Spot, where Monk and Trane had previously shaken jazz, was creating the biggest shock waves since the days of bop. Ornette had taken jazz freedom a step further than even the advances Miles had made with *Kind of Blue*. His improvisations seemed to be based on an indeterminate key with apparently no harmonic framework of any sort. Coleman believed in "playing the music and not the structure"—in other words, unfettered melodic improvising. Although his music confused and alienated many, he was almost immediately hailed as a new jazz messiah, even by such cultural icons as Leonard Bernstein, who ostentatiously hugged Coleman after one of his performances at the Five Spot.

Coleman immediately polarized the jazz community. Suddenly, those players who thought of themselves at the cutting edge by continuing to play the same old bop clichés were looked on as the new "moldy figs"—the term used in the Forties for those in the jazz community resistant to modern jazz. Coleman, if anything, exacerbated those divisions by giving his albums names like *Change of Century, Tomorrow Is the Question,* and *The Shape of Jazz to Come*. Some musicians, like the always prescient John Lewis, praised Coleman, while others, like the great trumpeter Roy Eldridge, who, although his style came to fruition in the Thirties, had come to admire bop, nevertheless had no use for Coleman's music. After jamming with Coleman's group, Eldridge told acquaintances, "Ain't nothing happening, baby." In his eyes, this music was a clear case of brand-new clothes for the emperor. Even the eternal iconoclast Charles Mingus, after first welcoming Coleman to the jazz community, turned against the saxophonist after playing with him. More than a few were fascinated with Coleman's music, however. As "far out" as it was, it also seemed at times like the most natural, even primitive, music imaginable.

One thing is certain: Coleman, the musicians in his band, and the young musicians influenced by him were all true musical and existential tightrope walkers, making one of the great gambles in the music of our time. This was the beginning of the Free Jazz movement. As John Litweiler points out in his book on post-Fifties jazz, *The Freedom Principle,* Free Jazz and Freedom, with the uppercases, was a specific movement fathered by Coleman, Cecil Taylor, and Coltrane. Although Ornette is often compared to the serialist composers, his music came from a very different direction and had, at least at first, no underlying theoretical principle such as the tone row. Coleman was a pure improviser (although he later proved to be a distinguished composer of pieces for string quartet and even symphony orchestra), and his ideas came strictly as an evolution of the jazz tradition. In essence, his music asked the question, Why can't we improvise the tonal logic of our music as a servant of our melodic and rhythmic imagination?

More than ever, the jazz improviser had to look within for the creation of his music rather than to structures imposed from without. And whether or not he deliberately intended to do so, his music moved jazz further away from European tradition and closer to its own essence. That "essence," or something close to it, was the object of John Coltrane's quest.

Coleman needed the blessings of the important jazz musicians on the scene, for something about him was different from the other major jazz innovators: in a music of alienation, he was an outsider. He had never worked his way up in the jazz community by playing and learning in the bands of recognized important jazzmen. Rather, he had "paid his dues" by mainly playing in R & B bands in his native Texas. Without having proven his ability to master the older forms, his innovations were met by some with distrust. But more than a few were thrilled and intrigued by Coleman's fresh musical thinking. Among those listening hard were Sonny Rollins, Jackie McLean, the MJQ's John Lewis, and, of course, John Coltrane.

About the time Coltrane was recording *Kind of Blue* with Miles's sextet, he was becoming increasingly restless. Although he loved Miles's music (at one time he said that he loved Davis's trumpet playing so much that he often thought of trying to imitate his boss's style), he began to feel that it was time he led his own group. At times when the Davis sextet was idle, he frequently played in a group, with Donald Byrd on trumpet and Art Taylor on drums, that he co-led with Red Garland. But that wasn't enough. In June 1959, when the sextet played the Blackhawk club in San Francisco, Coltrane told a reporter that he was thinking strongly of leaving Miles and forming his own group: "There's nothing definite yet, but I have been seriously thinking of it." Despite his occasional musical forays with his own groups, he inevitably returned to Miles, but not without some reluctance. At the end of that August the group played a gig opposite Maynard Ferguson's band. Wayne Shorter, who had become Coltrane's friend in Philadelphia and with whom he had often practiced (to the extent that early in his career Shorter was often wrongly described as a Coltrane imitator), was then playing in Ferguson's band, and he spent much time with his friend between sets. One night, in a rare outburst of pique, Coltrane said to him, "You want to be with Miles? You got it. I'm finished doing the Miles gig." Putting up with the vicissitudes of the ever-mercurial Davis was perhaps finally getting to him. Miles apparently refused to play any of his tenor saxophonist's compositions, and Coltrane by this point was probably tired of playing the same old tunes in the Davis songbook.

Furthermore, Coltrane was being pushed on all sides to form his own group, now that he was winning polls and reaping positive, at times glowing reviews and critiques even from some of those prominent critics, such as Nat Hentoff and Ralph J. Gleason, who had formerly written little good about him. In addition, and perhaps most importantly, he was intrigued by the new ideas floating around in jazz, particularly those of Ornette Coleman. While Miles did say admiringly that at least Coleman wasn't playing the clichés that had become so prevalent in modern jazz, he himself was not about to play music as free as Ornette's. Coltrane wasn't sure if he was ready either at this point, but he definitely wanted the opportunity to explore these radical new concepts. It was clearly time to move on.

The main thing keeping Coltrane from making the move was his own fear of the managerial hassles he would inevitably face in leading his own band. With Miles or Monk, all he had to concentrate on was his own playing, not hiring sidemen or getting booked or any of the details involved in being boss. Another reason was Miles himself. Miles used all his considerable powers of persuasion to hold on to Coltrane, the man whom he considered, as he told me two decades later, "the greatest saxophonist who ever lived." Coltrane finally worked out an agreement with Miles to stay with the sextet for a 1960 tour of Europe and, upon returning, to quit and form his own group.

Around this time Coltrane made a discovery that would be monumental to his career, both musically and in terms of his popularity as a performer. The soprano saxophone had virtually never been played in jazz since Johnny Hodges recorded with it in the Thirties and Forties. Before that, Sidney Bechet, a great influence on Hodges, had been the great master of the horn, which he played in addition to clarinet. Bechet got an unbelievably powerful sound out of the little instrument, overwhelming even the brass instruments in the New Orleans ensembles in which he usually played. The only musician to play it with any sort of regularity since was Steve Lacy, who had begun playing in Dixieland bands and had soon advanced musically so far that he became a member of Cecil Taylor's ultra avant-gardist group in the Fifties.

There are at least three divergent stories about how Coltrane discovered the soprano: According to one story Coltrane told a writer, a fellow musician accidentally left his soprano in the trunk of Coltrane's car returning from some gig. Coltrane started fooling around with the horn and found he could do things that he had been hearing in his head but was unable to play on tenor. Still another story, as told in J. C. Thomas's biography, is that Coltrane was discussing music with some other musicians and that Sidney Bechet's name happened to come up frequently in the conversation. The next morning, after hearing Bechet's sound in his mind all night, Coltrane drove straight to the Selmer saxophone factory in Elkhart, Indiana, and chose a soprano. Then again, according to Miles, the trumpeter bought Coltrane the soprano as a gift, believing that it would "revolutionize" Coltrane's tenor playing. If that was so, to a degree he was right.

Coltrane would later say that playing the soprano changed the way he played the tenor. In his autobiography, Miles writes that he would often say to Coltrane that the saxophonist was "in debt to me for as long as he lived. Man, he used to laugh until he cried about that, and then I would say, 'Trane, I'm serious.' And he'd hug me real hard and just keep saying, 'Miles, you're right about that.' But this was later, when he had his own group and they was killing everybody with their shit."

Taking up the soprano saxophone was much more difficult than it may seem to a nonplayer. Unlike the alto or even the baritone saxophone, technical prowess on the tenor could not be immediately transferred to the smaller horn. For one thing, it demanded a different embouchure (the method of holding the mouthpiece with the lips), one more like the clarinet than like the other saxophones. Just making this adjustment required many hours of practice. Also like the clarinet, the soprano was difficult to keep in tune. Despite these obstacles, the soprano opened up new vistas of improvisation and musical worlds for Coltrane to conquer.

In an interview years after he had mastered the soprano, Coltrane was asked, "Do you think that learning to play the soprano changed your style?" He answered, "Definitely, definitely . . . the soprano, by being this small instrument, I found that playing the lowest note on it was like playing one of the middle notes on the tenor—so therefore, after I got so that my embouchure would allow me to make the upper notes, I found that I would play *all over* this instrument, playing certain ideas which just went in certain ranges, octaves. But by playing on the soprano and becoming accustomed to playing on tenor from that low B-flat on up, it soon got so that when I went to tenor, I found myself doing the same thing. It caused the change or willingness to change and just try to play as much of the instrument as possible."

When asked if playing the soprano changed his rhythmic conception also, Coltrane replied, "I think so. . . . A new shape came out of the thing and patterns—the way the patterns—would fall . . . the patterns were one of the things I started getting dissatisfied on the tenor mouthpiece, because the sound of the soprano was actually so much closer to me in my ear. There's something about the presence of that sound, that to me—I didn't want to admit it—but to me it would seem like it was better than the tenor—I liked it more. I didn't want to admit this damn thing, because I said the tenor's my horn, it's my favorite. But this soprano, maybe it's just the fact that it's a higher instrument, it started pulling my conception." And how did he feel now? "Well, the tenor is the power horn, definitely; but soprano, there's something there in just the voice of it that's really beautiful, something that I really like. . . . now, it's another voice, another sound." Especially fascinating in these remarks is the degree to which such physical aspects of music making as an instrument's embouchure and the closeness of its bell to the player's ear could have such a profound impact on Coltrane's music.

Within a few years almost every tenor player would double on soprano in emulation of Coltrane. As many critics have pointed out, Coltrane's soprano work often seemed more conservative than his tenor playing. But his development of this new "voice" brought a new dimension to his art, added substantially to his popularity, and, owing to the unique sonority of the soprano, gave him the chance to explore the sound and feeling of Arabic and Indian music, which so fascinated him. Still, the search for that essence of musical and metaphysical truth, the quest for which was the core of his life, was pursued primarily on his tenor saxophone.

However he first discovered the instrument, Coltrane was mesmerized by the soprano, and during the long hours of traveling during the European tour he did little else but play endless scales on the little horn. Although he grumbled the whole time about wanting to go out on his own, his restlessness had no effect on his performance during the European trek. Cannonball was no longer with the group, having gone out with his own quintet featuring his brother Nat, and his absence gave Coltrane even more space to solo as his improvisations grew even longer. Although there are no official recordings of Miles's group on this tour, several bootleg recordings were made, some (though certainly not all) with superb sound quality. The bootlegs reveal that Coltrane's playing was now at a peak; in later years he would sometimes equal the strength and quality of his improvising here, but he would never surpass it. He was still using, now to brilliant effect, some of the harmonic devices he had discovered during the "sheets of sound" period. But his harmonic, vertical approach was perfectly melded with his melodic attack. Now he seemed to be able to explore every nook and cranny of both chord and melody; listening to him solo on "So What" or a blues like "Walkin'," one could expect to hear everything and anything—truly the "sound of surprise"—and be uplifted through the sheer joy of creation.

At moments Coltrane could be too close to his music and, as he himself had said, lack objectivity. For instance, one of the things he was working on was multiphonics—trying to play two or more notes on his horn at one time. In some of his solos he tries for minutes at a time to create multiphonics, fascinating to a student of the instrument but to others an example of "practicing on the stand," an epithet often hurled at him, usually unfairly but here all too true. One can also detect, at times, the tension brewing between Coltrane and Miles. Coltrane didn't want to go on this tour in the first place, and Miles was making it difficult for him to do what he knew Coltrane had to do, form his own group. Coltrane was a gentle man who found it hard to express his anger overtly. But at some points during a few of the concerts, particularly when he was soloing on "So What" or Miles's favorite blues at the time, "Walkin'," his playing is so adventurous that it borders on the outrageous. On a couple of versions of "Walkin' " that were covertly recorded, he stretches the boundaries so much that Miles interrupts his solo with the closing riff, obviously shutting Coltrane down before he went even further. Miles had always been an experimenter, but he would let the limits of his art be pushed only so far and no further. Coltrane knew this, and it is not reading too far to interpret some of his playing on the tour as a petition for his freedom, both professional and musical.

However, his playing at this time was nothing less than magnificent—searingly lyrical, with a new type of melodicism redolent simultaneously of both Arabic and African music and the "deep blues" of the Mississippi Delta. Yet his music continued to puzzle, if not outrage, many listeners. When the Davis group played certain venues in Europe, Coltrane's solos were often booed. Among the nastier comments of some of the European critics were: "They [Miles and Coltrane] made fools of us, and now they are probably sitting there behind laughing." "How new can an emperor's clothes be?" "It was something of a performance Coltrane gave us, playing chorus after chorus without swinging even one single note." In Stockholm, right before a concert that was broadcast (and very well recorded), Coltrane agreed to a radio interview. The first question his interrogator asked was, "Your playing has been called untenorlike, unbeautiful, un-just about everything you could think of. How do you respond to that?" Coltrane, obviously taken aback, does not and cannot answer such a question directly, but he does say, "Some of the critics seem to think it's an angry thing—some of them." When the interviewer asked Coltrane if he was angry, the answer was immediate, "No."

The group returned to the States, and at a gig in Philadelphia Miles did something shockingly out of character: he made a short speech to the audience. He announced, with obvious sadness, that this would be the last time Coltrane would be playing with his group. And except for one recording session, it was the last time these two geniuses would play together.

In some ways, Miles never recovered from losing Coltrane. For the next few years his musical direction seemed aimless. He replaced Coltrane with Hank Mobley, but he found no inspiration in Mobley's playing. He didn't pursue very far the ideas set forth in *Kind of Blue,* and even his own playing seemed to lose its pungency. Only in the mid-Sixties, when he formed his great quintet with Herbie Hancock, Wayne Shorter, Ron Carter, and Tony Williams, a group of young players unconnected to Miles's past, did the trumpeter find his way and again begin making truly thrilling and trailblazing music. But he never did completely forget the magnificence of his former saxophonist. Years after Coltrane's death, when Miles was leading a dense electric jazz-rock band, someone mentioned that he needed four or five saxophonists to fit into such music. With a sad look, Miles muttered, "I once had four or five saxophonists." And in Miles's coded tongue, it was clear whom he was talking about.

When Coltrane decided to form his own group, the only thing he knew for certain was that it would be a quartet. His solos were growing longer and longer and there was no need for another frontline soloist. After listening to Miles's talk of retirement, Coltrane's initial thought was to use Miles's rhythm section, or some of the other players he had been recording with, such as Art Taylor, Red Garland, or the bassist George Joyner. Things didn't work out with those musicians for a number of reasons: Miles really had no intention of retiring, and playing with him was still the most dependable and high-paying job in modern jazz; Art Taylor was getting ready to move to Europe; and Coltrane probably did not want to put up with the problems that Miles had had with a junkie like Red Garland. Coltrane decided on a fellow Philadelphian with whom he had occasionally played, Steve Davis, as his bassist. The first pianist was Steve Kuhn, who demonstrated with great enthusiasm his knowledge and love of the saxophonist's work: of all the pianists auditioned Steve was the only one to know all the changes of Coltrane's compositions. Stylistically, Kuhn was influenced by Bill Evans, perhaps not the best choice to accompany Coltrane: Evans tended to retard the beat when he comped. But Kuhn was (and is) a brilliant pianist, and he obviously loved Coltrane's music, so lacking anyone more fit, he was chosen.

Steve Kuhn was the only white musician Coltrane ever hired. Kuhn later recalled the unorthodox method Coltrane used to hire his musicians: "[When] I heard that Coltrane was leaving Miles Davis and looking for a band I called him up, saying that I didn't know if he knew who I was, but could we get together and just play a bit. I knew it sounded funny and that it wasn't the usual way of doing things, and I said so. He said he'd let me know. He called me back—I suppose he must have been asking around about me in the meantime—and said we'd rent a studio and play some. We played for about two or three hours.

Then we went out and had dinner. He was kind of quiet about things, as he always was about everything. We drove back to his house on Long Island and played some more, about four or five hours this time. Afterward, he and his wife drove me back to Manhattan, and when they left me off he said he'd call. Two days later he did call. He simply named a salary and asked if it would be all right. We opened at the Jazz Gallery."

Coltrane's first choice for drummer was Elvin Jones, of the musical Jones family, the other brothers being Thad, the magnificent trumpeter, and Hank, one of the most ubiquitous pianists in jazz. Because Elvin, whose lifestyle at the time was erratic, was serving time in Rikers Island for a drug bust, Coltrane took his second choice, Pete La Roca, a very underrated drummer who was working on polyrhythmic ideas parallel to, but quite different from, Elvin's.

In the spring of 1960 Coltrane opened with his new quartet at a downtown club called the Jazz Gallery, owned by the same men who ran the Five Spot. Like their other club, they booked major jazz musicians for several weeks at a time, rather than just a few days or a week like most other clubs. Coltrane was initially given an eight-week gig. He used the time to put his new group into shape, turning the engagement into a combination gig and workshop.

His opening was a great success, with many of the jazz elite attending what was later recognized as a milestone event. After a few weeks, Coltrane grew dissatisfied. The band was far from the group sound he was hearing in his head. He had to make changes, something this shy and gentle man was loath to do. In C. O. Simpkins's book, Coltrane's close friend Cal Massey tells him to get rid of Steve Kuhn for racial reasons, telling Coltrane, "Shit wasn't right . . . as soon as you get rid of that white boy on piano the group will improve." According to others close to the band, however, including Kuhn himself, that was not part of Coltrane's reasoning at all. Obviously, if Trane had been a racist, as some would like him to have been, he never would have hired Kuhn in the first place. This was a time of great racial tension in jazz, when the subject of "Crow Jim," reverse discrimination in jazz, was a regular topic of the magazines and among those in the jazz scene. Coltrane's racial conjecture would become increasingly a matter of discussion and conjecture as the decade advanced, so it is important to note how he handled having a white player in this early edition of his quartet. According to Kuhn, "As for my work with [Coltrane], I figured, I could do *anything*. But with the freedom I was allowed, I ran too much of the spectrum, and the result wasn't really together. Finally he gave me notice, saying that he had to and couldn't really tell me why. To tell you the truth, I was just about to give *him* notice, because I knew it wasn't working musically. . . . I was getting bored with my playing, so I was ready to quit anyway. I simply hadn't found myself stylistically, I was not supporting him, really. In a sense, I was competing."

Coltrane fired Kuhn in the gentlest of manners, a characteristic mode he would continue to employ when making either a professional or personal change in his life. He put his arm around Kuhn and said, "Steve, I think I'm going to have to give you notice." When Kuhn asked why, Coltrane replied, "I can't tell you how to play. There's something I want to hear that you're not doing." Coltrane was merely doing what everyone, including Kuhn, clearly knew had to be done for the good of the group. He obviously respected and continued to respect Kuhn. According to the pianist, "I would see Coltrane afterwards, of course. I remember once I ran into him on the street, and he said to me quite seriously, 'Steve, show me something new.' Imagine! Me show *him* something new. He never stopped searching. His total dedication never let up."

Coltrane replaced Kuhn with a young Philadelphian who had been playing with the Art Farmer-Benny Golson Jazztet, twenty-one-year-old McCoy Tyner. Coltrane had met Tyner five years previously, and even then was impressed with the pianist. Tyner and his wife were both Muslims, but not Black Muslims, and Coltrane was impressed with his devotion. The two spent time over the years discussing music and religion. In 1958 Coltrane recorded one of Tyner's compositions, "The Believer," for Prestige. Tyner's playing at first was very much in the mold of the predominant modern style, whose primary influence was Bud Powell. That is, the left hand would play sparse chords while the right played hornlike melodic lines. Playing in the Coltrane quartet, accompanied by the thunderous drums of Elvin Jones, Tyner became much more a genuine "two-handed" pianist, playing dense chords with both hands, for no other reason than simply to be heard. Tyner, whose playing obviously reflected the influence of Coltrane's particular lyricism, would eventually emerge as one of the two or three most important pianists of the past thirty years.

Tyner almost immediately fit in, his strong comping giving Coltrane the lift that he wanted. Since many jazz musicians in the "free" era avoided using the piano so as not to be tied to a harmonic framework, Tyner would eventually develop a method of comping that gave Coltrane a great deal of freedom rather than tying him tightly to a specific chord. With Tyner, Coltrane could play with a pianist and still be able to explore the musical unknown.

Although he was immediately happy with Tyner's playing, Coltrane did not feel ready yet to record his new band, since some parts and sounds still did not fit quite right.

Coltrane was torn about the music of Ornette Coleman, and he divulged his dilemma to George Russell, with whom he had a cordial and mutually respectful relationship. "I love what Ornette is doing," he told Russell. "But I'm afraid that if I go that way I'll lose my audience." Trane was aware of the exigencies of the music business, and now that he was a leader of his own group he was wary of challenging his audience too much. Having grown close to Ornette Coleman and his quartet, Coltrane decided to make an album of Ornette's music, although not with his own group. The resulting album, unblinkingly titled *The Avant-Garde,* contained three of Coleman's compositions, one by his trumpeter, Don Cherry (who played on the date), and a Monk tune, "Bemsha Swing." Besides Cherry and Coltrane, this pianoless group consisted of Ornette's drummer, Ed Blackwell, and either Charlie Haden or Percy Heath on bass. The album does not have a great reputation, for Coltrane does not really sound comfortable essentially taking the place of Coleman. On a tune like "Cherryco," which is supposed to be played completely free, Coltrane bases his solo on harmonic changes, thus negating the point of Ornette's innovations. The rhythm section work is subtle and throbbing, not the driving force Coltrane was used to and seemed to need.

Despite his good intentions, Coltrane was not yet ready for free jazz. Coltrane's playing may not be "free" in the Ornettian sense, but it is some of his most expressive, emotionally open, at times churning, yet lyrical music he had put on record to this point. The album includes Coltrane's first recorded solo on soprano saxophone, "The Blessing." Considering that he had been playing it for less than a year, the solo is remarkable for his control and already highly developed musical conception on the difficult little horn. Ornette's particular methods, compositions, sidemen, and so on, were clearly too far from Coltrane's particular conception, but his gusto in playing in this atmosphere is a strong clue to the musical places he was going.

7 the quartet

At least as important as the right pianist in a jazz group is the right drummer. Coltrane grew dissatisfied with La Roca, whose subtle playing lacked the sheer power he had grown used to from Philly Joe Jones or Jimmy Cobb. La Roca, who tended to play just a touch behind the beat, Coltrane thought, was the perfect drummer for a lyrical trumpeter like Art Farmer, with whom he had played for a number of years, but not for the driving, pushing rhythms of Coltrane. With Elvin Jones still in jail, Coltrane brought in Billy Higgins, who had played with Ornette Coleman, among others. The band in this formation actually recorded— not for Atlantic, for some reason, but for the rather sleazy Roulette label, rumored to be run by mobsters. The band recorded only three tunes, not nearly enough for an album. One can only glean so much from these numbers, but one thing is clear: in Billy Higgins, Coltrane had still not found a suitable drummer. That is not to cast aspersions on Higgins. If there could possibly be something called a lyrical drummer, Higgins was it. He was able to play with everything from Ornette's free jazz to Lee Morgan's funky semi-boogaloo "The Sidewinder." He clearly gave Coltrane adequate support, but as Miles used to put it, for Coltrane he lacked *"that thing,"* that indefinable something that excited the mind and made the blood run faster. Without *"that thing,"* jazz lacked the edgy atmosphere conducive to fresh musical ideas and innovation.

While touring the West, Coltrane learned that Elvin Jones was finally out of jail. Promptly, Coltrane let Higgins go, in his gentle way, and flew Elvin out to the group's next gig, in Denver. The very first night they played together, it was obvious to all observers that Elvin was the guy with *"that thing"* and then some. His explosive, polyrhythmic style was a perfect match for Coltrane's ferociously fiery solos. According to the bassist Steve Davis, "That first night Elvin was in the band, he was playing so strong and so loud you could hear him outside and down the block. Trane wanted it that way. He wanted a drummer who could really kick, and Elvin was one of the strongest, wildest drummers in the world. After the gig, Trane put his arm around Elvin, took him to a barbecue place around the corner, and bought him some ribs. Trane and Elvin were tight from then on." Saying that Elvin was a "wild" drummer misrepresents him. Like Coltrane, he was a great innovator who had developed his style through hard work and deep musical thought. It was through one of those great moments of serendipity that keep on recurring throughout the history of jazz that Coltrane hired Elvin just as the key aspects of his innovative drum style were coalescing, for Elvin's playing, more than that of anyone other than Coltrane himself, made this group so important.

When Elvin joined Coltrane, he was really known as the younger brother of Thad and Hank. His career, like that of so many jazz musicians, had been hobbled by drug addiction, and except for a few records, he was little known except to the cognescenti. Born the youngest of ten children in Detroit in 1927, Elvin Ray Jones could not avoid music in his large family. Detroit in the late Forties and Fifties, at the time Jones was maturing, was a fertile ground for jazz. Besides Elvin's brothers, the guitarist Kenny Burrell, the baritone saxophonist Pepper Adams, the tenor man Billy Mitchell, the vibraharpist Milt Jackson, and the pianist Tommy Flanagan were all important modern jazz musicians who came to musical maturity in the Motor City at around the same time.

After a stint in the army Elvin moved to New York, like all those others, to be close to the heart of his music. He played, as did every other jazz musician finding his way, in all sorts of musical settings, everything from backing third-rate Sophie Tucker imitators to an adventurously experimental quartet led by Charles Mingus. During all these gigs, Elvin, a brilliant and articulate man, was developing his own unique ideas on playing the drums: "I figured that a lot of things drummers were doing with two hands could be done with one—like accents with just the left hand on the snare, so you wouldn't have to take your right hand off the ride cymbal. It didn't seem to me that the four-four beat on the bass drum was necessary. What was needed was a *flow* of rhythm all over the set. I never learned any tricks, anything flashy—like juggling sticks or throwing them in the air. That kind of thing stops me inside. After all, Artur Rubinstein doesn't play runs on piano with his chin."

Unlike Coltrane, we can view the development of Elvin's innovative style only in glimpses, since he recorded sporadically from the time he first became a professional musician in 1949 until he joined Coltrane's group in 1960. Unfortunately, he never had the opportunity to play in a group like Miles's, where in a secure environment he could explore his ideas night after night. Before 1960 he was perhaps most famous for being one of the drummers on Sonny Rollins's classic *A Night at the Village Vanguard* album. Even in the mid-Fifties, however, it was already obvious from even one of those Prestige jam sessions (*Olio*, recorded in 1956) that his style was unique.

Jazz drumming had become somewhat formulaic by then, with almost every drummer playing a slight variation on the founding fathers of modern jazz drumming, Kenny Clarke and Max Roach. Those two great drummers had taken aspects of two of the greatest drummers of the Swing Era, Jo Jones and Big Sid Catlett, and simultaneously refined them and made them more complex. For instance, Clarke and Roach used the bass drum not to keep time—a steady pulse on the cymbals and high hat were used for that—but only for powerful accents, in the bop era called "bombs." By playing more complicated rhythms on the snare and tom-toms, they complemented the rhythmic complexities of Charlie Parker, Dizzy Gillespie, and the other great bop players. But since the Forties there had been few innovations.

While Art Blakey and a little later Philly Joe Jones did, through their vigorous, brash styles, push the drums into more dominating positions in the jazz group, their styles again were basically variations on the bop drumming of the Forties.

Listening to Elvin's early records, it is clear that, like Coltrane, he began as a talented bopper, but gave little indication of his future importance. It was when he decided to use the whole drum set as accompaniment, rather than just cymbals, snare, and bass drum, that he began to make discoveries. The primary discovery was that he could play remarkably rich polyrhythms, not dissimilar to West African drum corps, on a standard drum set, and thus create an incredibly rich rhythmic environment for a soloist with the skills to exploit it. He absolutely knew what he was doing and was totally in control of his "wild" and complicated rhythms. No one, including Coltrane when he first hired him, realized the extent to which Elvin would develop his style.

The pieces of Coltrane's group now seemed to be in place. After a few seasoning months of playing together on the road, Coltrane brought his new quartet into the Atlantic recording studios in October 1960. In shades of Miles's marathon Prestige sessions in 1956, within a few days Coltrane had recorded more than enough material to fill three albums. Perhaps the most remarkable aspect of the music recorded in those initial sessions is its accessibility. It is among Coltrane's most melodic work, at times joyously lyrical, and even the darker and harder-driving tunes have an open, inviting quality.

The first taste Coltrane's public got of his new group was one selection on the *Coltrane Jazz* album, a lovely straightahead blues entitled "Village Blues." The rest of the album, recorded in 1959 with Coltrane accompanied by the Miles rhythm section, Wynton Kelly, Jimmy Cobb, and Paul Chambers, was perhaps Coltrane's version of a typical Sonny Rollins album, containing obscure and offbeat pop songs ("Little Old Lady," "My Shining Hour") and even a Coltrane tune based on a typical Rollins phrase called "Like Sonny." [The most intriguing track on the album is a blues called "Harmonique," in which Coltrane demonstrates a technique he had been working to perfect, the creation of harmonics, blowing more than one note at one time. It is a startling effect, but in this context it is not much more than that and is regarded as something of a gimmick. But Coltrane would continue to develop harmonics and, within a few years, discover ways of using this technique beyond that of just effect, at times with devastating results.

The new quartet's first full album, *My Favorite Things*, was something of a sensation to the jazz world. Since the *Avant Garde* session had not yet been released, the title tune was the first time Coltrane's soprano saxophone was heard on record. No one could have asked for more unlikely material than this saccharine tune from Rodgers and Hammerstein's *The Sound of Music* for a supposedly hip jazz musician like Coltrane to play. Yet images of Julie Andrews and those lovable nuns and kids vanished moments into Coltrane's version. While retaining its waltz time, Coltrane played the tune using a pinched, almost nasal tonality, making it sound Arabic or even like an Indian raga. This Middle Eastern atmosphere was enhanced by McCoy Turner's hypnotic repeated piano vamp, the repetitious bass line, and Elvin's complex rhythmic figures, acting as sort of a tabla to Coltrane's sitarlike soprano. Since the tune is based on two alternating scales, it was perfect for modal improvisation. Coltrane first soloed on one scale, then reprised the tune, and then soloed on the second scale. But the technical aspects of Coltrane's performance were irrelevant to the general public, which reacted immediately to the bracing joy of Coltrane's solos. Too often this quality of joy, the pure joy of creation that is central to Coltrane's best work, is overlooked, especially in light of some of his later music. Coltrane's music might have lacked the wonderful humor of Monk or his friend Sonny Rollins, but he more than made up for it in his almost Mozartean celebration of life.

The most fascinating of the three albums culled from these sessions is *Coltrane Plays the Blues*. It is not known if Coltrane intended to make what is now known as a "concept" album, but listening to these six tracks is like a journey through the blues, from the most primitive to the "world beat" blues. The slow first track, "Blues to Elvin," the most basic, "deep" blues of the set, might well be a meditation on the earliest country blues (and brings to mind the comment of one critic that Coltrane's blues playing made his tenor saxophone sound like "an old country blues guitar"). Yet there is nothing atavistic in Coltrane's playing; as deeply funky as it is, it is still searching new music, as personally Coltranesque as anything he ever recorded, simultaneously old, thoroughly modern, and perfectly beautiful. It is a terrific track to play for anyone who says he doesn't "get" Coltrane. If he doesn't get "Blues to Elvin," he is either deaf or dead.

The second track is "Blues to Bechet," and, no surprise, it is played on soprano. Coltrane never tries to blatantly imitate Bechet—for one thing, his sound is narrow and serpentine, especially in comparison to the enormous, overpowering sound with its river-wide vibrato that Bechet was able to coax from this little horn. In the early part of his solo (played without piano accompaniment) he plays simple, basic, beautiful blues figures that recall in their feeling the early master. As the solo develops, Coltrane's ideas become increasingly complex, almost as if he were charting for the listener the direct link between such early players as Bechet and avant-garde players such as himself. The next track, "Blues to You," takes the basic blues even further. Playing at a fast tempo, Coltrane takes the idea of the blues to the outermost limits, at least the limits up until that time, vocalizing phrases, taking the saxophone, and human emotions, to their extremes and never looking back. Once again Tyner lays out, and the interplay between Coltrane and Elvin is more like a duet than a solo with accompaniment.

A year later, Coltrane would record a similar but even more adventurous variation of the blues that would become a seminal moment in jazz. At any gig where he was given the freedom, Coltrane would play a fast minor blues, eventually accompanied by, or to be more precise, intertwined with, only Elvin's polyrhythms. In his final sets, when only the faithful were left to persevere through a solo that could last anywhere from twenty minutes to two hours, Coltrane would always find something to say in the blues.

Two of the last three tracks on the *Plays the Blues* album are even more fascinating for what they say about the future of music. In "Mr. Day" and "Mr. Knight," blues played against exotic rhythmic backgrounds, Coltrane seems to be deliberately melding the blues with African and Middle Eastern rhythm and feeling. Both tunes use pedal points to create a hypnotic atmosphere, and Elvin shows his mastery of all sorts of rhythmic complexities; in "Mr. Day" the rhythm alternates between a fast $\frac{6}{8}$ and $\frac{4}{4}$. Not only does Elvin handle the alternations expertly, but on top of those rhythms he plays increasingly complex polyrhythms. Coltrane's playing in particular is ecstatic, as if finding some connection between different forms of music is a cause for celebration. Coltrane was obviously already listening to all kinds of music, but make no mistake, "Mr. Day" is jazz, great jazz. As he said around this time, although he was listening to music from all over the world, he always returned to the jazz tradition for his ultimate inspiration. Like a few other musicians, such as Yusef Lateef and Randy Weston and Ornette, Coltrane was fascinated by the possibilities of mixing Eastern, African, West Indian, and Spanish elements with traditional jazz elements, thus giving birth to what in the Seventies came to be called "world music." On *Coltrane Plays the Blues* the saxophonist had clearly made the heady discovery that the blues had some vital connection with music from exotic places all over the world, all of which had been created through a similar need of the heart.

The third complete album culled from these sessions, *Coltrane's Sound*, is perhaps the weakest of the three. It has its fascinating moments, though, and one such moment is Coltrane's version of that old classic "Body and Soul." Ever since the classic versions of this chestnut by Coleman Hawkins and Chu Berry were released in the Thirties, it has been looked upon as something of a standard for tenor players. Playing "Body and Soul" meant, in a way, that Coltrane was officially part of the pantheon of great tenor men. His version here is taken at a much swifter tempo than usual, and Coltrane makes the tune as uniquely personal a vehicle as Hawkins or Berry or any of the other great tenor men had before him, even considering Sonny

Rollins's superb unaccompanied version. Coltrane does what every great jazz musician can do with a tune no matter how familiar or shopworn: he makes it into a uniquely personal statement and lets us hear it anew, as if for the first time. The other tune of great interest is a gorgeous Coltrane composition called "Equinox," whose title reflects Trane's fascination with astrology. Again, over a repeated vamp based on the simplest of harmonic constructs, Coltrane plays a searching, heartbreakingly beautiful solo, simultaneously meditative and passionate.

The most amazing thing about these sessions is how much the group had coalesced in such a short time. Coltrane obviously had different aesthetic aims from Miles in putting together his group. McCoy Tyner's playing, rather than providing a buoyant contrast, as did that of Red Garland, is as forceful as that of Coltrane and, like Elvin's polyrhythms, heightens the density. Coltrane put his group together in pursuit of specific musical ends, rather than to display contrasts of light and shadow. He was clearly on a musical quest by this time, and on this quest he needed like-minded company.

Coltrane was less aware, or certainly less concerned, about the effect of his group on his audience than was Miles. The contrast of styles in Miles's great groups provided variety, a changing texture more immediately entertaining than the relentless thickness and density of Coltrane's music—which would grow even thicker when he added more musicians to the group.

There is another aspect of these initial recordings of the quartet which may on the face seem subjective, but I feel is obvious to anyone listening to these records. A hopeful feeling, a genuine optimism, runs throughout the initial quartet albums, even in the deepest blues, and most obviously in the classic version of "My Favorite Things." Coltrane was in a bright mood. Not only was he finally on his own, but in Elvin and McCoy he had found the perfect musical companions. He had also discovered a new road, one based on modes or simplified harmonic structures and on unlimited melodic development. For years he had eschewed his enormous melodic gifts, especially during the height of the "sheets of sound" period, and now he had rediscovered melody, unhampered by complex harmonic structure. It is almost as if a great fastball pitcher had, in midcareer, decided to forgo the hard stuff and become strictly a knuckleball pitcher.

Moreover, Coltrane was reflecting the times, for the early Sixties were a time of relative hope and optimism. There was a feeling of genuine progress in America, particularly in relation to America's disgraceful history of overt racism. Young politicians such as John Kennedy, who was elected only a couple of weeks after these sessions, were bringing a sense of rejuvenation into society after the gray Eisenhower years. New winds were already beginning to blow throughout the culture, and these records definitely reflect that mood. But this was also visionary music ahead of its time, and had eternal qualities that would make its vision of hope be felt for years to come. That is the essence of great jazz and great art: to be simultaneously of and beyond its times.

Coltrane's playing in these sessions is different, far more conservative than what he was doing in live performances, as the "bootleg" albums of his European tour with Miles, the same year as these sessions, reveal. On the face of it, this may seem surprising, since with his own group he could presumably play whatever he wanted. But Coltrane's records—and this would become increasingly obvious now that he had his own group— were statements intended to put into cogent and coherent form the ideas he had been relentlessly exploring in the laboratory of live performance. His best records reveal that, contrary to the complaints of many critics, Coltrane could be a master of form, even from a conservative point of view.

Was Coltrane in essence, as some critics charged, "practicing on the bandstand"? Coltrane responded to this charge a few years later: "They are right. But they should remember that I have been playing for almost 25 years. I have always practiced in public. But then, that's the wrong word. If you are playing jazz, you have to play what comes out at any moment—something you have never said before. So the word should not be 'practice' but 'improvise.' "

As straightforward as that answer might seem, there are different levels of freedom for improvisation. Coltrane was still improvising on these records, of course, but he exerted tighter control over his own self-editing. He was certainly well aware of how far he could take his music; he told a writer, "I want to progress, but I don't want to go so far out that I can't see what others are doing." That comment would eventually seem ironic, to say the least. The question of self-indulgence looms large over much of Coltrane's career, even among some of his stoutest supporters.

In the late Seventies Miles Davis, then in his "retirement" mode, was discussing the idea of an autobiography. "I couldn't do it," he said, "because I would have to put into it that [a major show business celebrity] is a flaming faggot."

"You don't have to write about him," someone replied, "how about somebody you respected, like Charlie Parker?"

"Charlie Parker was a greedy motherfucker. One night a lady brought us this corn bread backstage at the Three Deuces. He ate the whole damned thing and gave me one thin slice."

"Well, then how about Coltrane. He was a nice guy, right?"

With exactly the same inflection as he used with Bird, Miles said, "Coltrane was a greedy motherfucker. One time he had a big bottle of heroin and he took it all except for one little bit for me." Since Miles's memory is so faulty, and since the stories were mirror images of each other, and taking into consideration the mischievous look on his face as he told them, one would be well advised not to take either story literally. But then Miles got serious. "You see," he said, "when you're a genius on the level of Bird or Coltrane, you've got to be greedy. You just need more when your mind is working on that high a level."

I am not sure about Coltrane's "greed," but if one substitutes "self-indulgence" for "greed," then Miles's story may have relevance, especially to the later years of Coltrane's life. But there was no such self-indulgence in the first recordings of the quartet.

A few months before the quartet's initial recordings, Coltrane collaborated with the jazz writer Don DeMichael for an extraordinary "self-portrait" called "Coltrane on Coltrane," published in *Down Beat*. The good feeling that one hears in the music is borne out in Coltrane's own words. "The quartet is coming along nicely," he wrote. "We know basically what we're trying for and we leave room for individual development. Individual contributions are put in night after night.

"I want to broaden my outlook in order to come out with a fuller means of expression. I want to be more flexible where rhythm is concerned. I have to study rhythm some more. I haven't experimented too much with time; most of my experimenting has been in a harmonic form . . .

"But I've got to keep experimenting. I feel that I'm just beginning. I have part of what I'm looking for in my grasp but not all.

"I'm very happy devoting all my time to music and I'm glad to be one of the many who are striving for fuller development as musicians. Considering the great heritage in music that we have, the work of giants of the past, the present and the promise of those who are to come, I feel that we have every reason to face the future optimistically."

One of the most important elements in a supporting group for Coltrane, especially for the drummer, was the group's ability to accompany him in his increasingly longer solos. Coltrane's solos were now lasting as long as half an hour or even longer.

Coltrane was not the first jazz musician to take long solos. Far from it. Lengthy improvised solos were played in the early days of jazz, or at least since the Twenties and the first developed solos. Louis Armstrong himself could be heard playing ten- or fifteen-minute solos on a good night (and usually after he had smoked some marijuana). The place where long solos were heard most often was in the after-hours jam sessions, when musicians would join battle by playing the longest and most inventive solos. Of course, the general public had little idea what such solos sounded like, since musicians only rarely improvised at such length on the bandstand and records were only three or so minutes long. Perhaps the best-known long solo before Coltrane's was that of Paul Gonsalves with the Duke Ellington Band at Newport in 1956 linking the two parts of "Diminuendo and Crescendo in Blue." Gonsalves's twenty-seven choruses galvanized the crowd and created a near riot when fans began to dance in the aisles. The wonderful thing about his performance is that, unlike so many legendary jazz performances, it was recorded.

The difference between a solo like that of Gonsalves and those of Coltrane was that Gonsalves's was keyed to choruses and the harmonic structure of a tune. When he finished one chorus, he went back to the beginning and played another improvisation parallel to the tune and its chord changes. Most of Coltrane's long solos in the Sixties were modal, based on a simple scale or a couple of chords. He had to build his own structures on these stark outlines. When he was less inventive his solos sounded like a simple seesawing between two chords, but when he was inspired he built up long, hypnotic cycles rather than choruses. Using cycles rather than choruses gave him at once greater freedom and a greater burden in building structure into the vast architecture of these long solos, in which the cycles became more complex as time went by.

The other difference between Coltrane and, say, Gonsalves's Newport blowout was that Trane *consistently* played very lengthy solos, establishing the right for a jazz musician to develop his ideas on a larger canvas. The very idea that a jazz musician as a regular practice could improvise a solo as long as one of Mozart's or Beethoven's symphonies brought to jazz a new challenge. Unfortunately, most jazz musicians were simply unable to sustain a solo longer than a few choruses, and when they tried to emulate Coltrane, which in his wake too many did, the result was more often than not boredom and impatience for their listeners.

Despite his initial happiness with his group, Coltrane felt that something was lacking. He let Steve Davis go and hired as his bassist Reggie Workman, who had been playing with Roy Haynes's group. In addition, Coltrane felt that perhaps another instrument was needed. He loved the sound of Wes Montgomery, who at the time was just beginning to get national recognition, and asked the guitarist to sit in with the quartet when they played a club in San Francisco. Montgomery was an inventive though not experimental musician, and although he enjoyed the heady atmosphere of the Coltrane group, he decided it was not the place for him.

Perhaps another reason for his discomfort was the increasingly long wait he had to endure if his solo followed Coltrane's. In Elvin Jones Coltrane had found a drummer who could play not only with the polyrhythmic intensity he needed but also with the endurance he now required. Although he would oblige those fans who came to hear him play his "hit," "My Favorite Things," his solo on that piece alone could last twenty minutes or longer. Elvin's drumming increased in power, volume, and complexity as Coltrane stretched out in his solos, which now were stretching well past the twenty-minute mark. The drums and saxophone intertwined, building and burning to such a degree that most pieces became essentially duets between Coltrane and Elvin, even when McCoy and Workman were still playing. (Elvin mostly drowned out the piano and bass, anyway.) Even Coltrane was sometimes overwhelmed by his drummer. When someone asked him about the powerful effect of Elvin's drums, he replied, laughing, "Sometimes he's too much for me."

Coltrane made one final glimpse backward toward the past, toward the golden years with Miles Davis. Still cordial, Miles had helped Coltrane by arranging for the quartet to be managed by Miles's own lawyer and agent, Harold Lovette. In March 1961, in gratitude to the trumpeter, as well simply to reunite with his former comrades, Coltrane played on two tunes for Miles's *Someday My Prince Will Come* album. As Jimmy Cobb remembers it, the group, which then had the same rhythm section as when Coltrane had last been with Miles (Wynton Kelly, Paul Chambers, and Cobb), with Hank Mobley now in place in the tenor chair, was having problems working out the chord changes of the title tune. At least Mobley was having difficulties, even after a long, agonizing rehearsal. (One can only imagine Miles's state, since he hated any rehearsal.) Finally, when they seemed to have matters in hand, they began recording.

As Cobb recalls: "The red light was on in the studio, and we were right in the middle of the tune when Trane showed up. While we were playing, he put together his horn while Miles showed him the changes for the tune on a piece of paper. Coltrane put his horn in hand and he blew that solo that you heard [on the record], that incredible solo. To this day, I don't know how he was able to immediately play in exactly the right key, right in tune with the rest of the band, and handle the changes, which baffled Hank, never having seen the sheet music for the song before."

That is why Coltrane is called a genius. The solo is extraordinary. In some way it is a throwback to the "sheets of sound" period, being made up of coiling, arching arpeggios linked with achingly lovely melodic phrases. If Coltrane felt that the "sheets of sound" technique was not a thing of beauty in the past, here he definitely made of it something beautiful. In this brief musical miracle the feeling is so light and buoyant that the notes seem to spread wings and fly. Coltrane had once told an interviewer, "Jazz used to be happy and joyous. I'd like to play happy and joyous." Later on he would find that the deeper he dug, the less possible it was for him to play *only* joyous music. But here, on once again unlikely material, he created something as ecstatically life-affirming as anything in jazz.

Yet a poignancy also underlies the joy: Coltrane's melancholy at knowing that these techniques were now a part of his past. That melancholy extended beyond the "sheets of sound" to all of Western harmony and his fascination and deep involvement with its intricacies. Throughout his career Coltrane would look back at various stages of his musical development and wonder if perhaps one or another was where he should have stayed. Such nostalgia never lasted very long, however. He continued to forge ahead. He deeply believed that he had no other choice.

8 world music

In 1961, with only one more album due on his Atlantic contract, Coltrane was signed to a new jazz label. The new label, Impulse, was an offshoot of ABC-Paramount, and it was to be run by Bob Thiele, who had been producing jazz records since the Forties. Wanting Impulse to be in the forefront of jazz recording, Thiele chose Coltrane to give the new label credibility and add credence to its motto, "The New Wave of Jazz is on Impulse." Coltrane was given a fifty-thousand-dollar advance, spread over a five-year period—an excellent advance at that time for a jazz musician.

Coltrane decided that his first album for the new label had to be something more than just another quartet date. He turned to a musician who had become one of his closest friends, the reed man Eric Dolphy. Coltrane had first met Dolphy years before, when Coltrane had been touring with Johnny Hodges and was left stranded in Dolphy's hometown, Los Angeles. Coltrane was in bad shape at the time, strung out on dope. Dolphy, then a stranger, came to his aid, lending him money and helping him get back east.

Such actions were typical of Dolphy, who had played in several groups on the West Coast and was well known to musicians there for his saintly behavior, even when he had nearly nothing himself. Even though he had long periods without work, Dolphy would always come to the aid of fellow musicians, buying them groceries, if necessary, with his last few dollars. A prodigious musician, Dolphy played flute and bass clarinet, rarely used in jazz, in addition to alto sax. He did not gain national recognition until he joined Chico Hamilton's popular quintet of the Fifties, a group that featured the unusual instrumentation of Dolphy's reeds, guitar, cello, bass, and drums; a group so cool that it was more than occasionally precious. Dolphy can be seen playing both with the group and as a meditative lone flutist in the classic documentary on the Newport Jazz Festival, *Jazz on a Hot Summer's Day*. Dolphy left the group and settled in New York in 1959.

Dolphy had heard Ornette Coleman back in the Fifties when Coleman was living in Los Angeles, long before he had come to national prominence. Dolphy's style, originally heavily influenced by Charlie Parker, became more adventurous the longer he listened to Ornette. In New York he was hired by Charles Mingus, who had known Dolphy back in the Forties on the West Coast. Mingus's working group at the time was an adventurous quartet made up of Ted Curson on trumpet, Danny Richmond on drums (whom Mingus had trained to play polyrhythmically in the mode of Elvin Jones), Dolphy, and Mingus. The group made one classic album for the little Candid label, whose producer was the jazz critic Nat Hentoff. It is on this album that Dolphy's breathtakingly exciting mature style is first heard at its peak. Dolphy was once or twice compared to Sidney Bechet, and in the sheer audacity of his improvisations, their brashness and dominance and their feeling of utter exhilaration, they are indeed reminiscent of the great New Orleans musician. Dolphy's solos sounded as if they were neither completely "inside" or "outside," but seemed to career forward like a mad hummingbird, here alighting outside the harmony, there floating inside it. His playing seemed influenced by all sorts of extramusical sources: human speech, the sound of the wind, the singing and chattering of birds. As radical as his music often seemed, Dolphy did not consider his playing atonal. As he put it, "Yes, I think of my playing as tonal. I play notes that would not ordinarily be said to be in a given key, but I hear them as proper. I don't think I 'leave the changes,' as the expression goes; every note I play has some reference to the chords of the piece."

After leaving Mingus in 1960, Dolphy led an active career, judging from the number of records on which he appeared. Occasionally he would find himself playing in a situation where his iconoclasm was, as it had been with Mingus, encouraged and his imagination allowed to run wild. Such an occasion was when he played in George Russell's experimental group, with whom Dolphy made, sadly, only one album, the brilliant *Stratus Seekers,* on Riverside. Frequently, the effect of having Dolphy play in sessions made up of post-boppers was the same phenomenon we witnessed with Coltrane's performance in all those Fifties jam sessions—as if Dolphy had taken a ride backward by time machine in order to appear at the session. However, that was certainly not true for one album he played in during 1960—Ornette Coleman's shattering *Free Jazz.*

Coleman's term for the group of musicians performing in this session, a "double quartet," was literally true: there were two sets of horn men—Coleman and Don Cherry, Dolphy and the young lion trumpeter Freddie Hubbard (who was associated with hard bop, but was imaginative enough to play in many different settings)—and two rhythm sections. The tunes had no prearranged keys or chord changes, or any directions at all except for a brief opening "theme," so ambiguous in form that a soloist could do anything with it that he pleased. Sections where the group plays together alternate with solo sections, accompanied by both rhythm sections. In its use of ensemble improvisation the album suggests a throwback to New Orleans jazz, or rather a group of New Orleans jazz musicians under the influence of a strong hallucinogen. *Free Jazz* was reviled by many as well as hailed by those who saw in it a key to the future of jazz. The album's title would even be used as a name for the movement that it helped to inspire. John Coltrane must have listened long and hard to this record, but there would be no evidence of this until a few years later, when he would take Coleman's ideas a step even further.

Nobody was kinder to Dolphy when he came to New York

than John Coltrane, who remembered Dolphy's aid when he was stranded in L.A. There was more to their friendship, however, than mutual compassion. Dolphy was almost as obsessed with music as Coltrane was, and he spent almost as much time practicing. Both men had burning musical curiosities, and both were constantly in a state of artistic evolution. They loved to practice together, often playing spirited and exploratory duets.

Their common interest in music from all over the world gave Coltrane an idea. For his first album on Impulse, *Africa/Brass,* rather than just putting together another quartet date, the group would perform with a large brass section, arranged by Dolphy. The primary piece, "Africa," would be based on the music that both men had been listening to, that of South African pygmies. Coltrane had recorded pieces with Wilbur Harden with names like "Dial Africa" and "Tanganyika Strut," but these titles indicated only a generalized interest in African heritage; the pieces themselves owed no more to African music than most other jazz tunes. But "Africa" was different. It was true "world music." Coltrane had grown fascinated with the sustained drone heard in many world musics, especially that created by the tamboura of India. In order to simulate that sound, yet remain within the jazz tradition, he used two bassists, Workman and the brilliantly proficient Art Davis. While one bassist repeated a droning figure throughout the piece, the other played more freely around it. The meter was basically $\frac{4}{4}$, which Elvin played in such a way as to emulate the polyrhythms of African music. The result is stunning. Dolphy's brass arrangements wail like African chants, over which Coltrane plays magnificently. The result is not exoticism, but a genuinely new jazz.

In addition, Dolphy created an arrangement for a song that Coltrane had loved for a long time, the old British ballad "Greensleeves," and another arrangement for a minor-key blues with the not too imaginative title "Blues Minor."

As he was recording *Africa/Brass,* Coltrane also made his last record for Atlantic, *Olé,* whose title cut expressed Coltrane's interest in flamenco. He had already played flamenco-influenced jazz on *Kind of Blue*'s "Flamenco Skethes." Flamenco is the blues of Spain, even including African influences and the use of improvisation. Coltrane once again used the two bassists as well as Dolphy, this time playing flute, and Freddie Hubbard on trumpet. The result, though not as brilliant and adventurous as "Africa," again shows Coltrane's ability to use the folk music of other cultures in fusion with his jazz tradition. *Olé* also includes another piece influenced by African music, "Dohomey Dance," another fascinating exercise in polyrhythms, with the rhythm section segueing between a tricky $\frac{6}{4}$ time and $\frac{4}{4}$, and doing it brilliantly.

As powerful as both the *Africa* and *Olé* albums are, and as fascinating as they are in their bringing together jazz with exotic musics from various regions, it is amazing how little impression these records made on most of the critics of the day. In *Stereo/High Fidelity* magazine, one reviewer wrote of *Africa* that Coltrane needed editing, and could find little else of importance to say about this groundbreaking album. Reviewing the record in *Down Beat,* Martin Williams is more devastating: "Certainly no one could question Coltrane's particular skill as a tenor saxophonist. Nor that his ear for harmony, his knowledge of it, and his use of it, can fascinate. Nor do I question whether his playing is honestly emotional, if, to me, somewhat diffusely so.

"What I do question is whether here this exposition of skills adds up to anything more than a dazzling passionate array of scales and arpeggios. If one looks for melodic development or even for some sort of technical order or logic, he may find none here.

"In these three pieces, Coltrane has done on record what he had done so often in person lately, make everything into a handful of chords, frequently only two or three, and run them in every conceivable way, offering what is, in effect, an extended cadenza to a piece that never gets played, a prolonged montuna interlude surrounded by no rhumba or son, or a very long vamp 'till ready."

This review could not be overlooked by Coltrane or his supporters. They regarded it as the work of some uncomprehending ignoramus, though Martin Williams was perhaps the most respected of all jazz critics. Gary Giddins wrote about him, "Martin Williams is one of the most distinguished critics (of anything) this country has produced." Williams had produced a brilliant body of critical work on jazz, analytical yet passionate enough that his writing communicated the most subtle ideas even to those with little knowledge of jazz. Yet Williams had his limitations, of course, and perhaps the most glaring was John Coltrane. He simply never warmed up to Coltrane's music, although he couched his lack of enthusiasm for such an obviously important figure in what seemed carefully reasoned analysis. Despite Williams, *Africa/Brass* was a revelation to many in its linking of modern jazz and the music of Africa.

Coltrane was not alone in his interest in world music. In the early Sixties, folk music had become tremendously popular in America. Harry Belafonte had been selling millions of records with his music from the Caribbean, Miriam Makeba was singing the music of South Africa on a major label, and old English ballads like "Greensleeves" were gaining new popularity with the many folk singers and groups of the period. Record companies like Folkways flourished. The sambas of Brazil fused with cool jazz and created the fad called bossa nova. Something uplifting in America's outward look toward the music of the world, a sign perhaps that the country was overcoming its provincialism, can be heard in these albums. It is a mistake, however, to view Coltrane's exploration of non-Western musics as merely an attempt to be trendy. He was clearly trying to invigorate jazz with fresh, albeit actually ancient, musical concepts. He was also fascinated with those aspects of music that were universal and most deeply felt, no matter what part of the world they had been created in. Once again, it was part of his search, his quest for what he called "the essential."

Coltrane's exploration of the music of Africa, India, and the Middle East had significance far beyond the specific inspiration for pieces like "Africa" and, a little later, "India." By turning to non-Western sources in the creation of his music, Coltrane was making a statement with profound social and cultural as well as musical implications. He was also, no doubt, consciously trying to correct the direction of jazz.

If jazz is a meld of European and African (and other non-

Western) elements, in the Fifties there was a movement to put greater emphasis on the European elements. Probably the two most popular jazz groups, the Dave Brubeck Quartet and the Modern Jazz Quartet, quite self-consciously used classical music techniques such as fugues, rondos, and counterpoint; the MJQ would even perform works by Bach and other classical composers. The "chamber jazz" these groups produced was often good music, though at times precious. In addition, much West Coast cool jazz—music played mainly by white musicians—also employed classical techniques. Far more ponderous was the Third Stream movement, which attempted to combine jazz with modern classical music. Although he rarely spoke out on such matters, Coltrane made clear his dislike for the Third Stream. Miles Davis also disliked it, comparing Third Stream music to "looking at a naked woman that you don't like." By emphasizing its European elements, jazz began to lose touch with its folk roots and alienate a good deal of its audience.

By turning to Third World music, particularly that of India and Africa, Coltrane brought to jazz not only a new infusion of its non-Western folk roots, but a different perspective in the social and cultural relationship between the musician and his audience. Indian music, like jazz, is based on improvisation. Ragas, the most important Indian musical form, leave far less room for musical freedom than jazz. In his book *Musical Cultures of the Pacific, the Near East, and Asia* William Malm explains, "The art of Indian music has been called guided improvisation, by which is meant that at all times the musician must be guided simultaneously by the raga and the tala (Indian musical cycle of time). . . . The Indian musician . . . has before him a dazzling array of rhythmic and melodic possibilities, thanks to the thoroughness of the rules which serve as guides to his improvisations."

The Indian musician is thought of as being something more like a priest or a shaman than an entertainer. This stems from the early roots of Indian music, the Vedic hymns, sacred texts set to music. According to Malm, "Metaphysically, the physical vibrations of musical sound (*nada*) were inextricably connected with the spiritual world, so that the validity of a ritual and the stability of the universe itself might be adversely affected by a faulty intonation of sacred texts."

This spiritual framework as well as the improvisational nature of Indian music "results in a different kind of artist-audience relation. . . . The Indian audience reacts not to the challenge or reproduction but to the performer's ability to create his own music within given bounds." Performances of ragas, which, like Coltrane's longer solos, often last over an hour, may put the audience into something like a trance and create a bond between listener and musician quite unlike anything in Western music. Indian improvisation is far more restricted than that of jazz, particularly that of Coltrane, who could solo for hours based on a couple of scales. The idea of tala rhythmic cycles, the intertwined improvising of the primary instrument, say a sitar, and the tabla, must have amazed Coltrane in its parallel to the long improvisations he was making every night with Elvin Jones.

The point of the music was, to use a now hackneyed Sixties phrase, to "expand the consciousness" of the listeners, to create nothing less than a transcendant religious experience. The spiritual burden borne by the Indian musician is certainly something to which Coltrane could relate.

In African music, the relationship between the musician and the audience is even closer than that of India. Drums, of course, are at the heart of African music, and the drummer has a complex role regarding his music and those listening to it. In *African Rhythm and African Sensibility* John Chernoff writes, "In an African musical event, everyone present plays a part, and from a musician's standpoint, making music is never simply a matter of creating fresh improvisations but a matter of expressing the sense of an occasion, the appropriateness at that moment of the part the music is contributing to the rest. Just as anyone present must behave properly, so does the music become something which *behaves,* and the master drummer fulfills a complex social role. . . . African music is improvised in the sense that a musician's responsibility extends from the music itself into the movement of its social setting. . . . People pay attention in a special way, and a master musician uses his music to comment upon and influence the situation in much the same way that he comments on the rhythms of a supporting ensemble."

Coltrane's study of African and other non-Western music was a mainstay in bolstering his belief that the purpose of music transcends that of mere entertainment, and can actually socially transform its listeners.

Elvin Jones was keenly aware of African drumming, particularly that of West Africa. In the Fifties some bandleaders had attempted to streamline the rhythms of the drummer. Lennie Tristano, for example, gave the drummer the function of something little more than a metronome. But in the late Fifties a number of drummers turned to Africa for their inspiration. Art Blakey made a number of percussion records rooted in the African sound. But nobody employed the complex cross-rhythms so essential to African music more than Elvin Jones. Listening to him at full force, you could close your eyes and imagine you were deep inside an African rain forest.

The profundity of rhythm itself is perhaps the aspect of African music least easily understood by Westerners. African cycles of incredibly complex rhythms are parallel to, but quite different from, that of Indian talas. With the rhythms of the drums alone African musicians can make sophisticated, subtle, and quite personal statements readily understood and appreciated by their community. We feel rhythm in a far more visceral way than other aspects of music; it moves us physically at the same time we may be appreciating it intellectually. That accounts for its power, whether heard in an African ceremony or on an R & B record on a jukebox. Jazz has been criticized at times for the central importance of drums, as if it cannot be a truly great art form if it needs such brazen rhythm. Of course, the interplay between the drummer and soloist is at the very core of jazz, a technique inherited from Africa and other non-Western musics. There is as much subtlety in that interplay, on an intellectual, physical, and spiritual level, as in any other musical form. By permitting Elvin to play without restrictions, louder and with more rhythmic complexity than had ever been heard before in a jazz group, to the extent that Jones often seemed the center of musical activity whatever the soloist was playing, Coltrane acknowledged the African creed of the primacy of rhythm.

One thing that Coltrane was continually criticized for was repetitiveness, taking a phrase and playing it over and over. Consciously or not, Coltrane was emulating another aspect of African music. According to an African music scholar quoted in *The African Roots of Jazz,* by Kaufman and Guckim, "People unfamiliar with African traditional music, and hearing it out of context, sometimes find it too repetitious. The more clearly the listener can understand the music's function, the less likely to be his irritation, until eventually he realizes that repetition is one of the primary aids the music utilizes to fulfill its purpose." As Charnoff puts it in his book, "One of the reasons why repetition is so important in African music is that repetition of a rhythm often serves to clarify its meaning." Since the musicians of Africa are such an essential part of their society, and their music expresses everything from religious beliefs to the need for war, its clarity is all important. When music informs every aspect of life, it must be felt and clearly comprehended in mind, body, and soul.

Coltrane's interest in applying specific non-Western techniques to his own music was short-lived. He told an interviewer that no matter how far his musical curiosity might wander, his primary inspiration would be the rich tradition of African-American music. Although his study of world music changed his views on the purpose and possibilities of his own music, he remained committed to jazz. After all, in no other music, certainly not that of Africa or India, would he have such freedom to explore the outermost boundaries of improvisation. However, he would internalize many of the ideas he had gathered from different world musics, meshing the basic concepts and techniques with that of his growing musical conception.

The most profound concept of non-Western music for Coltrane was its cyclic, rather than linear, nature. Viewing the flow of music, as well as human life itself, in terms of cycles seems incompatible with a linear, Aristotelian worldview. These cycles, like the rounds of an infinite spring or a Möbius strip, have no beginning or end, no outside or inside. Certainly in these terms,

East is East and it at least seems impossible for its twain to meet that of the West. Yet Coltrane somehow melded the cyclic nature of Eastern music and thought with the elements of jazz, already a blend of East and West, and made it work. The more we listen to Coltrane, the more we Westerners are able to absorb the Great Cycles of the East into our linear minds.

Coltrane's greatest idol, Albert Einstein, changed the very idea of the universe from a linear model to a curved one. Coltrane surely appreciated in Einstein's theories their parallel to Eastern religion. The synchronicity between Eastern music and belief, the theories of modern physics, and his own discoveries through improvisation must have given Coltrane encouragement that he was on the right road, or should we say *cycle*, of his great quest.

If Coltrane was considered a great hero to those blacks involved in the Sixties cultural revolution, it was certainly not because of any statements he made on black nationalism. But by looking toward Africa and India for his inspiration and using the most profound aspects of their aesthetic outlook in the creation of his own music, he made a tremendous contribution toward black pride. He demonstrated that a serious musician did not have to look for inspiration only in the European musical tradition. Those who listened with sensitivity and acceptance to the cycles of sound and rhythm in his music had inevitably to open their minds to what was an indubitably black perspective on not just music but the universe itself.

Now that he was a leader in his field, Coltrane was spending a lot of time considering and reconsidering his musical methods, including some of the most basic aspects of his performance. In an extraordinarily revealing interview with the critic Ralph J. Gleason, he freely discussed the latest turns in his musical thinking: "I like to play long . . . the only thing is, I feel that there might be a need now to have more musical statements going on in the band. I might need another horn, you know. I ran across a funny thing. We went into the Apollo and the guy said, 'You're playin' too long, you got to play twenty minutes.' Well, at the Apollo we ended up playing three songs in twenty minutes! I played all the highlights of the solos that I had been playing in hours, in that length of time. So I think about it. What have I been doing all this time? It's made me think, if I'm going to take an hour to say something I can say in ten minutes, maybe I'd better say it in ten minutes. And then have another horn there and get something else. . . .

"I've been soloing for years and that's about all. I feel a need to learn more about production of music and expression and how to do things musically, so I feel a need for another horn for that reason. I could really go on playing like I am now, I enjoy it playing that long. It seems like it does me a lot of good to play until I don't feel like playing any more, though I've found out I don't *say* much more! Cut it right in half.

"On 'My Favorite Things,' my solo has been following a general path. I don't want it to be that way. . . . I wanted it to be something where we could improvise on just the minor chord and the major chord, but it seems like it gets harder and harder to really find something different on it. . . . I think that the $\frac{3}{4}$ [time signature] has something to do with this particular thing. I find that it's much easier for me to change and be different in a solo on $\frac{4}{4}$ tunes because I can play some tunes I've been playing for five years and might hear something different, but it seems like that $\frac{3}{4}$ has kind of got a strait jacket on us there!"

Gleason then asked Coltrane about his composing methods. Coltrane replied: "I've been going to the piano and working things out, but now I think I'm going to move away from that. When I was working on those sequences which I ran across on the piano, I was trying to give all the instruments the sequences to play and I was playing them too. I was advised to try to keep the rhythm section as free and uncluttered as possible and if I wanted to play sequences or run a whole string, do it myself and leave them free. So I thought about that and I've tried that some, and I think that's about the way we're going to have to do it. I won't go to the piano any more. I think I'm going to try to write for the horn from now on, just play around the horn and see what I can hear. All the time I was with Miles I didn't have anything to think about but myself so I stayed at the piano and chords, chords, chords! I ended up playing them on my horn.

"I tell you one thing. I have done so much work from within now what I've got to do is go out and look around me some and then I'll be able to say I've got to do some work on this or on that."

Some of these thoughts would find their way into his work, but others would be quickly forgotten. In particular, his vow to investigate shorter solos was germane only when he played in situations like the Apollo or certain nightclubs like the Village Gate, which didn't allow sets to last much longer than forty minutes, or the rare times he appeared on television. In most of his live appearances his solos, if anything, grew longer. His longest solos were usually no more than twenty minutes to half an hour long, but one afternoon in 1961, without a word to the band, he played one piece for over two hours. From then on, it was not extraordinary for him to solo for an hour or longer when in the proper setting and the right frame of mind, usually with the bulk of his very long solos a duet with Elvin. When interviewed a few years after Coltrane's death, Elvin was insistent about one important aspect of those long solos: no matter how caught up in the intensity of the moment Coltrane might have seemed, when he played a solo, no matter how long it was, Trane was always aware of exactly where he was in the cycle of each solo, and was always completely in control.

Coltrane's concerns about his improvisations on "My Favorite Things" were valid. Listening to various bootleg recordings of Coltrane concerts in the early Sixties, it is clear that in each performance his playing moves in somewhat the same directions as it did on the original recording. Nevertheless, any misgivings he may have had about waltz time did not prevent him from continuing to play pieces in time signatures other than $\frac{4}{4}$.

Before the late Fifties, any time signature other than $\frac{4}{4}$, or $\frac{2}{4}$, was extremely rare, with such novelties as Fats Waller's "Jitterbug Waltz" among the few exceptions. Then the middle and late Fifties saw a vogue in exploring other time signatures. Max Roach, for instance, recorded a whole album of jazz waltzes, and Sonny Rollins recorded his famous "Valse Hot." Dave Brubeck became a one-man crusader for odd time signatures such as $\frac{9}{8}$, $\frac{6}{4}$, and $\frac{7}{4}$. He even had a hit in 1960 with his saxophonist

Paul Desmond's "Take Five," which is in $\frac{5}{4}$. Brubeck pointed out that using such meters reflected the complexities of African drumming. Even black field hollers recorded in the South, he pointed out, were often in odd meters such as $\frac{5}{4}$. Brubeck sometimes fudged the issue, however, by playing the head in some odd time signature, then reverting to standard straightahead $\frac{4}{4}$ for the improvisations (although Desmond's "Time Out" is played, and improvised on brilliantly by Desmond, in $\frac{5}{4}$ throughout the entire piece).

The reason that $\frac{4}{4}$ has dominated jazz, at least since the end of the early jazz era, when $\frac{2}{4}$ lay at the heart of New Orleans jazz, is easy to understand. It has a forward motion that is most conducive to the momentum of an improvisor. It is said that jazz musicians, at least of the Swing Era, when the straightahead $\frac{4}{4}$ time came into vogue, were influenced by the sound and the headlong motion of railroad trains. Duke Ellington, for one, wrote several pieces based on the sounds of trains: "Happy Go Lucky Local," "Daybreak Express" (from which the saxophonist Jimmy Forrest appropriated the main theme and created the R & B hit "Night Train"), not to mention his alter ego Billy Strayhorn's "Take the A Train." Playing in other time signatures, especially triple meter, even a simple waltz, did not provide that sense of forward push. Clark Terry once compared rock and jazz rhythms: the rock beat, he said, is like jumping up and down while jazz rhythm—straightahead $\frac{4}{4}$ jazz rhythm, that is—had a sense of moving forward. It turned out to be not much of a surprise that jazz played in these odd time signatures with their feeling of rhythmic stasis would be especially popular to the generation weaned on rock. That is one of the reasons, besides its great beauty, that "My Favorite Things," and the other similar pieces Coltrane would play, struck a nerve with a new generation just then approaching jazz in the Sixties. It is also one of the ways that Coltrane would influence the jazz/rock fusioneers in the late Sixties and Seventies.

One thing mentioned in the Gleason interview that Coltrane did do was add another horn to the group. In mid-1961 Eric Dolphy joined Coltrane's band. Dolphy's effect on Coltrane ran deep. Coltrane's solos became far more adventurous, using musical concepts that without the chemistry of Dolphy's advanced style he might have kept away from the ears of his public. This was also a great opportunity for Dolphy, who gained not only great exposure but also the luster of playing beside the man many in the jazz world considered the single most important current innovator. Dolphy was not yet a completely mature stylist, as exciting as it was to listen to him. Although he was kicking down fences on jazz's frontiers, his own playing was often marked by sameness and rhythmic predictability. Regular work and the freedom that Coltrane allowed him was just what he needed to develop his already brilliantly promising improvisatory powers.

This new group, the John Coltrane Quintet, would tour extensively throughout both the United States and Europe in 1961 and the first half of 1962. As the tour progressed the musicians increasingly felt as if they were on a perilous mission fraught with danger. They were, consciously or not, spreading the message that jazz was going through a new stage in its evolution. Ornette Coleman rarely played outside New York once he moved east, and Coltrane, as an accepted member of the jazz establishment, could not simply be ignored. His music, he believed, deserved serious thought from his audience and the critics before any snap judgments were to be made.

The group created a furor wherever they performed. Even some supposedly hip jazz musicians were turned off. Wes Montgomery sat in with the group when they played San Francisco, but quit almost immediately, telling his friend Coltrane, "Now you guys are getting too far out for me." But it was the critics who were particularly savage. The bitterest attacks came when they played Los Angeles. There is an interesting parallel here to a similar crusade fifteen years earlier when a group including Dizzy Gillespie, Charlie Parker, and Milt Jackson brought the bop message to the West Coast by playing a club in L.A. for several weeks. Except for a number of forward-looking musicians and a small hipster clique, the boppers were either routinely disparaged or ignored. Coltrane, bringing a new radical musical message, was not prepared for the intensity of the attacks. Writing in *Down Beat,* John Tynan, then an associate editor of the magazine (which at the time was the only major jazz journal), wrote: "Go ahead, call me reactionary. I happen to object to the musical nonsense currently being peddled in the name of jazz by John Coltrane and his acolyte, Eric Dolphy. ▬

"At Hollywood's Renaissance Club recently I listened to a horrifying demonstration of what appears to be a growing anti-jazz trend exemplified by these foremost proponents of what is termed avant-garde music. I heard a good rhythm section . . . go to waste behind the nihilistic excesses of the two horns.

"▬ . Coltrane and Dolphy seem intent on deliberately destroying this essence [of jazz, swing]. They seem bent on pursuing an anarchistic course in their music that can but be termed anti-jazz. ▲

"Melodically and harmonically their improvisations struck my ear as gobbledegook. It is said that one of Coltrane's fondest desires is to play a chord on the tenor saxophone. In this aspiration I wish him lots of luck and concede that this ambition may account for most of the musical confusion. In this he earns my sympathy. . . .

✔"Coltrane is an artist to be sure (although his development these days would hardly appear to support that statement), and thwarted desire is, to an artist, life's cruelest blow. ▬

". . . The sincerity of Coltrane and Dolphy is not the question here. They may believe fiercely in the truth of their approach. They may be unalterably convinced that they are extending the horizon of jazz. They may swear they are probing toward New Frontiers in music. There is no evidence to doubt any of this. But the sounds they produce stand alone and apart from their intentions. And to these ears the sum of the sounds remain musical nonsense." ➤

Tynan wasn't the only important West Coast critic who felt this way. Leonard Feather, who had written negatively about Coltrane in the Fifties, quickly endorsed Tynan's point of view with at least as much vehemence. Concerning the obviously good intentions of Coltrane and Dolphy, Feather wrote, "Even Hitler was sincere."

Coltrane would have perhaps been better off if he had simply ignored these attacks. After all, what does the term "anti-jazz" mean in the first place? It is certainly a case of verbal "gobble-degook." However, Don DeMichael, who had coauthored with Trane the "Coltrane on Coltrane" piece, gave him and Dolphy an opportunity to reply to their critics in an interview for *Down Beat*. In the piece, titled "John Coltrane and Eric Dolphy Answer the Jazz Critics," the two musicians explained their methods, as much as such a thing is possible, in the calmest and most careful terms, considering how pointed their attackers had been. About the charge that the solos (including those of Dolphy and the rhythm section as well as his own) were too long, Coltrane replied, "They're long because all the soloists try to explore all the avenues that the tune offers. They try to use all their resources in their solos. Everybody has quite a bit to work on. . . . By the time we finish, the song is spread over a pretty long time. . . . It's not planned that way; it just happens."

What about editing? asked DeMichael. Many critics, even some favorable to Coltrane, had mentioned his need to edit his solos as he played. Coltrane answered, "There are times when we play a place opposite another group, and in order to play a certain number of sets a night, you can't play an hour and a half at one time. You've got to play 45 or 55 minutes and rotate sets with the other band. For those reasons, for a necessity such as that, I think it's quite in order that you edit and shorten things. . . . But when your set is unlimited, timewise, and every-thing is really together musically—if there's continuity—it really doesn't matter how long you play. On the other hand, if there're dead spots, then it's not good to play anything too long." This is a change in Coltrane's thinking since his interview with Ralph Gleason a few months previously. In that interview, he was won-dering if there was ever a need to solo at such length if it was possible to play a shorter solo and still express the same basic ideas. Obviously, he had come to the conclusion that when the player was inspired, his solo should be as long as he could sustain musical interest.

DeMichael asked Dolphy if he deliberately imitated the sound of birds, particularly in his flute solos. When Dolphy said that he did, DeMichael asked if such a technique was valid. "I don't know if it's valid in jazz," Dolphy replied, "but I enjoy it. . . . At home [in California] I used to play and the birds always used to whistle with me. I would stop what I was working on and play with the birds. . . . Birds have notes in between our notes—you try to imitate something they do and like, maybe it's between F and F#, and you'll have to go up or come down on the pitch. . . . Indian music has something of the same quality—different scales and quarter tones. I don't know how you label it, but it's pretty."

Finally, DeMichael asked the most basic of questions: What were Dolphy and Coltrane trying to do? After a half-minute of silence, Dolphy said, "That's a good question. . . . What I'm trying to do I find enjoyable. . . . It helps me play, this feel. It's like you have no idea what you're going to do next. You have an idea, but there's always that spontaneous thing that happens. This feeling, to me, leads the whole group. When John plays, it might lead into something you had no idea could be done. Or McCoy does something. . . . Or when the rhythm section is sitting on something a different way. I feel that is what it does for me."

After listening to Dolphy in "frowned contemplation," Coltrane gave a brief history of his association with Dolphy. Then, after a thoughtful pause, he said, "It's more than beauty that I feel in music—that I think musicians feel in music. What we know we feel we'd like to convey to the listener. We hope that this can be shared by all. I think, basically, that's about what it is we're trying to do. We never talked about just what we were trying to do. If you ask me that question, I might say this today and tomorrow say something entirely different, because there are many things to do in music.

"But, overall, I think the main thing a musician would like to do is to give a picture to the listener of the many wonderful things he knows and senses in the universe. That's what music is to me—it's just another way of saying this is a big, beautiful universe we live in, that's been given to us, and here's an example of just how magnificent and encompassing it is. That's what I would like to do. I think that's one of the greatest things you can do in life, and we all try to do it in some way. The musician's is through his music.

"This philosophy about music, life, and the universe," Coltrane said, is "so important to music and music is so important. Some realize it young and early in their careers. I didn't realize it as early as I should have, as early as I wish I had. . . ."

"When did you first begin to feel this way?"

"I guess I was on my way in '57, when I started to get myself together musically, although at the time I was working academically and technically. It's just recently that I've tried to become even more aware of the other side—the life side of music. I feel like I'm just beginning again. Which goes back to the group and what we're trying to do. . . . They respond so well that it's very easy to try new things."

Dolphy interjected, "Music is a reflection of everything. And it's universal. Like you can hear somebody from across the world, another country. You don't even know them, but they're in your back yard, you know?"

"It's a reflection of the universe," added Coltrane. "Like having life in miniature. You just take a situation in life or an emotion you know and put it into music. You take a scene you've seen, for instance, and put it into music. . . . Actually, while a guy is soloing, there are many things that happen. Probably he himself doesn't know how many moods or themes he's created. But I think it really ends up with the listener. . . . It's a sharing process—playing—for people."

"You can feel vibrations from the people," Dolphy said.

Coltrane continued, "The people give you something too. If you play in a place where they really like you, like your group, they can make you play like you've *never* felt like playing before."

Both Coltrane and Dolphy were puzzled by the term "anti-jazz."

"Maybe it doesn't swing," Coltrane offered.

"I can't say that they're wrong," Dolphy said. "But I'm still playing."

Did Dolphy *feel* that he swung?

"Of course I do," he answered. "In fact it swings so much, I don't know what to do—it moves me so much. I'm with John; I'd like to know how they explain 'anti-jazz.' Maybe they can tell us something."

Coltrane pointed out, "There are various types of swing. . . . In fact, every group of individuals assembled has a different feeling—a different swing. It's the same with this band. It's a different feeling than in any other band. It's hard to answer a man who says it doesn't swing."

As usual, the stinging criticism had made Coltrane thoughtful. Rather than being reflexively defensive about any of the jabs, he said, "Quite possibly a lot of things about the band need to be done. But everything has to be done in its own time. There are some things that you just grow into. . . . I've felt a need for editing and a need for ensemble work—throughout the songs, a little cement between this block, a pillar here, some more cement there, etc. But as yet I don't know just how I would like to do it. So rather than make a move just because I know it needs to be done, a move that I've not arrived at through work, from what I naturally feel, I won't do it. . . . There may be a lot of things missing from the music that are coming, if we stay together that long. When they come, they'll be things that will be built out of just what the group is. They will be unique to the group and *of* the group. . . . The best thing a critic can do is to thoroughly understand what he is writing about and then jump in. That's all he can do. I have even seen favorable criticism which revealed a lack of profound analysis, causing it to be little more than superficial. . . . Understanding is what is needed . . . the whole thing. In talking to a critic try to understand him, and he can try to understand the part of the game you're in. With this understanding, there's no telling what could be accomplished. Everybody would benefit."

This pacific attitude toward critics who had attacked him viciously is typical of Coltrane and his remarkably gentle and compassionate nature. In an interview a few years later, however, he revealed how upset he truly was. When asked about the critical attacks during this period, Coltrane replied, "Oh, that was terrible. I couldn't believe it, you know, it just seemed so preposterous. It was so ridiculous, man, that's what bugs me. It was absolutely ridiculous, because they made it appear that we didn't even know the first thing about music—the first thing. And there we were really trying to push things off. . . . Eric, man, as sweet as this cat was and the musician that he was—it hurt me to see him get hurt in this thing."

So how does this controversial music stand up a generation later? The group was well documented, with many bootlegs and the official recordings of the group made live at the Village Vanguard. It is clear from the bootlegs that Coltrane was playing his usual book with Dolphy, "My Favorite Things," "Blue Train," "Mr. P.C." (from the *Giant Steps* album). But for the group's stand at the Vanguard, and the live album that would be recorded there, Coltrane brought in some new and fascinating material whose inspiration came from an amazingly wide musical spectrum. One tune was based on an old Negro spiritual that Coltrane had found in a book of spirituals. The piece, simply called "Spiritual," has a stark and haunting melody, both sad and foreboding. On the version of the tune used on the original *Live at the Village Vanguard* album, the three improvisations by Coltrane, Dolphy, and Tyner are as basic and melodic as the original spiritual. It isn't reading too much into the piece—both the original tune and the improvisations—to say that it sounds like a melancholy meditation on the painful yet somehow triumphant past of African-Americans. It is also redolent, of course, of that great sanctuary, the black church, whose music had become increasingly a musical source in jazz by the late Fifties, part of the return to "roots." Horace Silver's "The Preacher," Charles Mingus's "Wednesday Night Prayer Meeting," Jimmy Smith's "The Sermon," and many other tunes from that era were all influenced by the sounds these musicians had heard as children—the rhythm of the preacher, the gospel music of the choir, the amens of the congregation. Coltrane, of course, had witnessed the music of his grandfather's church in his own childhood, and undoubtedly "Spiritual" was his way of tapping those potent memories.

From a place thousands of miles away from the American South Coltrane found the inspiration for another stunning piece. He had been listening to the music of Ravi Shankar years before the Beatles discovered the great sitarist's music. In "India" Coltrane once again used two basses to simulate the drone of the tamboura. The simple melody line was not from an Indian raga, but rather "Mr. Knight," from *Coltrane Plays the Blues*. Here again Coltrane finds the connection between the blues and the music of a seemingly distant culture. In a version released years after Coltrane's death, two added musicians play the Eastern oud and the oboe in a lengthy introductory passage before Trane, on soprano, and Dolphy, on bass clarinet, play the theme. In the improvisations on this piece one can hear most clearly Dolphy's influence on Coltrane. Coltrane's solo, like much of Dolphy's playing, is often made up of speechlike phrases, almost as if he were literally talking through his instrument. At moments the soprano's sound seems to twist and twirl in ecstatic glee. I suppose if one has rigid expectations of what music "should" or "shouldn't be," Coltrane's and Dolphy's use of these extra-musical devices and the strange and often bizarre places their solos wander to could be an affront, a challenge to what some believe to be right and proper in music and in art in general. Yet after several listenings to "India," the logic of these solos should become clear. If one lets down his guard and just permits the music to take him along, it is a bracing emotional experience. Both men have a well-defined sense of melody and musical form, and the fact that they were stretching the boundaries of their art here should have been a cause for exaltation rather than a reflexive negativity. Is there a line, though, in which the musician wanders too far from the aesthetic experience one demands from music? I think there is, and I think in later years John Coltrane *did* cross it, but not here.

Perhaps more controversial than "India" was the long blues "Chasin' the Trane" (don't blame Coltrane for that title—it was conceived by the engineer on the date). Played by Coltrane on tenor accompanied only by bass and drums, it is a sequel to "Blues to You" on the *Coltrane Plays the Blues* album. Coltrane talked about the "life" side of music as opposed to the "technical"; "Chasin' the Trane" is a definition of the difference. Coltrane's playing is the most intensely emotional of his career; he squeals, wails, and cries through his saxophone. Analyzing the tune technically is beside the point—it is an experience, a catharsis shared by Coltrane and his audience, and it is unlike anything that preceded it.

"Chasin' the Trane" is especially hair-raising because it is clear that Coltrane has dug deeply into his psyche to create this music—"cleaning the mirror," as he would put it a few years later. The music sounds as if it is a portrait of the raw stuff of his inner being, music so frankly confessional we feel slightly embarrassed listening to it. It is, in its subjectivity, in the tradition of the most innovative twentieth-century art and literature. This type of inner-driven improvising was key to Coltrane's quest. By looking within, he was trying to find a center of both that musical "essence" and the mind of God. From here on, most of his music would similarly be a result of his "cleaning the mirror."

Another piece from the Vanguard sessions, after the spirituals, Indian ragas, and blues, is based on, of all things, a theme by Debussy. The tune, "Impressions," is modal, based on the same modes as Miles Davis's "So What." The initial version—the Vanguard material was originally released on two separate albums, *Live at the Vanguard* and *Impressions*—is an example of the type of modal performance critics labeled "tedious." Played here only by Coltrane and the rhythm section for about fifteen minutes, it is monotonous and often pointlessly repetitive, not nearly as brilliant as many of Coltrane's performances of "So What" with Miles. It does sound here like a mechanical seesawing between the two chords or modes. Despite moments of lyrical beauty, it does not hold together like "Chasin' the Trane."

On the *Impressions* album, immediately following the fiery title piece comes "After the Rain," reflecting another side of Coltrane. The title is a perfect description of the mood, the calm in the air after an intense storm. It is such gentle, lulling music, so at peace with itself, especially after this version of "Impressions," that it is hard to believe that both pieces were played by the same musicians. But this lyrical piece reveals as much of Coltrane's inner state as those explosive works that are usually associated with his name.

Taken together as a single work, the Vanguard sessions must be counted as a Coltrane masterpiece, despite the monotony of the earlier version of "Impressions." ("After the Rain" was recorded in the studio after the Vanguard sessions.) Dolphy was the catalyst that had prodded Coltrane to advance the bold expressionism of his music, and to explore more fully what he called the "life side" of his music. The addition of Dolphy's horns brought new light and perspective to the music, changing its dimensions geometrically and providing fuel to Coltrane's pursuit of his quest.

9 a love supreme

In late 1961 Coltrane added the last piece to his classic group. Reggie Workman left the band for various reasons, and to replace him, Coltrane brought in Jimmy Garrison, a twenty-seven-year-old bassist who had formerly played with Ornette Coleman. Garrison, another Philadelphian, was part of a new generation of bassists, most of them influenced by Charles Mingus, who were changing the role of the bass in the jazz group. Before Mingus, the role of the bass was mostly that of timekeeper, except when the bassist soloed. Since Jimmy Blanton in the early Forties, the bass had assumed an increasingly assertive role, and with Mingus it became a melodic voice playing almost contrapuntally with the primary soloist. A young bassist named Scott La Faro took this concept even further in his work with Ornette and especially the first, and most innovative, Bill Evans trio, where at times he would forgo strict timekeeping altogether for a more interactive role.

Garrison had also worked briefly with Evans, although his concept of the bass was different from that of La Faro, who had tragically died in a car crash in July 1961. La Faro was a very fast player, and his sound tended to be much higher than one would expect, almost as if he were playing a cello instead of a bass. Garrison, in his own words "slowed down" La Faro's approach and developed a more traditional bass sound while still trying, like so many of his contemporaries, to free the bass from the straitjacket of strict timekeeping. He also had the physical strength to keep up with the lengthy solos of Coltrane and the rest of the group, an important consideration.

The new group, along with Dolphy, toured Europe shortly after the Vanguard sessions. Coltrane was still thinking of adding Wes Montgomery to the group, despite the guitarist's obvious discomfiture in that setting. "I very much wanted to have Wes here in England," he told the British writer Valerie Wilmer. "He's really something else because he can make everything sound that much fuller." Coltrane's tour was the talk of the European jazz world. While the group enthralled some European listeners, it puzzled and even infuriated others. At a Paris concert, some audience members even threw coins at the stage, a French method of showing extreme displeasure. Elvin Jones, for one, shrugged it off, saying, "We can always use the money."

Although Coltrane's music was generally afforded more respect by European critics than by American, perhaps no critic, European or American, was as avidly anti-Coltrane as Philip Larkin. In the early Sixties the famous British poet was given the job of reviewing jazz for a major London newspaper, the *Daily Telegraph*. At first careful about revealing his prejudices, he eventually came to write reviews explicit in their antimodernist bent. In the introduction to a collection of his jazz pieces, *All What Jazz: A Record Diary, 1961–68,* he described bop as "shallow and *voulu*. Worst of all was the pinched, unhappy, febrile, tense nature of the music." As much as he disliked bop, he utterly despised the music that followed bop, especially that of Miles Davis and his *bête noir* (pun intended), John Coltrane: "With Miles Davis and John Coltrane a new inhumanity emerged. Davis had several manners: the dead muzzled slow stuff, the sour yelping fast stuff, and the sonorous theatrical arranged stuff, and I disliked them all. With John Coltrane metallic and passionless nullity [I suppose he is referring here to the "sheets of sound" period] gave way to exercises in gigantic absurdity, great boring excursions on not-especially-attractive themes during which all possible changes were rung, extended investigations of oriental tedium, long-winded and portentous demonstrations of religiosity. It is with Coltrane, too, that jazz started to be *ugly on purpose;* his nasty tone would become more and more exacerbated until he was fairly screeching at you like a pair of demoniacally-possessed bagpipes.

"[Charlie] Parker," Larkin wrote, "was a modern jazz player just as Picasso was a modern painter and Pound a modern poet. . . . I went back to my books: 'After Parker you had to be something of a musician to follow the best jazz of the day.' Of course! After Picasso! After Pound! There could hardly have been a conciser summary of what I don't believe about art . . . 'modern' when applied to art has a more than chronological meaning: it denotes a quality of irresponsibility peculiar to this century. . . ."

It is doubtful if Coltrane ever saw one of Larkin's reviews. In a way, though, Coltrane did answer Larkin, or the many Larkins who were finding his music impenetrable. His coauthor of the "Coltrane on Coltrane" piece, Don DeMichael, lent him a book by the American classical composer Aaron Copland called *Music and Imagination.* In a lengthy and brilliantly articulate letter to DeMichael commenting on the book, Coltrane wrote, "If I may, I would like to express a sincere hope that in the near future, a vigorous investigation of the materials presented in this book and others related will help cause an opening up of the ears that are still closed to the progressive music created by the independent thinking artist of today. When this is accomplished, I am certain that the owners of such ears will easily recognize the very vital and highly enjoyable qualities that exist in this music. I also feel that through such honest endeavor, the contributions of future creators will be more easily recognized, appreciated and enjoyed, particularly by the listener who may otherwise miss the point (intellectually, emotionally, sociologically, etc.) because of inhibitions, a lack of understanding, limited means of association, or other reasons.

"You know, Don, I was reading a book on the life of Van Gogh today, and I had to pause and think of that wonderful and persistent force—the creative urge. The creative urge was in this man who found himself so much at odds with the world he lived in, and in spite of all the adversity, frustrations, rejections and so forth—beautiful and living art came forth abundantly . . . if only he could be here today. Truth is indestructible. It seems history shows (and it's the same way today) that the innovator is more often than not met with some degree of condemnation; usually according to the degree of his departure from the pre-vailing modes of expression or what have you. We also see that these innovators always seek to revitalize, extend and reconstruct the status quo in their given fields, wherever it is needed. Quite often they are the rejects, outcasts, sub-citizens, etc. of the very societies to which they bring so much sustenance. Often they are people who endure great personal tragedy in their lives. Whatever the case, whether accepted or rejected, rich or poor, they are forever guided by that great and eternal constant—the creative urge. Let us cherish it and give all praise to God."

These thoughts were perhaps engendered by the reviews of his *Live at the Village Vanguard* album. At this point, his music had become so controversial that *Down Beat* began assigning two reviewers to some of his albums, one sympathetic to Col-trane, the other not. The negative review in this case was written by his former supporter during the Fifties, Ira Gitler. Gitler had been an advocate of the radical musicians of the Forties and Fifties but, like so many critics, was intolerant of the artistic breakthroughs of the following generation; the music of the Vanguard sessions, particularly "Chasin' the Trane," was a land-mark to many of what would be called the "New Thing" mu-sicians, and a key to their music. Gitler wrote, " 'Chasin' the Trane,' a blues that consumes all of the second side [of the album], is more like waitin' for a train—a 100-car freight train—to pass. . . . Coltrane may be searching for new avenues of expression, but if it is going to take this form of yawps, squawks, and countless repetitive runs, then it should be confined to the woodshed. Whether or not it is 'far out' is not the question. Whatever it is, it is monotonous, a treadmill to the Kingdom of Boredom. There are places when his horn actually sounds as if it is in need of repair. In fact, the solo could be described as one big air-leak."

The other review, far more sympathetic to Coltrane, was written by Pete Welding, a critic who always was open to new musical ideas. After stating that the music is not altogether successful, he wrote: "The fault is less in Coltrane than in the task he has set himself. Perhaps the fullest appreciation of the monumental difficulties involved in the approach may be seen in the Coltrane-improviser that he so often is unable to bring it off, to control and direct it with the strength and sureness of purpose it needs.

". . . ['Chasin' the Trane'], with its gaunt, waspish angularities, its ire-ridden intensity, raw, spontaneous passion, and, in the final analysis, its sputtering inconclusiveness, seems more properly a piece of musical exorcism than anything else, a frenzied sort of soul-baring. It is a torrential and anguished outpouring, delivered with unmistakable power, conviction and near-demoniac ferocity—and as such is a remarkable human document. But the very intensity of the feelings that prompt it militate against its effectiveness as musical experience. It's the old problem of the artist's total involvement as a man supplanting his artistry, which is based after all, to some greater or lesser degree, in detachment."

Welding is right about "Chasin' the Trane." By the usual standards of Western music and theories of art since Aristotle, it is a very imperfect work, lacking the sense of balance and artistic detachment one expects of great art. Coltrane was breaking away not only from European musical concepts but also from the Western conceptions of the very function of art, the relationship between the artist and his audience, and the place of art in society. He and his music were moving toward ideas founded in his interest in non-Western art, philosophy, and religion.

Coltrane continued exploring the "life side" of his music even after his catalyst, Eric Dolphy, left the group in 1962. In spring of that year he recorded his first quartet-only album for Impulse, called simply *Coltrane*. (*Coltrane* was also the title of the first record under his own name for Prestige.) It was usually referred to by fans as "the Blue Album," owing to its blue-tinted cover photo of Coltrane.

"Out of This World" is the album's most famous cut, a lengthy version of a Harold Arlen standard, one of the very few modal show tunes. Coltrane completely transforms it, playing it in a hypnotic $\frac{6}{8}$ against a pedal point and a repeated piano vamp similar to that of his version of "My Favorite Things." Atlantic had muffled the sound of Elvin Jones's drums, but here they are recorded with something close to their proper dominance. Jones is incredibly aggressive and exciting—if you didn't know better, you would swear there were at least two drummers on the recording, so dense and powerful are his polyrhythms. After a dreamlike, off-tempo beginning, Coltrane doesn't so much play the tune as he deconstructs it, tearing into the exotic melody and interspersing cries, heartrending wails and dark bleats, rippling arpeggios and hypnotically repeated phrases, in a constant duet with Jones's explosive drums, building toward a series of shattering climaxes, unmistakably sexual in their intensity. Coltrane ends the piece as he began, out of tempo. The performance is reminiscent of both Arab and African music, a storm in a rain forest, and the visceral working out of some radical form of psychotherapy. Someone like Larkin or Gitler might have found "Out of This World" abhorrent, but nobody could call it dull. After repeated listenings, one finds here a carefully worked-out form, something lacking in "Chasin' the Trane'." But that is the difference between Coltrane's live performances and his recordings.

When playing in public, Coltrane explored ideas as far as he could take them. In the studio, he took the best ideas and put them together in relatively concise, cohesive musical statements. That is why he was so agonizing to record with—although he still improvised, he had certain aesthetic goals in mind, and he would record take after take until he realized them. The extramusical devices, while heartfelt, are also key elements of Coltrane's musical plan—the screams, wails, howls, honks, and cries extend the aural range, an important consideration when playing modal pieces. If Coltrane played these pieces, as some saxophonists did, in a well-modulated tone, the monotony of modality would become all too apparent. Stan Getz, for instance, disliked playing modal tunes, but given his style that is understandable. By extending his range and musical devices Coltrane could make the listener overlook the lack of harmonic variety in modal music.

*   *   *

With the growing success of his group, the shy, introspective Coltrane found himself becoming that unique entity, the American celebrity. *Newsweek* had a feature article about him in its music section. It was a rare occurrence for any major national nonmusic magazine to cover jazz in those days. The piece focused on Coltrane's soprano and especially on his "hit," "My Favorite Things." Coltrane told the newsmagazine, "It's hard to say whether I prefer the soprano or tenor. I find myself playing the soprano more and more, though. You can play lighter things with it, things that have a more subtle pulse. After the heaviness of the tenor, it's a relief to shift to the soprano." As for his constant innovation and change, he told the magazine that there were "quite a few avenues open for jazz and they're all going to be explored. I know that I'm going to try everything."

His life at this point was hardly that of a superstar. He was living in a small but comfortable house in Queens with his wife, Naima, and daughter, Toni, whose Muslim name was Syeeda. He had become a fanatic about nutrition and diet. Making fresh juice from various fruits and vegetables on his electric juicer became something of an obsession. Friends could count on being subjected to his latest blend whenever they visited. He also frequently dined at Indian restaurants, since his interest in the music and culture of that country had increased. He often fell victim to his sweet tooth, however, and despite his interest in good nutrition and regular workouts with weights, as the Sixties went by he was overweight more often than not. He was able to kick alcohol and heroin, but he could never get his craving for sweet potato pie out of his system.

When he wasn't working on his music he was reading, often voraciously, with the same steady commitment that he made toward his music. Most of the books that absorbed him were on religion and cosmic philosophy, everything from *Autobiography of a Yogi* to volumes on Einstein's theory of relativity, which remained a rich source of fascination for him. Most of his reading in religion was far from superficial. He read the Koran, the Torah, the Kabbalah, and, constantly, the Bible. He was fascinated with all sorts of mysticism but was also just as interested in scientific theory. His interests in cosmology had a parallel to his music: the outer realms of human thought and the bedrock reality of scientific inquiry.

Yet it is wrong just to view Coltrane as some sort of (non-Thelonious) Monk devoted only to his music and cosmic meditation. Everyone who knew him always remarked about his gentle, understated sense of humor. He could also be found devoted to such things as playing with his step-daughter and watching sports on TV, a favorite respite from his mental and musical wanderings.

Coltrane was consistently down to earth. Just before his death he gave a long interview to Frank Kofsky, a university teacher who was especially fascinated with the jazz avant-garde and its relationship to black nationalism. Kofsky was Jewish and also a dyed-in-the-wool Marxist. When he pointedly asked Coltrane if he was forced to record the album he made after *Coltrane,* an album of pretty ballads, by the greedy philistines who run record companies, the saxophonist's answer was so straightforward and direct, and completely apolitical, that he obviously threw Kofsky off stride. "Well, I'll tell you," Coltrane answered, "I had some trouble at that time. I did a foolish thing. I got dissatisfied with my mouthpiece and I had some work done on the thing, and instead of making it better, it ruined it. It really discouraged me a little bit, because there were certain aspects of playing—that certain fast thing that I was reaching for—that I couldn't get because I had damaged this thing, so I just had to curtail it."

The resulting album, simply called *Ballads,* was on the face of it a rather bewildering move for the man who had recorded the cyclonic "Out of This World" just a few months previously. There was even some speculation that Coltrane was having a change of heart about his musical route, and that making this record was his way of turning back. It is a simple album. On most tracks, Coltrane states the melody, McCoy plays an effusively romantic, almost florid, solo, Coltrane restates the melody, and that's it. No track is longer than five minutes, and only one is even somewhat uptempo, "All or Nothing At All," which Coltrane plays in a style influenced by Arabic music.

Every great jazz musician was a master of ballads, from Armstrong to Lester Young to Bird to Miles, and they all loved playing them. Coltrane was no exception. Playing ballads, and playing them well, making a personal statement, is considered by most musicians as one of the greatest challenges in jazz. Nevertheless, most early reviews of *Ballads* were negative, whether written by those who were usually pro- or anti-Coltrane. Yet many people find this album deeply moving. Coltrane barely improvises at all, almost as if he challenged himself to see how personal a musical statement he could make by sticking to the melody, with the exception of a few grace notes and simple, affecting phrases. The directness of Coltrane's sound, the feeling he injects into even a rather vacuous tune like "Too Young to Go Steady" with the simplest of musical materials, "the cry" at the center of his sound—all, as Nat Hentoff has pointed out, make *Ballads* as much a tribute to Coltrane's musical genius as any of his vastly more complex works.

Those who waited for him to deconstruct these tunes would be disappointed, but they were also missing the point. It reminds me of something Joe Zawinul said about first listening to Miles Davis's hypnotically repetitive version of Wayne Shorter's "Nefertiti," in which the horns repeat the exotic theme over and over while the rhythm section boils beneath them: "I was waiting for something to start happening, when I realized that the music had been happening all along." *Ballads* was clear proof, if any was still needed, that Coltrane's genius had many mansions. "Do not understand me too quickly," wrote André Gide; Coltrane could have used that quote as the only liner notes he needed for most of his albums. Incidentally, the *Ballads* album took on a life of its own, showing up frequently in several movie soundtracks, most recently in *The Fisher King,* as hip background music for scenes of romance and seduction.

If Coltrane's fans and critics were put off, or at least surprised, by the *Ballads* album, many of them were utterly shocked by the next album he released, recorded around the same time, *Duke Ellington and John Coltrane.* Bob Thiele, Coltrane's producer at Impulse, is associated with Sixties jazz because of his relationship with Coltrane and the other young lions he recorded because of Trane's endorsement and encouragement. His real roots, however, were in the jazz of the Thirties and Forties, when he made some classic recordings of Coleman Hawkins, Lester Young, and a number of other important musicians from that prebop period. His idol was Duke Ellington, and when he was given a chance to record with Ellington, he jumped at the chance. Rather than just recording Ellington in his usual settings, he paired the great composer, arranger, and pianist with three other important jazz innovators: Louis Armstrong, Coleman Hawkins, and John Coltrane.

Fans of both Ellington and Coltrane were less than happy with the idea of teaming these two. In a way, it made perfect sense, for despite the shortsightedness of each man's most fervent supporters, the two men actually had much in common. Both were restless musical explorers, constantly looking forward, unlike, say, Armstrong, who though he could still play magnificently, remained rooted in his past. Ellington, like Coltrane, believed in always moving forward and never dwelling in the past, just as he had also been intrigued by non-Western music and had also explored ways to meld Asian and African elements with jazz. Ellington was mainly concerned, though, with incorporating the general feeling and colors of Asian and African music rather than with any true technical fusion. His greatest long work from the latter years of his life, the *Far East Suite,* did capture some of the Asian landscape as filtered through this genius's consciousness, though anything by Ellington is ultimately of and about that unique musical universe only Duke and his musicians inhabited.

Ellington had become deeply religious in his later years, embracing a pantheism not dissimilar to Coltrane's, and the last major works of his life were his "Sacred Concerts," large-scale efforts to explore the idea of God through jazz.

Thiele put the two men into a setting that he thought both would find comfortable: a quartet, mostly playing tunes by Ellington and Billy Strayhorn. It may have been the simplest way of bringing these two men together, but you have to wonder what Coltrane would have sounded like playing with the Ellington band, with special pieces, such as the "concertos" he had written for various members of his band, composed and arranged for the occasion. Thiele's setting, a quartet alternating Ellington's and Coltrane's rhythm sections, gives only a brief glimpse of how Coltrane would have reacted in the realm of Ellington.

The album opens with the one genuine classic from this session, a ballad: Ellington's gorgeous chestnut "In a Sentimental Mood." Over a lovely Ellington vamp, Coltrane plays the melody with such "confidence" (as Coltrane had years previously described the playing of Johnny Hodges) that if you didn't know any better you could swear the tune was written specifically for Coltrane and this session. After a brief, abstract solo by Ellington, always the avant-gardist, Coltrane improvises over Elvin Jones's pulsating drums, Ellington returns to the vamp, and Coltrane repeats the melody, this time playing with such poignancy and melancholy nostalgia that more than one pair of eyes have become moistened listening to this lovely musical moment. It is quite simply that rarity in jazz known as a perfect performance. Johnny Hodges, who had known and played the song since its first performance, said, "As long as I've heard this song, I think Coltrane gave the most beautiful interpretation I've ever heard." One has to wonder if critics like Philip Larkin heard this piece as well as the *Ballads* album. It would have to complicate, if the critic were honest, the portrait of a musical brute which hostile critics had routinely painted of Coltrane.

The rest of the album is more pedestrian, although it is startling to hear an Ellington solo, no matter how short, as they all are on this album, follow one of Coltrane's. On a tune composed by Coltrane, "Big Nick" (named after a Philadelphia tenor saxophonist well known to musicians, though not to the public), Ellington plays his best solo, placing those dark, damp chords of his with a perfect sense of time and correctness. This tune, incidentally, does not sound at all like a Coltrane composition; it has a humorous flavor that is rare in his work, composed or improvised. Ellington's one tune written exclusively for this recording—"Take the Coltrane"—is more a sketch than a full-blown Ellington fantasia. It begins with Duke playing a short, typical solo, and then strolls (does not accompany) as Coltrane, who has been holding in his reins throughout most of the recording, finally lets go. He ranges so far that he might as well be on a different planet from Ellington. The fury engendered by Coltrane and Elvin on this track must have been quite a shock to the always blithe and collected Ellington.

According to Bob Thiele, the most important aspect of the session was Ellington's effect on Coltrane. Coltrane, as usual, wanted to play take after take of a tune until he was convinced it was as close to perfect as he could get. Ellington had an attitude closer to that of Miles Davis. He told Coltrane, "Why play it again? You can't duplicate the feeling." After these sessions with Ellington, Coltrane was less insistent about repeating takes, according to Thiele. Coltrane had been subjected to this philosophy of recording for years with Miles, however, so one must wonder about his changing so drastically after making one record with Duke.

Fans who saw Coltrane (along with Ornette Coleman) as the most iconoclastic musician in jazz were still reeling from the *Ballads* album and the album with Ellington when an even greater shock came along: yet another album of ballads. This time Coltrane co-led the session with a Billy Eckstine–influenced crooner from the Forties, Johnny Hartman. Hartman was an exceptional singer whose style was less mannered and more straightforward than that of Eckstine and whose career had taken some bad turns into obscurity. The resulting album, *John Coltrane with Johnny Hartman,* must be one of the prettiest albums of the Sixties. It is something more than that during "My One and Only Love," a tune adorned with a gorgeous Coltrane solo, once again with little improvisation, and Hartman's moving singing. The entire performance is genuine romance in its best and truest sense.

As lovely as all three of these albums are, and as much as they tell us about Coltrane as a musician and a man, his explanation for them—mouthpiece problems—only partially explains his state of mind during the second half of 1962 and the first few months of 1963. Not that mechanical difficulties are insignificant: obviously, the best improvising comes when the musician can let mind and heart freely create, unimpeded by any extramusical gremlins. But other factors, at least as significant, were also distracting Coltrane around this time.

The main distraction was his marriage, which was falling apart. According to J. C. Thomas, Coltrane had had a mistress since 1960. I mention that she was white and blonde only to counter the claim in Simpkins's book that he found white women totally unattractive. From all indications, however, it was not the mistress who caused the breakup of the marriage. Since Coltrane first met Naima in the early Fifties, he had gone through astonishingly broad and deep advances, both as a man and as a musician. The breakup was not acrimonious; rather, Coltrane, again according to Thomas, treated Naima almost as if she were a sideman whom he had to let go, gently explaining to her that he had to make a change in his life. The two remained close after their separation and divorce. Coltrane even wrote a tune for her, "Wise One," on the *Crescent* album, after they broke up.

Also troubling to Coltrane at this time were the problems he was having with Elvin Jones. He needed Elvin—there simply was no other drummer who could play with the polyrhythmic density he required. He also loved Elvin, not always an easy thing to do. When sober, Elvin could be a warm, brilliantly articulate, sensitive, and lovable person. But when he was high, particularly when he was drunk, it often was a different matter. He could be irresponsible, nasty, mean, and even violent. Coltrane's patience apparently knew no bounds. One night Elvin totaled Coltrane's car, which he had borrowed. When Coltrane heard that Elvin was all right he breathed a sigh of relief, without a trace of rancor, and said, "I can always get a new car but I'll never find another Elvin." After Coltrane's death, Elvin would tell an interviewer that he felt he had been touched by something supernatural when he was with the quartet, so angelic was Trane's treatment of other people as well as his ability to produce music on an unworldly plain.

But in 1963 Elvin had a dope habit again. He got busted, and an extremely distressed Coltrane felt his progress was being held up by having to use other drummers, even such superb players as Philly Joe Jones, Louis Hayes, and the drummer he used most of the time, Roy Haynes. Haynes was a youthful veteran, his career having begun in the late Forties playing and recording with Charlie Parker and the early Miles Davis. A fiery and free player, yet always supportive of the soloist, he was, and is, what is usually called a "listening drummer," one who is sensitive to the playing of the musician he is accompanying. He is quite simply a master, and Coltrane was lucky to get him for most of the period Elvin was locked up. Still, in listening to the few records the quartet made with Haynes instead of Elvin, as superb as many of them are, one can clearly hear the hole left by Elvin. With Jones, the group had become a whole greater than the sum of its parts but absolutely dependent on each of the four parts, Coltrane, Tyner, Garrison, and Jones.

When Elvin came back in the fall of 1963, Coltrane had worked out his mouthpiece problems and separated from Naima. By getting Elvin back, Coltrane could continue on his quest. Despite the relative conservatism of the three albums released in late 1962 and early 1963, Coltrane now had found his way again, and that way was forward, ever forward.

His solos became even longer, as he began reaching still deeper inside his soul and psyche for his inspiration. His audiences felt either mesmerized or assaulted, but were never apathetic. The experience of watching a man create, at a fierce tempo, an hour or hour-and-a-half solo (according to Elvin, at one matinee he played one piece for over three hours) in a twisting duet with a drummer who himself was as loud as many rock groups was a new sort of aesthetic experience in jazz.

Coltrane was now exploring the existential mode and the purpose of his role as an artist. Again we see how sensitive Coltrane was to the cultural and social ripples of his time, for in the Sixties he was not the only one attempting to revolutionize the experience of art. The Living Theatre, for example, wanted to break down completely the artificial wall between the "actors" and the audience, challenging the audience to participate directly in the theatrical experience. Avant-garde actors and directors wanted to provide more than an evening's entertainment; they wanted to shake up the audience, attack their emotions viscerally, often by leaving the stage and shouting directly into the faces of audience members. They provided a type of catharsis, for the actors and audience, undreamed of by Aristotle. The Sixties also saw a proliferation of "happenings," performances by dancers or actors or artists of a work that was part theater and part sculpture. In all the arts, reformers challenged basic assumptions on the nature and purpose of art. Was it enough to entertain your audience or should you try and transform them as well? Should the artist choose the emotions he expressed or just let feelings bubble forth freely, totally uninhibited? As a sensitive artist and man—remember Cecil Taylor's words that he had "a feeling for the hysteria of the times"—Coltrane certainly sensed the currents of change rippling through American culture in the Sixties.

One thing Coltrane was definitely aware of was the changes brewing in American society. The Freedom Riders, the forced integration of southern universities, the growing militance of many in the civil rights movement, all were upping the ante in the struggle of blacks for their civil rights. Many people, both black and white, felt a burgeoning sense of doubt about the American system itself, one that allowed such atrocities against minorities and the poor. As James Baldwin wrote, did blacks really want to be integrated into a burning house? The growing presence of the Black Muslims and their fiery advocate Malcolm X exacerbated these feelings of racial unease. John Coltrane virtually never spoke publicly about social or political issues— he once said that he could never make up his mind about anything except music—yet he was extremely sensitive to social change, especially when it involved blacks. Rather than make verbal statements, Coltrane used music to express the war in his soul, which reflected, among other things, the war in society. He always insisted that, despite the claims of many critics, his music was not "angry." Perhaps not, but it was so powerfully full of strong emotions, especially in the Sixties, that the listener was forced against a wall of feeling and made to confront its source.

On September 15, 1963, one of the most heartbreaking atrocities of the civil rights movement took place in Birmingham, Alabama. The Ku Klux Klan blew up a church and killed four little black girls. This depraved act caused a furious wave of shock and rage. In its aftermath, Coltrane wrote and recorded "Alabama," a Coltrane masterpiece. It is not only a beautiful piece of music, it is a profound meditation on the death of innocence and the seemingly endless tragedy of inhumanity. The piece, only a few minutes long, begins with the piano's ominous rumbling, before Coltrane states the melancholy theme. After a brief and, for Coltrane, melodically straightforward solo in tempo, Coltrane returns to the theme, seems to meditate on it, and then softly ends the piece. As LeRoi Jones states in his liner notes for the album on which "Alabama" first appeared, *Coltrane Live at Birdland,* before hearing this piece he never realized how beautiful the word "Alabama" was. Sidestepping any didacticism or preachiness, Coltrane approaches the subject with the insight of the true artist, and by so doing makes us feel the tragedy and, even deeper, the hope. That he could create such a stunningly beautiful piece of music out of these horrible events was indication of how profoundly compassionate a man and artist Coltrane really was. One is made to feel the part of Alabama that is in each of our souls. "Alabama" cries not only for the four dead girls, but for all of us.

Coltrane Live at Birdland is one of Coltrane's most accessible albums. Although only three of the five pieces were recorded at the fabled Manhattan jazz club, the whole album seems of a piece. Here, in the tradition of such lyrical soprano extravaganzas as "My Favorite Things," is "Afro Blue," composed by the Latin percussionist Mongo Santamaria, and a perfect vehicle for Coltrane in its harmonic simplicity. More exciting than any of the actual solo is the long tag, during which Elvin works up a lather around Coltrane's closing reiteration of the theme.

The most spectacular piece on the album is a new version, played on the tenor, of "I Want to Talk About You," which Coltrane had recorded five years earlier on the *Soultrane* album. After a fairly standard version of the lovely tune, he plays an unaccompanied coda—a rarity for Coltrane, although the specialty of his colleague Sonny Rollins, who often played an unaccompanied coda for ten or fifteen minutes. Coltrane's coda is dense aural fireworks, arpeggios exploding and lighting up the night. It is a true *tour de force,* and a remarkable display of saxophone technique and imagination. It is certainly a daunting lesson for anyone wishing to take up the instrument and genuinely master it.

If after the nostalgia of the ballads and the work with Ellington, Coltrane's supporters were hoping for important new advances, then *Live at Birdland,* even with "Alabama," was something of a disappointment. More was expected of Coltrane than of other musicians. He was never supposed to stand still artistically. Within a couple of years, however, many of his fans would wish that he *had* stopped developing around this period.

A new revolution was going on in jazz, the most fundamental since the bebop of the mid-Forties. At first hidden from the mainstream jazz audience, it was taking place in those small pockets in America, mainly in lofts in downtown New York, where the extremes of iconoclastic thought were easily accepted and even encouraged. The music was called the "New Thing," the "New Wave," or "Free Jazz." Freedom, musically and socially, was at the heart of the new movement. Its players were young men and women who had found their musical way in the wake of Ornette Coleman, Cecil Taylor, and, of course, John Coltrane. The music wasn't really atonal, it was mostly polytonal, but because of its constant dissonance, many thought the music to be atonal. It was usually characterized by its use of many of the extramusical effects, such as overblowing, shrieks, wails, and multiphonics, that Coltrane had begun exploring as early as his last year or two with Miles Davis, and most obviously in "Chasin' the Trane." The drummers went a step beyond Elvin Jones, playing "free" and often meterless rhythms, and the bassists were generally under the sway of Scott La Faro, playing melodically and rhythmically free rather than keeping time. Everyone in the "New Thing" movement looked up to Coltrane as a father figure. He returned their adulation with a fascination and then support of their music, which was unheard in most jazz clubs, with the exception of such Lower East Side havens as Slugs, on East Third Street. It was ignored by virtually all record companies, except for a small and very exploitative independent company called ESP, which recorded nothing but avant-garde jazz and occasionally experimental rock.

There are some parallels between the origins of the free jazz revolution and those of bop. By the early Sixties modern jazz, like swing in the early Forties, seemed to be foundering on its own clichés. For many, the music that escaped an excessive European influence tended toward heavy-handed funk, with little new to say. Many young and creative blacks were becoming increasingly aware of their African heritage and feeling rebellious toward Western culture, with which they felt they had been continually pounded. They now saw a non-Western perspective toward music as a vehicle for heightening a positive black self-image. They disavowed conventional—read European—harmony, rethought the place of rhythm, became less concerned with the comforts of pleasant melody, and did all this with energy made manifest through profound anger.

It is not hard to understand their rage after reading a statement such as that written by a man considered to be one of the great historians of our century, Arnold Toynbee: "The black races have not contributed positively toward any civilization." There is no point in even offering a rejoinder to such a thoughtless and plainly silly comment. But reading statements like Mr. Toynbee's, who is, sadly, not in an intellectual minority, one can understand the fury of the "New Thing" musicians' desire to play a music that denied all the aesthetic assumptions of Western art.

Many of the musicians who had been part of the postbop movement were now making strong racial statements, both verbally and in their music. Charles Mingus wrote a poisonous paean, half played, half shouted, to Arkansas Governor Orval Faubus called "Fables of Faubus," Max Roach made an album of his magnificent "Freedom Now Suite," and Sonny Rollins released his own "Freedom Suite." When Rollins first released his suite, a work about the trials and hopes of his people, his producer insisted on releasing the album with a reassurance to white listeners that the suite wasn't about black people, but about freedom in some general, abstract way. Mingus wasn't able to release "Fables of Faubus" with its shouted lyrics when it was first recorded for Columbia. That version had to wait until he recorded the piece for Nat Hentoff's adventurous but short-lived label,

Candid. Other jazz musicians, such as Miles Davis and Ornette Coleman, who also made strong statements about America's racism in the late Fifties and early Sixties, were often branded black racists, even though they played with and frequently hired white musicians, a point usually overlooked by their critics in the jazz magazines. Such was the state of racial politics in jazz by the time of the birth of the "New Thing" movement.

One figure who was a key part of the "New Thing" deserves to be singled out, partly because his career was so different from those of the other musicians of the movement. About a generation older than the young lions of the Sixties, he always insisted that Coltrane "stole" his musical concepts. He was the late Sun Ra, born Herman Sonny Blount around 1915 in Birmingham, Alabama. It is impossible to verify the facts of his early life because for about the last thirty or forty years he insisted he was born on some other planet, usually Saturn. He definitely did play piano with a Fletcher Henderson band in the Forties, and by the mid-Forties his arrangements were so original that most musicians, even a virtuoso such as Coleman Hawkins, found them nearly impossible to play. Sometime in the Fifties he put together his own band, which he called, variously, the Solar Arkestra, the Myth-Science Arkestra, the Astro-Intergalactic-Infinity Arkestra, and so on. In the Fifties the band played advanced bebop. Ra, long before anyone else in jazz, used a number of drummers and percussionists to create dense polyrhythms. Sometimes during a performance, the band would lay down their instruments and play various exotic percussion instruments from every corner of this planet and maybe a few others. By the early Sixties the band's music was often highly dissonant and sometimes genuinely atonal, with a frequent use of group improvisation—that is, the entire band screaming, yelping, and shrieking at once. Ra was the first major jazz musician to use electric instruments, often wowing the crowd by playing with his back to his instrument and his hands behind him pounding on a synthesizer or sometimes two instruments which Ra renamed the "Flying Saucer" or some such. Ra was also a great showman. After several minutes of bone-shattering music from the farthest point of the avant-garde, the band would break into singing one of Ra's wonderful tunes, such as "Space Is the Place," "Next Stop Jupiter," or, my favorite, "Outer Spaceways Incorporated": "If you find earth boring / just the same old same thing / come on sign up with Outer Spaceways Incorporated." Ra was probably also the first to use a light show while his band played, often showing films of outer space or of Egypt or, in the early Seventies, the first men on the moon, for whom he wrote a catchy ditty called "They're Walking on the Moon." He also had a small troupe of dancers who toured with the band and who would dance indescribably wild choreography while the band played.

It all sounds a bit too ridiculous to be taken seriously even by someone like John Coltrane, but beneath the fun and show of a Sun Ra performance there was almost always some serious, and often innovative, music making. Sun Ra simply had the misfortune to be always a bit ahead of his time in his pioneering of mixed media as well as in his musical advances. As well as being hopelessly, wonderfully weird, Ra always had excellent musicians in his band. They had to be in order to play Ra's charts. Many members of his band remained with him since the Fifties.

Sun Ra's charge that Coltrane stole some of his ideas is unlikely—many similar ideas were floating in the winds in the late Fifties and early Sixties. One of the mainstays of Ra's band was the tenor saxophonist John Gilmore, who Miles Davis was going to use when he was first putting together his mid-Fifties quintet. Gilmore joined Ra's band in Chicago, and the band eventually wound up in Philadelphia when Coltrane was living there. There were similarities in their styles, but that hard, steely sound was becoming something of a trademark of many saxophonists in Philadelphia, many of whom have remained obscure. Of course Coltrane had his influences, and Sun Ra was definitely one, just as Ra was undoubtedly influenced by Ellington, Basie, Lunceford, and Monk, and later, no doubt, by Cecil Taylor and the early Ornette Coleman. In the latter part of Sun Ra's career, he was more likely to play big band charts from the Thirties and early Forties, albeit with his own weird panache, than his further-out stuff.

In the mid-Sixties Ra was living communally with most of his band on the Lower East Side. One of the leaders of the "New Thing" movement was a tenor saxophonist named Archie Shepp, who became a good friend of Coltrane's. Shepp had played with Cecil Taylor and became a regular on the loft scene, as well as something of a spokesman for this latest generation of musical rebels. Shepp had quite an original musical conception: influenced by the advanced postbop tenors Coltrane and Rollins, he had also listened, and listened closely, to such prebop tenor saxophonists as Ben Webster and Paul Gonsalves. Shepp frequently emulated Webster's huge sound, particularly on ballads, but most of the time was involved with what was frequently called at this time "energy music"—fiercely dissonant shrieking and screaming played against violently aggressive drums. It is not hard to see the original model for this music: Coltrane and Elvin's roiling musical whirlwind, particularly "Chasin' the Trane" and the even more intense and often frenetic work that followed it.

Even more provocative than Shepp's music were his controversial statements and stands. Although coming from a middle-class background (his first model for tenor sax style was Stan Getz), he had, during the course of his career, become a staunch black nationalist and an unblinking Communist. He insisted that his music was inseparable from the racial and social revolution that he believed was brewing. He often read his poetry at his concerts, much of it burning with black rage and revolutionary fervor, some of it bordering on self-parody.

Many of the young lions of the "New Thing" movement were, to one degree or another, in agreement with Shepp. Not that protest was anything new in jazz: black music was born out of revolt. Even Louis Armstrong sang of racial protest. Armstrong's version of Fats Waller's song "(What Did I Do to Be So) Black and Blue" was central to Ralph Ellison's novel *Invisible Man.* If Sun Ra seems like a cosmic joker, look again. Beneath the stellar trappings is a new racial myth: blacks as alien to this evil planet. According to Ra and specifically laid out in an incredible full-length movie, *Space Is the Place,* the planet will be destroyed by the Creator after Ra helps all the decent blacks (read: those who have not colluded with the evil whites) escape on his giant flying saucer and return to their true home. It is easy to smirk at Ra's fantasy, but he was making a sincere attempt to construct new myths to replace those that were left behind in Africa when blacks were brought in slave ships to this country and cut off from their native culture.

Another musician who was a central figure in the "New Thing" movement was the saxophonist Albert Ayler, who was also fascinated with other-worldly myth. Ayler, like Sun Ra, was truly one of a kind, and during his brief, cometlike appearance on the jazz scene he managed to infuriate at least as many as he mesmerized. One of the fascinating things about the ultra-avant-garde Ayler was his use of older musical forms, some predating jazz. He often began a piece by playing on his tenor saxophone, with a huge vibrato, an old folk song or nursery tune, the type of thing you swore you have heard sometime in the past, but you just can't put your finger on. After playing this ancient tune with reverence, he would suddenly start tearing it apart, playing phrases faster and faster until he reached an elongated shriek that would twist and writhe with changing sonority. His rhythm section usually consisted of the freest of drummers, particularly Sonny Murray, and a Scott La Faro-esque bassist such as Gary Peacock. Together they would play with absolutely nothing that could be called a regular pulse, simply drums pounded seemingly at whim and the bass doing anything but keeping time. The piece would usually end with Ayler returning to the ancient ditty, as if the insanity in the middle had never happened. He also liked, along with larger groups, to play old New Orleans marches. Other times, often with his trumpeter brother Don, he would just play completely free, totally "outside," both of them screaming at once over a hyperactive free rhythm section.

Ayler gave his pieces names such as "Ghosts" (apparently based on a nineteenth-century European nursery song), "Spirits Rejoice" (based on "La Marseillaise" and "Maryland, My Maryland"), "Angels," and "Witches and Devils." One description of an Ayler group was "a Salvation Army band on LSD," although more than a few fans insisted on his genius.

Like Coltrane, Ayler considered his music to be spiritual revelation, and his purpose was far greater than that of mere entertainment. As John Litweiler writes in his book on post-1960 jazz, *The Freedom Principle,* "Ayler felt that the objective of his music was to purify, to lead people into spiritual communion. 'The music which we play today will help people to better understand themselves, and to find interior peace more easily.' " Of course, many listening to his music would argue that it produced emotion far more akin to inner turmoil, or even torment, than inner peace.

Looking at Ayler today, he seems to have been something unique in the history of black music, a jazz dadaist. Like the original dadaists, he wanted to shake things up, to make jazz musicians rethink their entire process of music making, and to help them escape from the European mode of thinking that had increasingly dominated much of the jazz of the Fifties. His music was useful in the way it changed one's concept of what music should be, not unlike the work of John Cage, though Ayler had a somewhat different agenda. In its time, his music was important and useful and, in limited amounts, certainly entertaining, but it seems dated now.

One of the musicians who was shaken by Ayler's musical vision was John Coltrane. Ayler's most famous statement was "It's not about notes anymore." Ayler's chief concern was that of pure sound, sound unsullied with melodic direction or harmonic structure. This type of musical thinking would eventually be central to much of Coltrane's later music.

Coltrane was seriously listening to his younger colleagues in 1964, but his music was at this point only obliquely influenced by them. The early effect on Coltrane of the "New Thing" was more in the form of pressure to change, to complete his search on the particular musical avenue he had been exploring with his quartet since its inception in 1960. Then he would move on.

This pressure came not just from the new generation of radical jazz musicians but also from the changing social atmosphere of the Sixties. Beginning with the assassination of Kennedy and continuing with the arrival of the Beatles, the increasingly ugly confrontations faced by blacks in their battle for civil rights, and the growing American military presence in Vietnam, an increasing urgency for change filled the air, a rising fever to which an artist like Coltrane was certainly sensitive.

Coltrane was now recognized by anyone even vaguely aware of jazz as the single most important jazz musician of his time, even more so than Ornette Coleman. He won every poll on both tenor and soprano saxophone, and his group routinely dominated the polls, with Elvin and McCoy becoming increasingly important figures themselves. Miles Davis was in 1964 almost considered a relic of the past. Until 1963 Miles was still basically playing postbop with pretty much the same repertory of tunes, except for the addition of a couple of modal pieces. His former sideman John Coltrane was overshadowing him now, and Miles knew it.

Miles, incidentally, had a theory about the New Thing: It was all the fault of a sort of conspiracy among racist white critics. In his *Autobiography,* he writes, "I think some of pushing the free thing among a lot of the white music critics was intentional, because a lot of them thought that people like me were just getting too popular and powerful in the music industry. They had to find a way to clip my wings."

Of course, Miles's basic premise is ludicrous: many, if not most, critics, almost all of them white, abhorred the so-called "free jazz" and certainly were not reticent to put their opinions in print. Actually, probably the two most avid supporters of the "New Thing" were Amiri Baraka (then LeRoi Jones) and A. B. Spellman, both black.

In 1964 Coltrane released two albums that summed up all his work with the quartet up to that time. The first, titled *Crescent,* was recorded in spring of that year. For a variety of reasons, this became the favorite album of critics like Martin Williams and Whitney Balliet who rarely found favor for Coltrane's work. One of his most accessible albums, it is beautiful, at times stunningly so. Coltrane does not improvise on the only piece that runs over ten minutes, and the blues on the album, the sort of thing that Coltrane would play for a half hour or more in a club, is only three and a half minutes long. The album has a haunting air of contemplation and dark-hued lyricism. Coltrane seems to be compressing many of his ideas and musical avenues, particularly lyrical modalism, expressed on earlier albums. *Crescent* is further proof for those that needed it that he could play with taut cohesion and discipline when he wanted to.

Crescent is a unified work only in terms of mood. There is no question, however, about the concept of *A Love Supreme,* the album that was recorded a few months later, in December 1964. This work was conceived as a whole in one night, and it became Coltrane's most popular, if not his greatest, album. What can be said about an album that has been so widely discussed and analyzed? It is one of the few jazz records that is often owned by people with only a general interest in jazz.

A Love Supreme has been described as a prayer, a work of devotion, a meditation on God, but it is much more than that. It is a searingly confessional, frankly personal piece based on Coltrane's quest to reach and find God through seeking within. In the liner notes Coltrane describes his religious awakening in 1957 when he kicked drugs and alcohol. One can hear the pain of Coltrane's struggle and the bliss, the moments of confusion and of resolve. *A Love Supreme* is divided into four sections: "Acknowledgement," "Resolution," "Pursuance," and "Psalm." The first section is a modal tune on which Coltrane plays tenor over a pedal point, then begins to sing/chant "A Love Supreme," which he does repetitively till the end of the section. It is startling to hear this shy man sing in this manner, but it is indicative of the depth of his religious feelings. He told Naima that from now on 90 percent of his playing would be prayer. One night he called her from Los Angeles just to tell her, "God is! I know that now!"

If one has any doubts about Coltrane's sincerity, listen to "Psalm," the last section on *A Love Supreme*. Played at a dirge-like tempo with no harmonic movement at all, it creates the impression of perfect stillness, like a man on his knees with his head bowed. It is utterly radiant and transcendent, at times pleading, almost sobbing in its need to be with God. It is one of the few works of art that, like the Sistine Chapel or Chartres

Cathedral or Bach's *St. Matthew Passion,* is itself a religious experience. *A Love Supreme* affected, and maybe even changed, lives. It still does. Two or three years ago, Bono, of the Irish rock group U2, announced his discovery of it and its powerful effect on him.

Coltrane was not worshiping the Christian version of God, or the Muslim or Hindu, but rather all of them or, more precisely, a personal synthesis of those ideas basic to all religion. According to J. C. Thomas, at this time he was particularly under the influence of the Kabbalah, the ancient book of Jewish mysticism. He was also heavily influenced by the writings of Paramahansa Yogananda, the author of *Autobiography of a Yogi,* and especially by the philosophy of Jiddu Krishnamurti. It was Krishnamurti who wrote these lines, which Coltrane must have found particularly pertinent: "Religion is not a matter of dogmas and beliefs, of rituals and superstitions; nor is it the cultivation of personal salvation, which is a self-centered activity. Religion is the total way of life; it is the understanding of truth, which is not a projection of the mind."

Many critics pointed out that the music on *A Love Supreme* was not much different from most of Coltrane's work since he began the quartet. Again, the music was mainly modal, often using pedal points, and most of the tunes had that by now familiar Coltrane Middle Eastern flavor, played over Elvin's dynamic West African–influenced drums. However, Coltrane also recorded at the same time a track that added to the quartet his new friend and colleague Archie Shepp and the bassist Art Davis. Coltrane originally wanted the track released with the rest of *A Love Supreme,* but it apparently did not fit on the record and was not included. It eventually was somehow lost. As it stands, besides being a powerful emotional and spiritual statement, *A Love Supreme* is, much as *Giant Steps* had been earlier, Coltrane's summary of his work of the previous few years. Undoubtedly, the lost pieces with Shepp were indications of where he was now heading, just as "Naima" and "Syeeda's Song Flute" had been on *Giant Steps.* Like *Giant Steps, A Love Supreme* transcends its moment in time and its particular place in Coltrane's career. Almost thirty years later it remains one of the most moving and genuinely spiritual documents of our century.

It is significant, and once again indicative of Coltrane's uncanny inner gauge to the temper of the times, that *A Love Supreme* was recorded at the end of 1964. That album is, among so many other things, something of a retrospective of those first few years of the Sixties, a unique time of hope, of the New Frontier and the Great Society and Martin Luther King's dream.

In 1965 that dream began to turn into a nightmare. By early 1965, as the war in Vietnam began to escalate, as the civil rights movement became dominated by the call for "Black Power," as Malcolm X was assassinated and riots tore up the inner cities, as the country's young began to feel a profound disaffection toward a society they viewed as sterile and corrupt, the Sixties really began to heat up. And John Coltrane, who more and more saw unity between his political and social life, his spiritual journey, and his musical search, now buoyed by the enormous surge of change in the air, was pressing forward in his quest into even deeper and more perilous waters.

part two
pursuance

10 ascension

Anyone even vaguely sensitive to the social, cultural, and political climate of America in 1965 had to be aware that the times, in Bob Dylan's immortal words, truly were a-changin'. The civil rights movement was becoming polarized, with many groups ousting whites in order to foster black self-determination. The greatest spokesman of that self-determination, Malcolm X, was assassinated by either Black Muslims or the FBI, take your pick. The Vietnam War had its first real escalation, and protests began to spread among students and others. Pop music was beginning to reflect the advent of the counterculture: Bob Dylan went electric, shocking the folk establishment, and the Beatles began their first experiments with psychedelic rock, recording *Rubber Soul*. America was becoming increasingly polarized in terms of race, the war, and the growing "generation gap."

The hope that blacks had felt earlier in the decade was souring, replaced by a mood of growing impatience. The situation in the northern cities, it came to be recognized, was at least as bad for blacks in its own way as that of the South. To many blacks, the promises of Lyndon Johnson's "Great Society" were basically empty as long as racism was so entrenched in American society. Their rage exploded in riots throughout the country, the worst occurring in the Watts area of Los Angeles. Black Panther Eldridge Cleaver's statement drew the line for the growing polarization, and it singed many consciences: "If you are not part of the solution, you're part of the problem." The "New Thing" musicians, playing a music that often sounded like the soundtrack to a race riot, were affecting, one way or another, virtually every thinking musician in jazz. One's reaction to free jazz became something of a litmus test of political and social as well as musical sympathies. For John Coltrane, 1965 would be a year of momentous transition.

As Coltrane looked around his world in early 1965, he must have been reassured that his struggle was not in vain, that the world, or at least his musical world, was changing and that he had been a large part of that change. It must have been a bit lonely in the Fifties when Coltrane was one of the few jazz explorers willing to climb as far out on the limb of improvisation as he had. Now it looked as if his musical progeny were about to dominate, and profoundly change, jazz in many different ways. In October 1964 a club on New York's Upper West Side held a series of concerts of the best of the New Thing musicians. The series was called the "October Revolution," and despite the difficulty of much of the music, most of the concerts were packed. Perhaps now, these new young lions thought, our music will finally be heard in places other than in private lofts, coffeehouses, or other obscure venues. The way they saw it, getting their music heard was as much a social and political act as it was a musical one.

The New Thing music was becoming more "outside"—more tonally and rhythmically free, certainly discordant to most ears, making it even less accessible to the bulk of the jazz audience. Their attitude was so radical that they refused to even call their music jazz, preferring "black classical music" or "African-American music," or some other more dignified term instead. Using the word "jazz," originally a slang term for sexual intercourse, was part of the same syndrome as "riding in back of the bus," Charlie Mingus once said, a way of segregating and diminishing the accomplishments of blacks. When Coltrane was asked in an interview what he thought of the phrase "new black music" in place of the word "jazz," he replied, "Phrases, I don't know. They don't mean much to me because usually I don't make the phrases, so I don't react too much. It makes no difference to me one way or another."

Coltrane could note the effect that aspects of his playing and, to some extent, that of his colleague in musical adventure Ornette Coleman were having on virtually every jazz musician with open ears. Even the playing of Stan Getz, the most popular tenor man of the Fifties and usually considered the paradigm of cool saxophonists, changed dramatically. Getz's admiration for Coltrane could be heard in his own improvising, which, while remaining clearly identifiable and personal, became far more fiery and intensely expressive. His tone hardened and his rhythmic attack pushed the beat rather than straying behind it. He even recorded with Elvin Jones and hired Jones's occasional substitute in the Coltrane group, the brilliant and dynamic Roy Haynes, to play in his regular working group. It became increasingly difficult to find a saxophonist, ranging from formerly "cool" players like Art Pepper and Lee Konitz to full-fledged members of the post-bop generation like Hank Mobley and Jackie McLean, who was not being influenced by Coltrane in one way or another.

And the influence did not extend only to saxophonists. Coltranesque runs could be heard in the trumpet playing of Freddie Hubbard and even the organ playing of Larry Young. Modal improvisation became almost as common for a while as that based on chords had been, and most players began improvising, for better or worse, at much greater length. The new tenor sax players on the scene differed from each other mainly in the degree to which their style was based on that of Coltrane. The best young tenor men, like Joe Henderson, Archie Shepp, and, especially, Wayne Shorter, who had practiced with Coltrane in Philadelphia, were strongly influenced by Trane in terms of general approach and dynamics, while remaining intransigently original players.

Art Pepper was a particularly interesting case. As one of the best of the West Coast jazz saxophonists, certainly the most dynamic, he was jailed in the beginning of the Sixties for a narcotics violation. When he was released a few years later, he found that jazz had been transformed almost as much as it had been in the Forties after the bop revolution. He even gave up his primary horn, the alto sax, and took up the tenor, with a changed, intensely expressive style complete with Coltranesque tonal distortions, wails, and shrieks. When he eventually returned to alto, his style was still a changed one; now, with the new emotional freedom of the Coltrane era, he was finally able to express the pent-up emotions he had felt as a junkie and convict.

The New Thing movement had special implications for black players, whether veterans or new on the scene, since it had powerful political and social overtones. In the Forties, when Charlie Parker played at a "jazz at the Philharmonic" concert, with a number of players still ensconced in late swing style, the pianist John Lewis pointed out that "Bird makes them all sound like old men." Besides his musical innovations, Bird represented a new social attitude shared by the new generation of boppers. Musicians who remembered that previous revolution understood well the penalties of lagging behind in the course of jazz's constant forward momentum.

Some attempts to join the avant-garde were unsurprisingly faddish. In the early Sixties Jackie McLean, a wonderful musician, would on some occasions interrupt an otherwise superb solo to let loose with a squeal so shrill it seemed only half an octave below a dog whistle. That long-held shriek apparently served no real musical purpose, but merely announced the player's fellowship with the New Thing-ers and with all the political and social baggage that went along with it. I don't wish to single McLean out. He made some superb records in the Sixties, using modes and shifting tempos and meters, and mostly his soloing was, as always, wonderful—which made that long-held squeal he would invariably throw into his solos at this time, when it was irrelevant, even more irritating.

Sonny Rollins, an adventurous musician since he first began to play professionally as a teenager in the late Forties, for a short time also aligned himself with the new avant-garde. In 1962 Rollins hired half of Ornette Coleman's band, including the highly iconoclastic trumpeter Don Cherry. Rollins only occasionally engaged in screams or sputterings, and only then for color and drama, but his solos began to grow even longer than before, and he ventured farther out of the harmonic structure. Rollins's imagination had always ridden free and wide: "Music is an open sky," he once said. His live album with this band, *Our Man in Jazz,* is a classic, one of the few records where one can hear the many levels of Rollins's genius, his humor, his constant risk taking, his deconstruction of melody, his rhythmic genius. He was still in his free mode, though with a different band, when he recorded with the father of the jazz saxophone, Coleman Hawkins. You might think that Rollins would restrain himself in such patriarchal company, but his playing was truly free—not predictable shrieks (although he did create all manner of sounds with his horn when it was relevant) but genuine stream-of-consciousness, anything-goes improvising.

Surprisingly, Hawkins showed that he too had been listening to the new breed and especially to Coltrane. It was Hawkins, with his vertical style, who had profoundly influenced the early Coltrane, especially during the beginning of Trane's "sheets of sound" period. Now, in the last few years of his life, he would play Coltranesque runs and yet, as always, remain true to his own muse.

Rollins came down to earth and began playing more conventionally by 1965 or so, but he would always retain some of the ideas he had explored during his flirtation with free jazz. It is hard to think of any musician more free than Sonny Rollins on a good night, no matter what he is playing.

Many of the white liberal critics were alarmed by the influence of this new generation of musical radicals, since, even more than with the boppers, the New Thing was closely associated with black political and social militance. Unknown to most white fans and critics, the truth is that many jazz musicians, long before the New Thing, harbored far more anger and resentment toward American racism than most other blacks, mainly due to their experiences traveling through this country and their sophistication from traveling abroad. Rarely did they discuss racial matters with critics, almost all of whom were white. When interviewed by a fellow black musician, however, as in the drummer Art Taylor's book of his interviews with several well-known colleagues, *Notes and Tones,* their comments on racism in America and its music business were frank, blunt, and as angry as many of the New Thing players of the Sixties. A white man who had been deeply involved in the jazz scene for many years told me he hated Taylor's collection of interviews because of its "racism." But it was just jazz musicians talking far more honestly and openly than usual.

Looking back, the cause of such rage is hardly a mystery. The viciousness of Southern sheriffs with their dogs and their firehoses made many blacks question not only Martin Luther King's policy of nonviolence but the idea of integration itself. The cries of "Black Power" that were beginning to dominate the civil rights movement could be heard echoed in the screaming intensity of the avant-garde jazz movement. Coltrane could now look out at his audience and see young black brothers thrusting their fists into the air when he played his furiously boiling hour-long solos.

In 1964 a series of panel discussions about race and jazz held at Greenwich Village nightclubs opened the eyes and scared the hell out of those who were unaware of the growing black fury. A nightclub now seems an odd place for a discussion of American racism, but in the Sixties it made perfect sense, so closely was the music tied to the political and social currents of the time. The first couple of forums were held at the Village Vanguard. The panel included Archie Shepp, LeRoi Jones, Nat Hentoff, and some others. Jones, a longtime Coltrane booster, had become a strong supporter of the new avant-garde (his two books on blues and jazz, *Blues People* and *Black Music,* are classics of social and cultural criticism). Many musicians looked on him as a sort of poetic spokesman, even occasionally having him read his poetry on some of their albums. Although early in his career Jones had been part of the Greenwich Village poetry scene, and good friends with many white bohos, he had grown increasingly separatist, often stridently so. Both Jones and Shepp were vitriolic toward all the white participants, treating them with utter contempt. When a Jewish man in the audience began comparing the plight of blacks to the Holocaust, Shepp erupted with,

"I'm sick of you Jews and your six million dead." Shepp might have had a point, of course, if he had said simply that the suffering of one group in the past has little relevance to the daily pain of another. But the way he said it antagonized and infuriated most of the audience—which might have been his intention.

At a subsequent meeting at the Village Gate, the panel included Hentoff and Jones once again, along with Cecil Taylor. Jones showed up late and told the audince that he was moving permanently uptown and never wanted to have anything to do with whites again. When a sincere young white person asked him what she could do to aid the black cause he said, "Kill yourself and save us the trouble. You are all rotten fruit." Taylor, on the other hand, expressed the ironic double edge of the avant-garde players. He asked the owner of the Gate, Art D'Lugoff, point blank why he was never hired to play at his club. This was the dissonant chord that Taylor repeatedly struck throughout the evening—the lack of work for him and other members of the avant-garde at the mainstream jazz clubs. Here was the irony facing the members of the New Thing: although they were racially militant, they were dependent on the white listeners who made up the largest segment of their audience, as well as white club owners and record company executives, for a living. For Taylor, as for a number of other New Thing musicians, his right to earn a living by playing his music was a political issue in itself.

To Jones (who in 1968 would discard his "slave name" and become Imamu Amiri Baraka), black music was directly a result of repressed rage. Whites enjoyed the music, but could only appreciate it on a certain level, since they had no real understanding of the furious source from which it sprang. Nowhere did he express this idea more eloquently than in his play *Dutchman*. This one-act drama is about a confrontation on a New York subway car between a black man and a seductive white woman. The tension builds until the black man, Clay, finally explodes under the duress of the woman's inherent racism. At one point he says to her, "Old bald-headed, four-eyed ofays popping their fingers . . . and don't know what they're doing. They say, 'I love Bessie Smith.' And don't even undersand that

Bessie Smith is saying 'Kiss my ass. Kiss my black unruly ass.' . . . Charlie Parker? Charlie Parker. All the hip white boys scream for Bird. And Bird saying, 'Up your ass, feeble-minded ofay! Up your ass.' And they sit there talking about the tortured genius of Charlie Parker. Bird would've played not a note of music if he just walked up to East Sixty-seventh Street and killed the first ten white people he saw. Not a note!"

Consciously or not, Jones was simply giving a twist to the Freudian view of creativity, that it springs from subconscious repression. Why was Charlie Parker's need to create different from that of any other great artist? Was Jones implying that blacks would have no creative urge if it weren't for their repressed rage? Would Mozart never have written a note of music if, say, he had killed the first ten Frenchmen he saw walking down the street? Racial oppression, with its resultant anger and frustration, was no doubt one of the elements that produced so many black musical geniuses in the twentieth century. But saying that oppression is the sole reason for black creativity is vastly oversimplifying the complex causes of the creative impulse and demeaning to those great black musical artists. Don't forget the testimony of John Coltrane, who hated it when some critics called him an "angry tenor man." He said that the only one he was ever angry at was himself, when he fell short of his artistic goals.

If anger was not the root cause for the musicians of the New Thing to be drawn to their art, rage was definitely a central theme of their music—as well as the other side of that coin, joy and ecstasy. The distinction is clear: music can use anger as its subject, just as it can use love or spirituality as its subject. The shrieks and screams that were so ubiquitous among the new wave of free jazz musicians were not only expressions of fury but also cries of ecstatic release.

How much did political concerns dominate the thinking of John Coltrane? He seemed to stand at the center of all these controversies sweeping through jazz, both musical and political. When he talked about his goals, the spiritual aspects of his quest were always paramount. In the Sixties polarization was so extreme that even stating that one believed in such simplistic pieties as peace and love carried all sorts of political and social baggage. Coltrane's beliefs and his life quest were, at heart, truly revolutionary, but they were revolutionary in the terms of Krishnamurti—that the true revolution, and hope for change in the world, was the revolution within. Since Coltrane, along with Ornette Coleman, were the fathers of the New Thing, they had to be torn between the rage of some of their young colleagues and the growing intensity of their own spiritual paths. Coltrane's study of religion, both Eastern and Western, must have given him insight into the self-defeating futility of hate and violence.

If Coltrane never made any statements that could really be construed as militant, the fact remains that he turned the tide of jazz from West to East. His involvement in the music of non-Western countries was clearly a statement about the value of non-European cultures, particularly those of Africa and India. Coltrane never denied, either verbally or inherently in his work, the value of Western music; he simply made clear the equal value of non-Western art. This in itself contributed to black pride, as well as raising whites' consciousness.

At that time increasing numbers of young Americans, of all races, were turning to the East for spiritual inspiration. There was a growing feeling that Western culture was becoming degenerate, with its values based on materialism, its destruction of the environment, and its one-dimensional lifestyle. Intuition, ecstasy, and spiritual passion were replacing, among large numbers of the young, the goals of security and material wealth. Coltrane may have had little directly to do with the creation of the counterculture, but the non-Western alternatives both in his music itself and his worldview reflected and contributed immeasurably toward the Sixties zeitgeist.

Coltrane's involvement in matters of the spirit might seem to contradict his standing among militants as a political and social totem. In the Sixties, however, religion, particularly esoteric religion, was not considered incompatible with strong anti-establishment social and political attitudes and viewpoints. The synergy between religious vision and political and social revolt was strengthened among many by the increasingly pervasive use of psychedelic drugs, particularly LSD. The use of LSD, especially before it was made illegal, was not seen as a way of simply getting high, but rather a viable method of attaining spiritual ecstasy and gaining personal, religious, and even social insight. When Timothy Leary and Allen Ginsburg decided to save the world through acid, jazz musicians, including Dizzy Gillespie, Charles Mingus, and Roland Kirk, were among the first cultural figures they turned on. Jazz musicians were a perfect choice, since most of them had smoked that mild psychedelic marijuana for years. The beats had viewed the jazz musician as a modern holy man and shaman, someone well experienced in exploring his psychic interior, as well as having extraordinary creative powers. The use of acid was rampant among many involved in the New Thing movement by the mid-Sixties, as well as among those in the burgeoning counterculture. In those early days of the counterculture, before it took on the trappings of a fad and media event, those involved in its creation were spiritual seekers not unlike Coltrane. They too had been heavily influenced by many of the same sources, including Krishnamurti, yoga, astrology, the Kabbalah, and the Tibetan Book of the Dead.

John Coltrane began using LSD fairly regularly some time in 1965. Although it has been stated by some that he took it only when he recorded *Om* later that year, he actually took it far more often during the last few years of his life, according to a number of people, including a member of the quartet who would prefer, like others, not to be quoted directly on this subject. One friend of his remembers that Coltrane would get so disoriented from acid during some gigs that after intermission he had to be guided back to stage. And Miles Davis once told me that "Coltrane died from taking too much LSD." He did not mean this literally, of course, but rather in terms of the music of the last few years of Coltrane's life (the very few times Miles tried psychedelics he reacted very badly, including once having to be treated for heart palpitations). For Coltrane and his quest, LSD was a remarkable tool to dig deeper into his own being so he could discover the essential and absolute truth at the center of his being.

Discussing Coltrane's frequent use of LSD makes it too easy for many of his critics to find new reasons to dismiss his late work. Coltrane's music was undoubtedly influenced by his use of psychedelics, but he was a great enough artist to put these experiences into artistic perspective, at least most of the time. Not all of his late work was successful, and some of it was incoherent and ill-conceived, but there are many moments of astonishingly powerful and cohesively realized music and lengthy passages of great beauty. Trying to find facile explanations for the interior source and artistic direction of an artist as complex as Coltrane is futile.

Coltrane's LSD experiences confirmed spiritual insights he had already discovered rather than radically changing his perspective. After one early acid trip he said, "I perceived the interrelationship of all life forms," an idea he had found repeated in many of the books on Eastern theology that he had been reading for years. For Coltrane, who for years had been trying to relate mystical systems such as numerology and astrology, theories of modern physics and mathematics, the teachings of the great spiritual leaders, and advanced musical theory, and trying somehow to pull these threads into something he could play on his horn, the LSD experience gave him visceral evidence that his quest was on the right track.

Books, however, continued to be the main source of Coltrane's intellectual and spiritual search. He read everything from biographies of other artists to books on esoteric philosophy and religion. One book that particularly fascinated him was *Autobiography of a Yogi* by Paramahansa Yogananda. Yogananda's life was also a quest for the ultimate truth, not unlike that of Coltrane. Yogananda believed that the secret of life could be attained through "scientific" methods and that the road to God was attainable like every other secret of nature. Eventually Yogananda, heeding his guru, came to America to spread his knowledge of yoga, which he did very successfully. Like Coltrane, Yogananda actively sought the blending of East and West spirituality.

Coltrane was also fascinated with the works of the Indian philosopher Jiddu Krishnamurti. Krishnamurti believed himself to be, basically, a revolutionary, but a revolutionary of the human spirit. He believed that each person must look within and work for personal change in order for the world at large to change. He wrote, "War is a result of our so-called peace, which is a series of everyday brutalities, exploitation, narrowness and so on. Without changing our daily life we can't have peace, and war is a spectacular expression of our daily conduct." He also wrote, "That human beings should behave in the bestial manner is revolting . . . one dominant race exploits another, as is shown all over the world. There's no reason, sanity, behind all this greed for power, wealth, and position. One must be an individual, sane and balanced, not belonging to any race or any particular ideology. Then perhaps sanity and peace will come back to the world." For Coltrane, whose life was about looking within and creating music with his inner discoveries, Krishnamurti's philosophy must have been a genuine revelation.

Since Coltrane rarely spoke about matters other than music, no one was certain of how much he shared the views of LeRoi Jones or Archie Shepp. Did he have as much open resentment against whites as they did? It's hard to believe that a man obsessed with unity could have such resentments. According to the white man with whom he worked most closely over the course of the Sixties, Bob Thiele, the A & R man at Impulse, he did not. According to Thiele, "I honestly can't say if [Coltrane] was militant or if he hated me or didn't like working with me—the impression I had was the opposite, that he did enjoy working for me." The same was not true of Archie Shepp, whom Thiele also produced for Impulse. Although they worked on several albums together, the tension reached a point where three-quarters through one session, Thiele said to Shepp, " 'You're under contract to the company, but they're going to have to get somebody else to work with you.' I just couldn't make it, and that was strictly on the personal, social level. That was the problem, it wasn't about music. . . . The musicians feel that the record company stands for everything that's white and the producers are ripping off black musicians. They're always talking about how they would like to see the record companies owned by black people, and one of my sarcastic remarks is, 'Well, then, record for Motown,' but the one black company in the record business doesn't really record black jazz music."

Regardless of Coltrane's political and social attitudes, the influence of the New Thing could be increasingly heard in his music. Now that he had completed the work he had begun since the first days of the quartet with two summarizing masterpieces, *Crescent* and especially *A Love Supreme,* he was free to explore fresh territory. He had not yet discovered that "essential" that he was searching for. As worthwhile as the music might have been, he still had not reached the end of his quest.

He was not yet ready to change course completely. By simply keeping the quartet together he kept a foot in the musical past. As adventurous as their work was, neither McCoy Tyner nor Elvin Jones were free jazz players. As 1965 progressed, Coltrane's music would become increasingly "outside," although he obviously was finding it difficult to give up the logic and lyricism of the music he had made until that year. He had become a man divided.

His confusion, or at least his divided loyalties, can be heard on the album he recorded in February 1965, only two months after recording *A Love Supreme.* The album, *The John Coltrane Quartet Plays,* at first glance would seem to be Coltrane simply treading water, with may be even a few commercial considerations. The first tune is "Chim Chim Chiree" from Walt Disney's *Mary Poppins,* another Julie Andrews classic. Like "My Favorite Things," Coltrane plays the simple melody over Tyner's vamp, although here the vamp is ominous and dissonant. In place of the ecstatic joy of "Things," his playing now is much freer and, complementary to Tyner's vamp and Elvin's churning drums, it has a feeling of mounting darkness. After Tyner's solo, Coltrane plays again, this time playing so fast that it sounds as if his soprano had suddenly exploded into hundreds of burning scraps of metal. This explosion of sound has no melodic direction; it is pure sound and fury in the mode of a spectacular fireworks display and a bit scary as well. The next tune, despite being titled "Brasilia," has nothing apparently to do with Brazilian music. It is another long modal piece with Coltrane on tenor. His playing is once again much freer than anything he had done before, suggesting the full chromaticism toward which he was headed. It is almost as if he longs to fly free, but the rest of the group, acting like gravity, is keeping him on the ground. Also evident is the long way he had come since the first recorded version of "Impressions," a piece similar to "Brasilia" in its modality and tempo. While that first "Impressions" had long dull patches, and at times seems oddly thin, "Brasilia" is dense with cohesively patterned ideas and is totally gripping throughout.

The next tune is a total surprise, Nat King Cole's hit "Nature Boy," though I doubt that Cole would have recognized it after the first few bars. Of course, "Nature Boy" has a quasi, some would say very quasi, Eastern-sounding melody and is basically modal, so in many ways it would seem perfect for Coltrane. One comes to this performance expecting the same approach he had been using on such tunes for the past few years, but such expectations are smashed. Coltrane once again uses another bassist on "Nature Boy," but rather than using it to "elasticize" the time as he had done in such pieces as "India," he has the second bassist, the redoubtable Art Davis, use the bow, producing an eerie effect almost like a swooning second tenor sax. Coltrane's playing has a disturbing, pleading quality, like a man sinking into musical quicksand.

The last piece, "Song of Praise," seems at first similar to the "Psalm" from *A Love Supreme*. But instead of the feeling of complete spiritual resolution and surrender of that prayerful piece, "Song of Praise" is more complex in mood and becomes instead the prayer of a man still searching. Instead of utter serenity, a feeling of restlessness, doubt, and inner turmoil pervades. The piece is not as perfectly constructed nor as awe-inspiring as the "Psalm"; the experience of listening to it is disturbing. This is clearly the work of a man desperately searching for inner peace and frustrated by the barriers keeping him from his goal.

Listening to *The John Coltrane Quartet Plays* it is obvious that despite the spiritual revelation of *A Love Supreme*, Coltrane is still not satisfied; he is still seeking. It is also obvious that as an artist he must move further into the musical unknown and, like Albert Ayler, perhaps beyond notes themselves. That imperative is in further evidence in a recording of "Nature Boy" made by the quartet at a New Thing concert given to benefit

LeRoi Jones's new Black Arts program in Harlem. Here Coltrane only vaguely alludes to the original tune before plunging into even freer playing than on the original recording. Incidentally, it should be noted that LeRoi Jones/Amiri Baraka held his benefit not in Harlem but at the Village Gate. Despite the fact that Jones was regularly railing against whites in his writing, in order to get a substantial audience for the New Music, the concert had to be held in Greenwich Village so that white jazz fans, who were still the bulk of the audience for the avant-garde, would comfortably attend.

It is hard to remember the masochism of the Sixties, when whites seemed almost to enjoy, or at least accept as their due, the virulent attacks of militant blacks such as Jones. Jones had a regular column in *Down Beat* in which he used racial epithets ("gray" or "gray boys") for whites, who formed the largest part of the magazine's readership. Jones regularly disparaged the magazine for which he was writing as well as its publisher and editors. That virtually all of the writers for *Down Beat* since its inception had been white was disgraceful, but for those editors to purge their guilt by allowing Jones to regularly condemn them and attack them, and all other whites, with racial slurs in its pages was a phenomenon that could only have existed in the Sixties. This same masochism probably had something to do with the appeal of the New Thing in its most extreme forms to some in the white audience.

Despite such social factors as white masochism and the support of young black militants, the avant-garde jazz players had a difficult time finding large-scale acceptance, or even an audience as large as that of the generation of hard boppers that had preceded them. Coltrane became the main benefactor of the new free players. Without the active encouragement of such an important "mainstream" musician as Coltrane, the New Thing movement would never have had nearly as much influence on both jazz and its audience. Trane convinced his producer, Bob Thiele, to sign a number of the young lions of the new avant-garde, including Archie Shepp, the altoist Marion Brown, Pharoah Sanders, and Albert Ayler, to record on Impulse. With increasing frequency one or more of these players would sit in with the quartet in clubs or concerts. When Elvin Jones, who disliked the playing of most of the free jazz players, saw Shepp or Pharoah Sanders stroll onto the bandstand after a long Coltrane solo, he would think, "Oh, no, here comes *another* one of those motherfuckers." As much as Jones loved Trane, he was finding it increasingly difficult to stomach his boss's new directions and cohorts.

In spring of 1965 Coltrane recorded the pieces that would eventually be posthumously released on the album *Transition*. On the longest pieces on the record, "Transition" and "Prayer and Meditation," it is clear that Coltrane was in the middle of a major change of style and that he was not ready to make a complete break with tonality and enter the realm of pure sound. The quartet was now perhaps holding him down, preventing the rocket of his imagination from shooting through the stratosphere.

One track, "Dear Lord," is one of the simplest and prettiest pieces he had ever recorded. "Transition," on the other hand, is a furious solo. "Dear Lord" is the peaceful side of the search for God, and "Transition" the darker, terror-laden side. "Transition," like much of Coltrane's work in the last years of his life, is often difficult to listen to; it seems to tear apart one's nervous system. Yet Coltrane's playing is brilliant, and despite the length of the track, he plays with a sure sense of form. Techniques such as multiphonics have been perfected and used as part of a musical whole rather than just for effect. Coltrane had obviously made great strides in modal improvisation since the early Sixties. Although he still uses repetitive phrases, there is never a moment of monotony in "Transition"; it is a gripping piece of music. Listening to "Transition," it is hard not to hear confusion, frustration, and even rage, maybe at himself, maybe at God or at least the difficulties of the path to God. Yet the more one listens to "Transition" the more one hears a diamond-hard beauty unlike anything else in music. That something so roiling can also have such beauty is one of the paradoxes of Coltrane's art. A lot of great twentieth-century art, since it reflects its time, seems to confront and challenge its audience: *Guernica, Finnegans Wake, The Rite of Spring*. Like those modern masterpieces, much of Coltrane's work from around this time has a modern grandeur unlike anything that has come before it.

"Prayer and Meditation," a lengthy suite, while equally intense, is far more accessible and often very moving, with a more lyrical beauty than "Transition." It is a hard-won beauty, however, both for musician and listener and therefore seems especially rewarding. Clearly Coltrane's vision of his pilgrimage to ultimate spiritual knowledge was not always filled with rose petals and incense. There was terror in looking for God within, and danger in the seeking. Finding God was a matter of catharsis as well as joy. The pieces on *Transition* are expressions of a man in the midst of change, deeply aware of the spiritual consequences of his direction.

The event that signaled Coltrane's full embrace of the New Thing and its players was the recording of *Ascension*. *Ascension* is an overwhelmingly powerful piece of organized sound. It is, however, ultimately a failure. An audacious failure—even fanatic Coltrane haters like Philip Larkin at least agreed about the saxophonist's sheer audacity in recording a piece of music like *Ascension*—but it is a failure nonetheless. *Ascension* marks a great turning point for Coltrane, however. With this album, he finally became a full-fledged member of the free jazz avant-garde, with no turning back. Whatever doubts he had about this move, musical or in terms of keeping his audience, he finally decided that he had no choice, he had to continue forward and explore these new, free, musical concepts, many of which had fascinated him since he first heard Ornette play at the Five Spot. As George Russell put it, "[When he recorded *Ascension*], that's when Coltrane turned his back on the money." The great inner debate he had described to Russell yeas before was finally settled. Despite the risk of losing his audience, he would plunge full force into free jazz.

For *Ascension*, Coltrane assembled half a dozen of the leading young players he had currently been listening to, together with his own tenor sax, the other members of his quartet, and the bassist Art Davis, and he had them play in alternating passages of completely free, raw, and raucous group improvisation and individual solos backed by a rhythm section. As one of the musicians on the date, Marion Brown, described *Ascension*'s making: "We did two takes, and they both had that kind of thing in them that makes people scream. The people in the studio were screaming."

Maybe so, but after several minutes of *Ascension* what should have been a bracing performance becomes merely numbing. The ensemble improvisations, while having a blunt power—shrieking, screaming, ripping through the air and one's eardrums, tearing apart the fabric of what polite culture accepts as music— nevertheless begin to sound alike, and even at times contrived. The solos of the very free players, like Pharoah Sanders and Marion Brown, and even the increasingly free Coltrane himself, sound out of place backed by the quartet rhythm section, which was still stubbornly postbop. One of the soloists is, inexplicably, Freddie Hubbard, who was never a free player. He sounds more comfortable than the other soloists with the rhythm section, however, since he, like them, is a postbopper rather than a free player.

Nobody, not even Coltrane himself, gets to really stretch out owing to the time limits of recording. Coltrane takes the first, and easily the best, of the solos. The rest, even Pharoah Sanders's piercing-shriek improvisation, come as anticlimax. In the end, when members of the rhythm section are all playing their solos, *Ascension* simply deflates.

The inspirations for *Ascension* were Ornette Coleman's far more successful *Free Jazz* recording and, most likely, some of the work of Sun Ra and his Arkestra. *Ascension* was a noble attempt to put the sounds of the New Thing into a larger musical setting and to present thicker and more varied tonal colors than are possible in small group jazz, while at the same time keeping the music basically improvisational. One aspect of jazz that seemed to have disappeared temporarily was true group improvisation, the heart of the New Orleans style that had dominated jazz until Louis Armstrong's magnificent trumpet improvisations of the mid-Twenties had made the individual solo the prime currency of jazz. Many musicians and critics of the Sixties believed that true jazz was that of the improvising ensemble of early jazz, and that the basically solo art it had become since was a debasement, virtuostic but lacking the dense colors and communal feeling of New Orleans jazz. The free players of the Sixties began to bring group improvisation back to jazz from a new vantage point. Once again by looking back, as far back as some of the musical traditions of Africa, jazz moved forward.

Ascension does not wear well; unlike the best of Coltrane's work, it seems dated, an artifact peculiar to a specific time in American music and society. As Martin Williams pointed out at the time, *Ascension* was perhaps more important as a social document than an aesthetic one, and perhaps should have been heard by policemen, politicians, social workers, and such. One can argue that in *Ascension* one can hear the aesthetic of the race riots. It undoubtedly belongs in a Sixties time capsule, since it so perfectly captures much of the furious temper of the times. Whether you liked it or not, when *Ascension* was released you had the feeling that you had to listen to it carefully as a sort of rite of passage, that it simply could not be ignored.

Some found other uses for this noisy album. The drummer Art Taylor, who had frequently played with Trane in the Fifties, told me how he pulled back the arm of his record changer, turned up the volume, and had it play over and over while he was away from home as revenge against obnoxiously noisy neighbors. Somehow, I don't think Coltrane exactly intended this use for *Ascension.*

Recorded with just the quartet on the same day as *Ascension*, but released on another album long after, is one of Coltrane's stunningly lyrical pieces, once again with a perfectly descriptive title: "Welcome." "Welcome," unlike *Ascension*, seems to lovingly embrace the listener with its warmth. To paraphrase Andre Gide, "Do not understand Coltrane too easily."

Coltrane's intentions in his immersion in the New Thing were misunderstood by a great many in the jazz community, including people who had at one time loved his music and sympathized with his musical quest. Many found his music becoming close to unlistenable, despite his goals. The irony is that the New Thing players were directly influenced by Coltrane, without whom, as well as Ornette, there would not have been a New Thing. When Coltrane appeared at a jazz festival in Chicago held by *Down*

Beat magazine, many booed and walked out when he and Archie Shepp launched into a long, wailing, screaming duet. Some critics called it among the ugliest music they had ever heard. Even the work that he had done with Eric Dolphy seemed tame compared to much of his work in this period. I think even Coltrane was even wondering what would have happened if he had gone further beyond the original intentions of his search. Don't forget his words of a few years previously: "I want to progress, but I don't want to go so far out that I can't see what others are doing." With such music as his duet with Shepp, he was getting dangerously near the edge.

Despite Coltrane's friendship with Shepp, it was Pharoah Sanders who became a regular part of the group around this time. Born Farrell Sanders in 1940 in Little Rock, Arkansas, he moved to California's Bay Area, where he first played professionally, like Coltrane, mainly in rhythm and blues bands. He came into contact with a number of the burgeoning avant-garde players, including the altoist Sonny Simmons, Ornette Coleman, and, briefly, Coltrane. His first break in jazz came when he joined Sun Ra's band. He began his jazz career as a Coltrane acolyte. "John," he told an interviewer, "has influenced me in my playing much longer than I've been playing with him. See, John is the kind of person who is trying to create something different all the time. . . . The way John and I play—it's different, we're both natural players and we have our own way of doing things. Somebody like John is playing things on his horn that make you think a lot of things and he makes me think about doing something in my own way."

About Sanders, Coltrane said, "Pharoah is a man of huge spiritual reservoir. He's always trying to reach out to truth. He's trying to allow his spiritual self to be his guide. He's dealing, among other things, in energy, in integrity, in essences. I so much like the *strength* of his playing . . . it's been my pleasure and privilege that he's been willing to help me, that he is part of the group."

Pharoah's usual solo at this time consisted of deep growls and an earsplitting drawn-out shriek that would develop into multiphonics as it progressed. If a shriek could be beautiful, then that was the sound Pharoah produced on his saxophone. He would not really perfect this scream until after Coltrane's death. The sound he makes on *Ascension* and other albums such as *Live at Seattle* is a shriek in progress. Despite its volume and power it is more noise, at this point, than music. A Sanders solo at this time in his career would begin in climax and build from there, driving many listeners quickly out the door. At heart, though, Sanders was as lyrical a player as Coltrane, and a superbly convincing blues player—aspects of his talent that would not emerge until after Coltrane's death, when he led his own group.

Now that a player as radically committed to the New Thing as Sanders was in his group, there was no turning back for Coltrane. Why it took so long for him to finally commit himself to free jazz, I think is connected to his basic feelings about music. Music, for Coltrane, was more than a source of entertainment. Influenced by the Indian and African attitude toward music as central to one's life, religion, and community, Coltrane's commitment to free jazz was a spiritual and ethical choice as much as an aesthetic one.

Yet he definitely had his doubts. Red Garland, Coltrane's friend and pianist from the Miles days, told an interviewer about seeing Coltrane playing at a club one night around this time. Garland, always the joyous melodicist, disliked Coltrane's new music intensely. Between sets Garland bought Coltrane a drink (probably orange juice) at a nearby bar. When he asked him if he really liked this new music, Coltrane seemed less than certain. He told Garland that he often thought he should return to his former style of the late Fifties and early Sixties. Such stories should be regarded skeptically, not because Garland was lying, but because any thoughtful artist who becomes involved in a radically new aesthetic naturally alienates a large part of his audience. That artist is bound to have second thoughts at times. Additionally, his friend Garland must have certainly brought back strong memories of the joyous music the two men had once made together. The idea of someone like John Coltrane retreating is unthinkable. The notion ran against his grain. He had to move forward, as nostalgic as he might be for the sheer beauty of his former musical conception. And as worried as he might have been about losing some of his audience, he had to find that "essence," that sound which would have him directly encounter the mind of God.

Now that he was committed to this radical course, Coltrane must also have given deep thought to the sociopolitical implications of the New Thing movement, an inescapable issue to anyone trying to sort out the multiple meanings of the new music. Even though Coltrane had his own spiritual agenda, he could not ignore the social issues. There were those in and around the movement, often with their own agendas, who relentlessly tried to paint him into a corner on the subject. Besides LeRoi Jones, the foremost critic of the political and social content of free jazz, there was Frank Kofsky. Kofsky was white and Jewish and wrote reams of seemingly endless articles, most of them published in the short-lived magazine *Jazz,* about black militancy and the "New Music," many of which reappeared in his book *Black Nationalism and the Revolution in Music.* Kofsky, a Marxist, heard in avant-garde music the screams of protest of the black masses. He regarded the New Thing musicians as the leading edge of that inevitable revolution which so many in the Sixties were convinced was right around the corner. Kofsky, an intelligent man and a scholar, realized that too exact an equation between radical politics and music was misleading, but the thrust of his argument was that the New Thing was the musical counterpoint to the ideas and rhetoric of Malcolm X and other black militants.

For a while, Kofsky was quite controversial and, among some in the jazz scene, influential. At the time, those advocating "Black Power" were in need of defending, since that term, which implied that blacks could never be truly equal in our society unless they had political and social power equal to that of whites, was twisted around by politicians and the press as somehow meaning a threat of violence against whites.

Kofsky was the scourge of any critic who had ever been less than sanguine about the New Thing, railing at their supposed racism and parochial points of view. To a degree he had a point. Too many critics ignored the racism of American society and its effects, in economic terms as well as in the serious acceptance of the musicians and status of jazz by the guardians of our society's cultural institutions. A few critics were exceptions, of course. Nat Hentoff, for one, often wrote on the social issues of jazz, and Martin Williams, for whom Kofsky had a special grudge, saw the value of *Ascension* as political statement and warning. Kofsky often seemed opportunistic, embracing Malcolm X whole-heartedly *before* Malcolm went to Mecca and, after seeing Muslim worshipers of all colors, radically changed his racial perspective. Until then, Malcolm X preached that whites were literally devils. Did Kofsky think that he was somehow exempted from this designation because of his politics?

Kofsky's main heroes were Malcolm X and John Coltrane, which must have confused the latter. Trane spent most of the late Fifties and early Sixties *denying* that he was an "angry tenor." In an interview, Kofsky made a major point out of Coltrane's having gone to see Malcolm X speak once when Malcolm had broken with Elijah Muhammad and his strict racist doctrines. Coltrane told Kofsky that he had wanted to hear Malcolm speak out of curiosity and that he had been "impressed." Anybody who ever heard Malcolm X was impressed, even William F. Buckley. When Kofsky asked Coltrane pointedly about the "relationship between some of Malcolm's ideas and [Coltrane's] music," Coltrane answered, "Well, I think that music, being an expression of the human heart, or of the human being itself, does express just what is happening. I feel it expresses the whole thing—the whole of human experience at the time that it is being expressed." His comment is hardly a ringing endorsement of Malcolm X.

Coltrane never named a piece after Malcolm X or dedicated one to him, as did some other musicians in the New Thing movement. He did write a piece for Martin Luther King, Jr., however. That may not mean much now, but in the polarized politics of the Sixties, when some black radicals tried to portray King as an Uncle Tom, it had great significance. King, of course, believed in integration and nonviolence, and much of his philosophy was adapted from Gandhi. It is no surprise that the gentle, introspective, profoundly religious John Coltrane would sympathize with someone like King and King's mentor, Gandhi, rather than the separatist views of Malcolm X. If Coltrane had any specifically political views, they are largely a mystery. He told Kofsky that social awareness was part of the content of his art, as it would be with virtually any artist, but clearly the whole of that content is much greater than this one part. Regarding Coltrane, Kofsky is like the protagonist of Nabokov's great novel *Pale Fire:* annotating the eponymous poem, written by a famous deceased poet, he interprets the meaning of the poem completely in his own terms and concerns, totally missing the poet's very personal true intentions. Not once does Kofsky address the spiritual aspects of Coltrane's music, a subject that Coltrane discussed repeatedly and that is patent to anyone even vaguely aware of Trane's artistic philosophy. The reason why the Marxist Kofsky ignored this particular subject is no mystery.

In an interview with McCoy Tyner, Kofsky again tried to elicit political rage, virtually putting words in the pianist's mouth. At one point he asked, "Malcolm X's autobiography reveals that he was a jazz lover and a close friend of many jazz musicians. Do you think this is just an accident or that there is some deeper significance about this—that this says something about the nature of jazz and the nature of Malcolm X?" How can one man's taste in music reveal anything about "the nature" of that music? What if Malcolm also happened to like Strauss waltzes? Further along in the interview Tyner, too, expresses awareness of social inequities. Once again, Tyner's conception is wider and deeper than Kofsky's narrow perspective. When Kofsky asks him if he would categorize his work as "new black music," Tyner replies, "It's not an accurate title. . . . Number one, I don't like to categorize myself or my music in any respect, because I feel that music, number one, is universal; and that at least the way I feel is that I'm motivated by different aspects of life. I'm not motivated by [political considerations]."

There was a subtle strand of racism in Kofsky's attitude toward black musicians. In Ralph Ellison's novel *Invisible Man,* the anonymous hero is befriended by apparently sympathetic white Communists. After a while, he comes to understand that he is invisible to them, too; he is a symbol of suffering and oppression to be used for their own revolutionary purposes, but not a whole, real, flesh-and-blood man. A great artist's agenda, like that of John Coltrane, is far more complex than any narrow social or political viewpoint, although that viewpoint may certainly be a part of it. To Frank Kofsky, Coltrane was an invisible man, in whose music he heard only what he wanted to hear.

Later in the Sixties, Kofsky almost completely stopped writing about black music because he had found his new revolutionary hero: the white hippie! Kofsky began writing reams of his dense prose about these hippies and acid rock and how *they* were the new catalysts of the revolution. His heroes became Janis Joplin (whom many resented for her blatant ripoff of black blues style, particularly that of Bessie Smith), the Grateful Dead, the Beatles, etc. In one piece he goes on and on about how sexy Grace Slick and Janis Joplin were, particularly noting Joplin's shapely legs. Kofsky might have raged against racism, but he saw nothing wrong with a little sexism.

One aspect of Kofsky's writings should be taken seriously, however, because it affected Coltrane and every other serious jazz musician. Kofsky was one of the few white critics to attack the racism that kept jazz a second-class cultural citizen. Jazz is second class at the record companies and at most of the exploitative jazz clubs. It is not treated with the same respect, including endowments and media coverage, as the other arts. Things have improved since Coltrane's death, but not by nearly enough. Musical achievements in the face of such pervasive racism make a man like Coltrane, and all the other great jazz musicians, even more heroic. Despite such towering obstacles, he pursued his musical quest stoically.

11 meditation

Finding a proper place to present his new music was a genuine problem for Coltrane in 1965. With the large number of musicians often playing with him, including two drummers, a larger venue than a club was needed. Coltrane's popularity had also reached such a plateau that he had to play larger clubs than, say, the Village Vanguard just to accommodate his new audiences. Playing in larger clubs often meant stifling his creativity, however. The larger the club, the more likely it was for management to "turn over" the crowd after each set in order to collect the often pricey admittance fee. Thus the musicians were made to play shorter sets, often no longer than half an hour. Of course, half an hour is what Coltrane needed just to warm up. At the barnlike Village Gate on a double bill with Thelonious Monk in 1965, what should have been a transcendent night of music turned into a sad disappointment for Coltrane. He was visibly dispirited, made to play within the rigidly enforced half hour time allotment. Most of the playing was done by McCoy Tyner, with Coltrane taking only perfunctory solos.

In the fall of 1965 Coltrane played a concert in Seattle that was recorded by Impulse and released as *Live at Seattle*. The music was wildly free. Pharoah's shrieking reached brain-damaging intensity, frequently in his duets with Coltrane and at times with the bassist Donald Garrett, who was doubling on bass clarinet and making raucous clamoring noises as well. Critics like LeRoi Jones actually criticized Coltrane for the comparative conservatism of his playing, since his solos then still had a ragged melodic inventiveness rather than just a prolonged scream or wail.

While in Seattle, Coltrane recorded what was undoubtedly the most bizarre album of his career, a genuine artifact of the Sixties. Entitled *Om,* it was apparently made while the entire band was tripping on LSD. It begins with Coltrane and a couple of the other musicians chanting lyrics from the Tibetan Book of the Dead, a Sixties psychedelic favorite. In Buddhist theology, *Om* is the first and last word, the vibration that brought the universe into existence. It is usually used in meditation by intoning it, stretching out its sound: "Ommmmmmmmm." But here the musicians shout the word with an eerie inflection, as if they were in a bad horror movie. Then the entire Coltrane group, including Pharoah and a flute player named Joe Brazil, rip into a raging group improvisation, the usual shrieking stuff, which runs for a while and gives way to a Coltrane solo. While the solo is not unlike much of Coltrane's "free" work from this time, it is played with the horrifying intensity of, for lack of a better term, a bad acid trip. After a surprisingly cohesive Tyner solo, there is a drawn-out flurry of bells, percussion, and flute. The record ends with more chanting from the Buddhist text, including a line about clarified butter, before ending with more moans and shouts of "Om." Coltrane, clearly embarrassed by *Om,* instructed Bob Thiele that he never wanted it released. It was too tempting in the hallucinogenic Sixties not to release such genuinely psychedelic music, and shortly after Coltrane's death the album was released. A copy was almost immediately placed in the window of the Haight-Ashbury Psychedelic Shop, although its content was hardly the melodies of happy tripping.

Coltrane's trek further and further "outside" was a reflection of his sheer bravery, for the New Thing was under increasingly fierce attack, and not just from critics. Musicians, even such once-daring innovators as Miles Davis, Charles Mingus, and Thelonious Monk, now had little use for New Thing jazzmen.

One evening at a club, Mingus had a band of apparent New Thing musicians play behind a screen. After several minutes of collective noise not unlike much free jazz, Mingus lifted the screen to reveal young kids trying to blow instruments or play drums or piano for the first time. He would rail against the avant-garde to his audiences regularly. "They can't even play bebop tunes from twenty years ago," he would say. The usually taciturn Monk expressed disdain when he was played an Ornette Coleman record as part of a *Down Beat* "Blindfold Test."

Miles regularly spoke out against the New Thing players, too. When Archie Shepp tried to sit in with his group, Miles walked off the stand rather than play with the young tenor man. After listening to a Cecil Taylor record, Miles said, "Take it off! That's some sad shit, man. Is that what the critics are digging? The critics better stop having coffee. If there ain't nothing to listen to, they might as well admit it." At another time he said, "Look, you don't need to play weird. That ain't no freedom."

Miles had even grown to dislike Coltrane's group, including Trane's own playing. In his autobiography he wrote, "At first the [Coltrane quartet] was all right. Then they became a cliché of themselves and wasn't nobody playing nothing for me but Elvin and Trane. I didn't like what McCoy was doing after a while because all he was doing was banging the hell out of the baby grand piano and that wasn't hip for me. . . . But all Trane and them were doing was playing in the mode and I had already done that. . . . The way that Trane played after a while got monotonous . . . if you sat and listened to him for too long."

Miles must have felt some jealousy: Coltrane, his acolyte and former employee, had overtaken him in the Sixties as the dominant and most influential jazz musician. Furthermore, Miles invariably felt that the playing of musicians who had been in his groups dissipated in quality when they went on their own, and he never quite forgave Coltrane for leaving his group.

Another former colleague, the pianist Bill Evans, caught Coltrane playing at Birdland around this time. Between sets, Evans suggested to Coltrane that perhaps not all emotions were worth expressing in one's art, that the artist had the burden of selecting those emotions he considered most beneficial for his audience. Coltrane had actually said something similar a few years earlier when he told an interviewer that jazz should express joy as it had in its past and that he wanted to bring joyous expression back to the music. Another musician puzzled and troubled by Coltrane's music was the sitar player Ravi Shankar. Coltrane had briefly studied Indian music with Shankar, and the two had become friends. While visiting America around this time Shankar heard Coltrane perform. About his experience he said, "I was much disturbed by his music. Here was a creative person who had become a vegetarian, who was studying yoga and reading the Bhagavad-Gita, yet in whose music I still heard much turmoil. I could not understand it."

One cannot listen to Coltrane performances such as *Live at Seattle* without wondering about this question of Coltrane's choice of emotional expression. The music often sounds like a spiritual holocaust and seems far from Coltrane's original joyous intentions. That feeling of joy is evident in much of his early work, including such groundbreaking work as the original "My Favorite Things," "India," and even "Chasin' the Trane." Angst, confusion, even rage are as legitimate emotional bases from which to create art as joy, love, and hope. If one insists, as some critics do, that playing these furious sounds is catharsis, one has to wonder if an artist's emotional catharsis and release, unreflected through the artistic process, is really art.

Some of these questions were raised again with the release of the soaringly powerful *Meditations*, recorded in November 1965 and basically a sequel to *A Love Supreme*. Coltrane used for the album his working group at the time: the quartet plus Pharoah Sanders and the drummer Rashied Ali. Although it has the similar roiling textures of many of Coltrane's late performances, *Meditations* is far more successful as an expression of the new free jazz than *Ascension*. Like *Ascension*, *Meditations* has sections of group improvisation (albeit with only the two horns of Coltrane and Sanders), but unlike *Ascension* these sections seem organic rather than regularly spaced portions of chaos. Everything in *Meditations* has artistic purpose, and although it is at least as shattering to the nervous system as *Ascension*, it rewards those willing to listen to it with genuine revelation, both musical and spiritual. Certainly not everyone agreed about this. Philip

Larkin called side one "the most astounding piece of ugliness I have ever heard."

The first piece, "The Father, the Son, and the Holy Ghost" (according to word in the jazz community, Coltrane was the Father, Pharoah the Son, and Albert Ayler the Holy Ghost), begins with a singsong melody reminiscent of some of Albert Ayler's compositions. Coltrane takes a strong solo that, although quite free, is not without a kind of granite lyricism. He then gives way to Pharoah, who makes the most wrenching elongated scream of his career up until then. The scream here fits into an overall design; it works to heighten the atmosphere, to build a sustained climax, and is quite effective, even moving. The drumming is so dense behind the solos that the rhythm seems all over the place, a rhythmic environment so molten that the soloists seem transported into the sky. The second half of the suite is far calmer, beginning with a lengthy bass solo. Pharoah takes another scream-solo, not unlike his previous one—as a matter of fact, not unlike virtually every solo he recorded with Coltrane's group. Here, another elongated scream seems irrelevant. The last piece, "Serenity," is as calm and lovely as one would expect from its title.

Who would expect the fury of the first fifteen or twenty minutes of this work, given the title *Meditations*? Coltrane's spiritual vision certainly was complex, and his soul's journey not an easy or safe road. His vision of God and his universe is not one of angels peacefully plunking harps amid billowy clouds in a static, calm sky. To Coltrane, the universe is a place of explosive dynamism, of stars bursting apart and reuniting, of atoms and molecules in a constant state of wild flux, with a God who is not peacefully sitting on his throne under shade trees but constantly in motion, changing the universe and being changed by it. The road toward this God, and toward a life that is part of "the force which is truly good," is twisting and dangerous, requiring great strength and resilience. Meditation, looking deeply within, is not a substitute for Valium. Perhaps Coltrane was thinking of the writings of Krishnamurti when he conceived *Meditations*, for it was Krishnamurti who wrote, "Meditation is never-ending movement . . . [it] is emptying the mind of the known . . . [it] is always new. . . . It has not the touch of the past. To meditate is to transcend time . . . [it] is the awakening of bliss; [it] is the summation of all energy. . . . This meditative mind is the religious mind—the religion that is not touched by the church, the temples or the chants. . . . The religious mind is the explosion of love."

Meditations has some lyrical moments, but Coltrane was feverishly working to find truth in his music, and not just to make pleasant listening. As he told Nat Hentoff, who wrote the liner notes, "Once you become aware of this force for unity in life, you can't ever forget it. It becomes part of everything you do. In that respect, this is an extention of *A Love Supreme* since my conception of that force keeps changing shape. My goal in meditating this through music, however, remains the same. That is to uplift people, as much as I can. To inspire them to realize more and more of their capacities for living meaningful lives. Because there is certainly meaning to life."

As Coltrane told Hentoff, *Meditations* was another step in his eternal quest: "There is never any end. There are always new sounds to imagine, new feelings to get at. And always, there is the need to keep purifying these feelings and sounds so that we can really see what we've discovered in its pure state. So that we can see more and more clearly what we are. In that way, we can give to those who listen the essence, the best of what we are. But to do that at each stage, we have to keep on cleaning the mirror." Hentoff then writes, "And that is what *Meditations* is about—cleaning the mirror into the self, going as far through the looking glass as possible each time. Making music as naked as the self can be brought to be."

This process of "cleaning the mirror" meant going beyond merely making pretty music. Some remarks of Picasso, as quoted by Max Harrison in his book *A Jazz Retrospect*, may offer some understanding of this difficult process: "When you begin a picture, you often make some pretty discoveries. You must guard against these. Destroy the thing, do it several times. In each destroying of a beautiful discovery the artist does not really suppress it, but rather transforms it, condenses it, makes it more substantial. What comes out in the end is the result of rejected discoveries."

As might be expected, *Meditations* immediately drew intense critical reaction. While some critics lamented Coltrane's full commitment to the New Thing, others, like LeRoi Jones, felt that Pharoah dominated the record, and that Coltrane had not ventured as fully "outside" as he should. Jones wrote, "The *Meditations* band brings Trane back to absolute contemporary expression, though Trane himself, it would seem, is content to 'scream' less, and prefers the older rhythmic feeling and his gorgeous lyric sweep, anyway. I would like to hear Trane come full out, as flag for the heavy Pharoah. Then the music would reach still another level. Right now, Pharoah is doing the pumping." Jones apparently felt that anything short of a sustained scream was reactionary music making.

Screaming saxophones, and screaming itself, were actually nothing new in black music. Rhythm and blues saxophonists had used screams for decades before the advent of the New Thing. In jazz itself, these types of freak effects were especially ubiquitous in the Forties and early Fifties, when "battles" between saxophonists, usually tenor saxophonists, gained great popularity. Players like Illinois Jacquet and Arnett Cobb gained notoriety, especially in their "Jazz at the Philharmonic" performances, for what many critics considered to be poor taste and blatant pandering to their audience by their frequent use of such shriek effects. After all, making these noises does not really take great skill—it is simply a specific technique based on overblowing and false fingering known to most saxophonists. But certain segments of the audience would mistake these effects for orgasmic emotion and cheer on the saxophonist who screamed the loudest.

Most of those who in the Sixties were enthralled with such similar freak effects by Albert Ayler or Pharoah Sanders probably had no use for Jacquet or Cobb, whose playing otherwise was one step removed from rhythm and blues and not even vaguely "free." Their shrieks did not seem dissonant like that of the New

Thing screamers, and were an obvious expression of joy rather than any form of protest.

The screams of the young militant free jazz players of the Sixties was commonly interpreted as black rage expressed in the most directly confrontational manner. Jean Genet's play *The Blacks,* which gained great popularity in the Sixties, also expressed the fury of black people toward whites. Genet insisted that whenever the play was performed, there had to be at least one white person in the audience, even if it was an effigy. One wonders if the harsh sounds produced by the New Thing players were similarly intended to unsettle and discomfit white ears. Hearing these screams brings to mind the agony of the slave ships, the whips of the plantation owners, and the wails of women watching their men being lynched. At a time when many white liberals felt a masochistic (though not entirely wrongheaded) need to relieve their guilt, the music of the New Thing seemed to have an inspired timeliness.

Certainly one reason for the use of these techniques was a rebellion against the European instrumental heritage. When Ayler or Sanders shrieked and wailed, they were reinventing what was deemed the "proper" method of playing on their instruments, as well as exhibiting a totally new black musical aesthetic.

It is impossible to separate free jazz from the Sixties—no other decade could have given birth to this music. Many called New Thing jazz "energy music"—it captured the electric feeling of the barrage of events in that decade. Screams, shrieks, and howls seemed the best way of expressing the experience of living in the Sixties. The indignation of the detractors of the New Thing, those "straights" and "squares" who just didn't get it, made those who supported it feel even stronger about the music; in the polarized Sixties, those who denounced the New Thing were viewed by its fans as being of the same reactionary stripe as those who supported the war in Vietnam, were wary of "Black Power," and who drank martinis instead of smoking pot.

Still other dimensions of the New Thing scream are less apparent to most whites. The screams were also resonant of the black church at its most intense moments, when members of the congregation would shriek, moan, and howl as their souls were seized by the spirit. In the Fifties Charles Mingus recorded such wonderfully exciting pieces as "Better Git It in Yer Soul" and "Wednesday Night Prayer Meeting," in which he used his own voice to simulate the black church experience. There was, then, a precedent for using the most intense sounds of that experience in jazz. Certainly, Mingus's precedent comes to mind especially when several musicians scream together, as on *Ascension* and during performances of Sun Ra's Arkestra. For Coltrane, these effects were undoubtedly expressions of the agony and ecstasy of his inner spiritual pilgrimage.

Still another way of understanding the "Music of Scream" is the psychological theory of the "primal scream," as formulated by Dr. Arthur Janov in the Sixties and popularized by John Lennon and Yoko Ono. Very briefly, the theory holds that we are each suppressing an enormous amount of rage and frustration dating back to earliest childhood, and the best way of exorcising that anger is to let one's most primitive and earliest emotions prevail and to actually scream, as long as one wishes, until the anger is dissipated. The application of this theory to the use of these extra-musical effects I think takes on great significance when we remember that it was John Coltrane who first began using them in such pieces as "Chasin' the Trane." Coltrane was relentlessly digging inside his mind and soul for inspiration, using the landscape of his inner being as the subject of his music. It should be no surprise then, according to Janov's theory, that ultimately he would find at the center of his psyche a wild scream wanting release. Both Lennon and Ono recorded albums inspired by their sessions with Dr. Janov; Lennon's album *Plastic Ono Band* is considered one of his best. With John Coltrane, such release would be felt as partly the orgasmic joy of the rhythm and blues tenor that he had played at the beginning of his career, and partly the anger of a modern, aware African American.

Perhaps the most important single factor affecting the direction of Coltrane's music was his desire to create pure sound, modulated and controlled in terms only of range and timbre and free of specific pitches. The quest for that ultimate music, that "essence" that he constantly said he was searching for, was the motor that drove him more than any other. After obsessively rooting through all the possibilities of harmony in his "sheets of sound" period, and then searching through the cycles of pure melody in his modal period from 1960 to 1964, he still had not found that ultimate musical "essence" he had been searching for since 1957. Now he had finally come to the point where the only answer could be found in pure sound, unfettered by melodic or harmonic direction. These screams, howls, and shrieks were pure sound, pure emotion, the last frontier of music. Coltrane had come to agree with Albert Ayler that it was time to go "beyond notes."

In our own present time, when credulity is in such short supply, the pursuit of such an idea would be the stuff of ridicule. There is little doubt that frequent intake of powerful hallucinogens went a long way toward making such concepts seem worthy of pursuit in the Sixties. There was much more to it than that. John Coltrane could take a concept that seemed abstract and remote, and in the course of exploring its possibilities continue to, at least much of the time, produce magnificent music. The sort of bravery Coltrane exhibited in reaching so deep within, and expressing himself so nakedly, is sadly missing from our own time, when musicians are heartily applauded for essentially rehashing musical ideas from the quests of the past rather than reaching for those new, and sometimes scary, goals that lie just outside one's grasp.

Coltrane's personal life in 1965 was going through a change almost as momentous as that of his music. A few years previously he had met a young black pianist named Alice McLeod at a party. The two struck up a casual friendship. In 1963 Alice was playing with the West Coast vibraphonist Terry Gibbs's group, which was sharing the billing with Coltrane's group. Trane was immediately impressed by her obvious musical talent—not only was she a uniquely personal pianist, but she even duetted with Gibbs on his vibraphone. Like Coltrane, she was a deeply spiritual, introspective person, who viewed her music as a road to

God. A few months later, after his separation from Naima, he moved in with her. In 1964 they had a son, whom they named John Coltrane, Jr. They didn't marry until 1966, however, owing to divorce difficulties. In an interview, Alice made a strange comment about their union: "I think John could have just as easily married another woman. . . . Not myself and not because I was a musician but any woman who had the particular attributes or qualities to help him fulfill his life mission as God wanted him to."

It sounds as if Coltrane needed a spiritual assistant more than a woman to love, almost as if he were above carnal passion. The two would have three children during the short time they were together, almost as if Coltrane knew his time for living was short. Mrs. Coltrane, a genuinely spiritual woman who now leads a Vedantic center in California, still emphasizes that Coltrane's life was totally devoted to finding that universal sound, almost as if he were beyond fleshly concerns.

Coltrane's determination to pursue his quest made him something of a warrior, a warrior of the spirit, one who took up the good fight every time he played. As Alice Coltrane said, "When John left for work, he'd often take five instruments with him. He wanted to be ready for whatever came. That was characteristic of John. His music was never resigned, never complacent. How could it be? He never stopped surprising himself."

After John and Alice were married, they moved into a large house in an upscale area of Long Island. Coltrane was now making more money than just about any other jazz musician, despite the often extreme adventurousness of his music. With that money he created a stable, even bourgeois, environment, a safe haven where he could pursue his quest through music and his avid study of esoterica.

Reading increasingly took up his free time, and many of the books he read were directly related to his music. With his holistic, relativistic perspective, he was always open to all sorts of connections to his music. Alice Coltrane said about his music from this time, "A higher principle is involved here. Some of his last works aren't musical compositions. I mean they weren't based entirely on music. A lot of it has to do with mathematics, some on rhythmic structure and the power of repetition, some on elementals. He always felt that sound was the first manifestation in creation before music."

The Jewish mysticism of the Kabbalah was quite influential in Coltrane's music of these later years. Several of his compositions would be based on its numerological systems. He also tried to apply Einstein's theory of relativity to his music. Coltrane must have been especially fascinated with the scientist's quest to develop a unified field theory that could explain both gravity and electromagnetism with one set of laws. Einstein once said, "God doesn't play dice with the universe," something with which Coltrane would readily agree. Both men were searching for the same thing, what Coltrane called the "essence," the ultimate vibration.

Coltrane's study of yoga caused him to work at good health and to become a vegetarian, knowing that he could not play on the level required for his quest unless he was strong. His true strength seemed to come from his mind. Charles Mingus, Jr., tells of a time when his father visited Coltrane on a day when the saxophonist was working out. He was curling a weight of 150 pounds with one arm. When Mingus pointed that out to him, Coltrane was surprised; he hadn't been aware of the tremendous weight he was lifting and curling with just a single limb. "It was," according to Mingus, "like a mother who somehow finds the strength to lift a car off her child in an accident. Coltrane wasn't that physically strong—but his mind was incredibly powerful."

Despite Coltrane's devotion to his health, he had tremendous difficulty controlling his weight, even to the extent of having two wardrobes, one set of "fat" suits and another set for when he had his weight under control. His use of the latter became increasingly rare as the Sixties wore on. The cause of his weight problem was his love of sweets, which also wrecked his teeth. Sweet potato pie alone probably accounted for a good deal of his struggle with his weight and the seemingly endless trips to the dentist. Coltrane felt so embarrassed about his teeth that he rarely smiled when he was photographed. This has lead many to believe that he was a continuously driven, darkly serious man constantly filled with angst. He did have a gentle sense of humor and he loved to laugh, only never when he was being photographed. Jimmy Garrison had one of the very few pictures of Coltrane smiling, and he would tell anyone who saw it that that was the real John Coltrane.

Despite these down-to-earth problems, during his lifetime Coltrane was looked on by some as a supernatural figure, a saint or prophet. Many who saw him as a mortal looked on him as a rara avis, a man gifted with a special genius and unique powers. There were a few debunkers, though, probably the most outrageous of these being James Lincoln Collier, the author of a number of jazz biographies and *The Making of Jazz,* a jazz history. According to Collier, Coltrane was a certifiably neurotic, if not near-psychotic man, driven by inner demons rather than a search for God. Collier points at Coltrane's extreme gentleness—even when faced with recalcitrant sidemen, especially the frequently late (and high) Elvin Jones—his binges of gorging on sweets, and his "compulsive practicing. At times Coltrane would walk around the house all day, playing. . . . Most of us have oral cravings: we smoke or snack or drink or chew gum. But in few people are the cravings this severe; the pacifierlike quality of the saxophone is too obvious to miss. Coltrane, clearly, was suffering from a larger load of anxiety than most of us are called upon to bear."

Coltrane's obsession was with music itself, not his mouthpiece. Nor does his voracious reading fit into Collier's cozy psychoanalytic theory. Here was a man who spent his life doing what he loved most, making music, who made great contributions to our culture, who was gentle with everyone around him, a man who was loved by his associates, even the cantankerous, suspicious Miles Davis. For Collier, such a decent guy simply *had* to be neurotic.

It is facile to attribute Coltrane's musical obsessions, his wish to evolve spiritually, to emotional instability. Coltrane was nothing other than a flesh-and-blood mortal, and much of his music in the last couple of years of his life was disturbing and self-indulgent. Perhaps that is inevitable when, in Browning's phrase, one's reach exceeds one's grasp. Heaven in one form or another, after all, was Coltrane's ultimate goal. That Coltrane had his demons is obvious to anyone who listens to his music, but through art he exorcised those demons and presented to the world the great gift of his music as well.

12 out of this world

As a producer Bob Thiele gave Coltrane a unique opportunity: to record as frequently as he felt he had something to say. Coltrane recorded more in that transitional year of 1965 than anytime since 1956–58, a period when he recorded, in Sonny Rollins's term, "promiscuously." Unlike those years, now he was leading the sessions. Much of the 1965 work was not released until after his death; there was just too much material for a record company to release while he was still alive. Quite a bit of the work he recorded at this time is tantalizing in its revelation of musical roads he was pursuing but never got a chance to explore fully.

One piece that stands out immediately is "Living Space," which can be found on an album called *Cosmic Music,* as well as with a collection of previously unreleased material that wasn't made available until the Seventies. Alice Coltrane added strings and percussion posthumously. The collection released a few years later called *Feelin' Good* includes the piece in its original form, with just Coltrane and the quartet. The tune's original title, "The Living Room Rug," refers to the source of inspiration: the pattern of a carpet in the Coltrane household. If, as seems plausible, this meditation on a rug was psychedelically induced, then here is an example of music produced under the influence of acid that, rather than being frenzied and chaotic, is calm and richly lyrical. Coltrane heightens the "spacy" feel of the piece, played on soprano, by overdubbing, "doubling the melody at the unison and the octave," as stated in the notes. "Living Space" is a rare example, at this early date, of a jazz musician doing what many rock musicians were exploring headlong: using the studio to produce musical sounds virtually impossible to duplicate in live performance. In rock's psychedelic era, overdubbing all kinds of sounds became almost *de rigueur,* as well as using overdubs to create vocal harmonies, adding bass lines, etc. Overdubbing does create philosophical complications in the recording of jazz, since jazz is supposed to be totally spontaneous, music of the moment. Coltrane does not overdub his superb improvisation on "Living Space," just the statement of the theme. Some jazz musicians, such as Bill Evans and Jimmy Raney, overdubbed themselves two or three times, Evans producing a whole album of such peformances, called *Conversations with Myself,* which was just that. It was a very rarely used technique in jazz, except occasionally to overdub obvious mistakes. Coltrane's use of the electronics of the studio exhibited a direction he perhaps might have pursued if he had lived a few years longer. This type of effect would become increasingly prevalent in the late Sixties and early Seventies, a time that the critic Robert Palmer has aptly called "the Sergeant Pepper era of jazz." Coltrane's use of overdubbing on "Living Space" produces a hushed, holy atmosphere unlike anything else in his work.

Listening to "Living Space" makes one even more aware of Coltrane's achievement as a composer. Even if he had never improvised a note, themes like "Space" and "Lonnie's Lament," "Resolution" from *A Love Supreme,* "Giant Steps," and "Naima" would have made him an important figure in jazz.

The title tune of the *Feelin' Good* collection is the Anthony Newley tune from *The Roar of the Greasepaint, the Smell of the Crowd.* It is one more example of Coltrane's ability, like that of all great jazz musicians, to take a simple pop tune and make it into an imperishable thing of beauty. Although it was recorded in 1965, the year of Coltrane's increasing commitment to free jazz, "Feelin' Good" demonstrates his reluctance to turn his back completely on the glowing lyricism that had once been so central to his art.

The gem of this collection is a piece labeled "Untitled," a lengthy, straightahead modal piece not unlike "Transition" or "Brazilia." Here Coltrane's mastery is undeniable. No dull or empty stretches mar this fiery, hypnotic performance, a superb example of what George Russell called "supravertical" playing, producing the illusion of harmony on a melody instrument. Such a performance strikes wonder that Coltrane could create such indelible beauty out of such volcanically intense material. It is almost impossible to be objective about Coltrane's music at this level—one has to be put in its trance and swept along in order to understand what he is doing. Trying to stay outside the music, objective and critical, is to miss the point, and perhaps even be put off by it. That is the level of power of Coltrane's music at his 1965 peak—it is a visceral experience, and it can be understood only by one's whole being, body, mind, and heart.

Also from 1965 is a live recording of "My Favorite Things" from the quartet's appearance at the Newport Jazz Festival that year. One can almost gauge Coltrane's artistic frame of mind, as well as the social and cultural tenor of the times, from simply following in sequence all the recorded versions of "Things." Here, although the music is still lyrical, the atmosphere is tense, reflecting the restrictive time limits at the original Newport Jazz Festivals, the darker political and social climate in 1965, and perhaps most importantly, the growing unease within the group.

Tyner and Jones were having difficulty adjusting to the changes in Coltrane's own playing. At the same 1965 Newport Jazz Festival, Coltrane played a tune called "One Up, One Down," which would be released on an album titled *New Thing at Newport,* on which could also be heard Archie Shepp's performance with his own group at the festival. More than ever, Coltrane is using freak effects, screams, long-held honks, lines that seem completely free of any reference to chords or even modes, and incessantly repeated figures played against the rhythm section rather than with or above it. Other Coltrane performances from 1965, such as the posthumously released "Sun Ship," are almost brutal in their tearing, rending sonic violence. Coltrane was exploring deeper and deeper into his inner landscape, at times producing work of almost frightening intensity. Listening, one cannot help being as disturbed as Ravi Shankar was, while at the same time marveling at Coltrane's sheer courage in reaching down so far and exposing himself so nakedly to his audience. Only through such intense digging could he reach, at last, the source of his quest, and bring together synergistically all the elements, from Einstein to Jewish numerology, that had acted as roadmarks for his journey.

Moreover, both Tyner and Jones were uncomfortable with some of the musicians now sitting in regularly with the group. As 1965 progressed, Coltrane's group became almost a caravan of the New Thing. By fall he had added a second drummer, Rashied Ali, to the group. In a review in *Down Beat*, A. B. Spellman, one of Coltrane's and free jazz's most outspoken supporters, described a typical performance of the Coltrane group at this time. Playing at the Village Gate in addition to the regulars of the quartet were Pharoah Sanders, Archie Shepp, and the avant-garde altoist Carlos Ward, as well as Rashied Ali. "Trane," Spellman wrote, "with his *Ascension* record date and with the augmented quartet he uses in the clubs is not only creating a band with more power than Con Ed but is also introducing some of the best of the New Jazz musicians to the World of the Living Wage and thereby performing a double service. . . . On this night, the two sets consisted of long interpretations of one tune each: *Afro Blue* and *Out of This World*. The difference between the two sets was that Jones didn't show for the first, and the first was, to my ear, far better.

"Coltrane played the theme on soprano and Shepp, in very good voice, took it from there. Shepp's style is reiterative—a kind of supercharged theme and variations. He stated a motif, broke it down to its elements, and returned to it every few bars. . . . Shepp is a bluesy player who roars his masculinity. . . . [Ward] seemed to be neither a screamer nor a singer, but a talker. He seemed to be engaged in some kind of a dialog with himself, playing a rapid series of terse, self-contained, but related phrases. . . . Sanders followed Ward, and he is the damndest tenor player in the English language. He went on for minute after minute in a register that I didn't know the tenor had. Those special effects that most tenor men use only in moments of high

orgiastic excitement are the basic premises of his presentation. . . . Trane soloed on soprano which, as usual, seemed a few
months behind his tenor. . . . No one was ever idle—a man
would finish his solo and pick up a rattle, tambourine, or some
other rhythm instrument and start shaking away. The reeds also
were free to provide filler or comment for the soloist, and the
effect was of an active, highly charged environment."

Coltrane's addition of Rashied Ali to the group was viewed
by Spellman as a way of creating "an ever evolving groundswell
of energy that will make the musical environment so dangerous
that he and the others will have to improvise new weapons
constantly to beat back the Brontosaurs." When both drummers
played simultaneously, "One simply couldn't hear anything but
drums. . . . I had no idea what the soloists were saying, and I
doubt that the players could hear each other. Garrison . . . was
completely swallowed up. At one point I saw Coltrane break
out a bagpipe . . . and blow into it, and damned if I heard a note
of what he played."

Coltrane's inclusion of both Ali and Jones in the group reflected his indecisiveness about plunging completely into the
New Thing. When Frank Kofsky asked about the addition of
Ali, Coltrane said: "I was trying to do something. . . . There was
a thing I wanted to do in music, see, and I figured I could do
two things: I could have a band that played like the way we [the
quartet] used to play, and a band that was going in the direction
that the one I have now is going in [referring to the free jazz
group he led in the last year and a half or so of his life]. I could
combine these two, with these two concepts going. And it could
have been done."

These words are similar to those Coltrane spoke in an interview around 1958, when he had rejoined Miles's group and was
experimenting with Miles's new modal approach. There too he
was torn between Miles's purely melodic approach and the harmonic "sheets of sound" direction he had been taking since his
stint with Monk. Back then, Coltrane had wanted to have it
both ways, and he often did in some of his more successful solos.
Here, things did not work out so well. Miles has often been

compared to Hamlet, I suppose because of his brooding nature. Coltrane had a lot more of Hamlet in his soul than Miles. Miles never had trouble making decisions, and once it was made he never wavered. Coltrane thought about things so deeply that he often seemed to have trouble with simple choices.

This new approach was doomed. The two drummers created an impenetrable wall of sound, and Elvin Jones hated it. Being one of the most complex and dynamic drummers in the history of jazz, he certainly didn't need any other drummer. In particular he disliked Ali's free rhythmic style, which he believed interfered with his own playing rather than adding to it. Ali's free rhythms were actually better suited to most of the New Thing players, but they destroyed the intense concentration Jones needed to play the complex but precise polyrhythms at the heart of his style.

Coltrane was reluctant to give up the brilliant Jones, with whom he had created such magnificent music. He must have recognized that in order to play the new music he had to have a drummer even freer than the polyrhythmic Elvin. Jones's playing was still steeped in the postbop period. When he finally left Coltrane, he used solid hard bop musicians, a number of them influenced by the Coltrane of the Fifties, rather than anyone connected with the avant-garde.

With the permanent addition of both Rashied Ali and Pharoah Sanders in the fall of 1965, both Tyner and Jones began to make serious noises about leaving the group. Tyner told an interviewer, "I didn't see myself making any kind of contribution to that music. At times I couldn't hear what anybody was doing! All I could hear was a lot of noise. I didn't have any feeling for the music, and when I don't have any feelings, I don't play." Tyner, too, never played free jazz when he went on his own, but was heavily influenced by Coltrane's modal music.

If even as stalwart a Coltrane supporter as A. B. Spellman had difficulty listening to this band with two drummers, then the music obviously had major problems. It was difficult for Tyner and Jones to leave; playing with Coltrane was one of the steadiest and best-paying gigs for a jazz sideman, and they still loved their boss and the great music they had made in the past. But there was growing tension within the group, a tension that could also be heard in the music.

A concert was held in Lincoln Center in 1966 called "Titans of the Tenor," and for once it seemed that such a swollen title would live up to its name. The participants were to include Coleman Hawkins, Sonny Rollins, and John Coltrane, generally considered to be the three most important stylists on the tenor saxophone, along with Lester Young. More or less standing in for Lester Young at the concert would be one of his most formidable students, Zoot Sims. With the inclusion of Shepp, one could see the entire panorama of jazz tenor saxophone from its beginnings in the Twenties and early Thirties right through to the current New Thing. Adding to the excitement was the rumor throughout the jazz community that Rollins would sit in with Coltrane for the first time in public since the two men recorded "Tenor Madness" in 1956. This last notion boggled the mind. Attending this concert was virtually mandatory for anyone with the slightest interest in America's greatest music.

The concert did not quite live up to one's greatest hopes, however. For some reason, probably a hassle with the promoter, Shepp dropped out. Added to the bill was the Clark Terry–Bob Brookmeyer group, one of the few combos in jazz without a saxophone. As for the momentous Rollins–Coltrane jam . . .

Hawkins opened the show, playing "In a Mellotone" backed by the Terry–Brookmeyer rhythm section. For a man fast losing his grip on life, Hawkins was magnificent, his sound as huge and gorgeous as ever, his melodic invention and vital sense of drama equal to anybody half his age. Despite a standing ovation, he refused to play a second number, but not because of temperament—he simply didn't have the energy. After some straightahead swing from Zoot with Terry and Brookmeyer, Rollins appeared with his group and with an unannounced guest, Yusef Lateef. Rollins hardly played for the short span of time he was onstage; he let Lateef do most of the blowing, frustrating his fans once again. At the end of the set, after a short version of "Autumn in New York," he announced he would return with John Coltrane's group. They were really going to do it! After so many changes in each man's music, could they find some common ground? What did they have to say to each other here in the mid-Sixties?

After an intermission, Coltrane brought on his group. There was an immediate commotion in the audience: where were Tyner and Elvin Jones? The answer was that this was Coltrane's new group. Replacing Tyner was Coltrane's wife, Alice; Rashied Ali had the drum chair all to himself; Jimmy Garrison was still the bassist. In addition, Coltrane brought onstage several ringers, including Carlos Ward, Pharoah Sanders, and Albert Ayler and his brother, the trumpeter Don Ayler. The crowd quieted as Coltrane played "My Favorite Things" on soprano. The dynamics of the group were quite different from the original quartet. Ali's rhythm was much freer and abstract than Elvin's but not nearly as loud or as dominant. Still, Mrs. Coltrane's piano accompaniment was largely drowned out by the ensemble and seemed basically irrelevant. She did not solo.

After a short soprano solo, Coltrane gave way to the Ayler brothers. Don and Albert took center stage and proceeded immediately to intertwine the sounds of their instruments into a lengthy, blaringly abrasive squeal-shriek, which in the echoing acoustics of Lincoln Center's Philharmonic Hall seemed even more acutely an assault on one's nervous system. After only a few moments, a large part of the audience, many with looks of horror on their faces and hands on their ears, fled the hall. Among those who stayed could be heard a smattering of boos and catcalls as the other players joined in for some collective screaming. The thing that kept most of them there was sheer curiosity as to how Sonny Rollins would join in the fray. As the group fulminated on, more people began pouring through the exits, keenly disappointed. When it finally came to an end, less than half the original audience remained in the house, and no Sonny Rollins appeared. Years later, a member of Rollins's group at the time told me that after only a minute or two of listening to the Coltrane ensemble's collective shrieking, Sonny shook his head and said, "Let's go." He had heard more than enough. At the time Rollins was playing with a straightahead postbop group, and although his playing was still adventurous and he used all kinds of extramusical effects in his improvising, he never exhibited interest in the white noise then *au courant* among the avant-garde.

The new group came as something of a shock to many of us who had long followed Coltrane. How could he let go of such apposite sidemen as Tyner and Jones? Yet such change was inevitable. Coltrane simply had to continue exploring this new music, which meant including a number of young players in the group and a drummer sympathetic to them. Now that he had left Coltrane, Elvin accepted an invitation from Duke Ellington to play with his band. Ellington had enjoyed playing with Jones on the record he had made with Coltrane, and Elvin, like every musician in jazz, revered Duke. After traveling to Europe to join the Ellington band, Jones, ironically enough, discovered that Ellington wanted him to play with another drummer. Jones tried for a short while but had to quit—that was the main reason he had left Trane.

Coltrane's replacement of Tyner with his wife is notable for a couple of reasons. For one, most of the New Thing musicians did not use a piano at all. The piano was used in jazz to lay down the chords on which the soloist improvised. Since the avant-garde players were not improvising on harmonies (an artifact of the European culture most of them were rejecting), they had no use for a piano. By continuing to use the piano in his group, Coltrane demonstrated that he was not ready to completely discard all of the so-called European elements of jazz; by retaining the piano he could even again play chordally if he decided that would, after all, be of value.

The other notable point is his forthright decency in using his wife. Sexism was a major force in jazz. Musicians who angrily and repeatedly decried racism and injustice thought nothing of their own often dreadful treatment of women. Miles Davis, for example, a man who complained loudly about racial intolerance and mistreatment, nevertheless regularly beat the women—all of whom he called "bitches"—in his life and never allowed the girlfriends or wives of his musicians backstage before a performance, believing, perversely enough, that the influence of females affected their playing for the worse. Most male jazz musicians at heart did not have faith in female players, and rarely used them, unless they were singers. Coltrane's employment of his wife, especially in playing such difficult music, was more evidence of his genuine belief in the unity of all humanity.

A large part of his audience was disappointed by the dissolving of the great Coltrane quartet. Wherever he went, Coltrane had to face the burden of trying to play completely new music with such a brilliant and popular legacy of great music in his past. As even-tempered as he was, he began to lose patience with clubowners and patrons who asked, and even demanded, that he play music from his past, occasionally from far in his past, such as selections from *Blue Train,* recorded almost a decade earlier. For any genuinely creative artist a decade is a long time in his artistic development, but for Coltrane, whose change of style was measured in months and sometimes in weeks, the idea of returning to the music of nine or ten years past was absurd. Since his career was tied directly to a quest that was personal and metaphysical as well as musical, such demands must have been severely disappointing to Coltrane. They showed that a large segment of his audience was ignorant of the enormous amount of sacrifice and continual inner growth, as well as the purely physical wear, that went into developing an art that he believed would yield great spiritual revelation and ultimate insight into the nature of man and his universe, rather than just a moment's entertainment.

It is amazing how well Coltrane was able to retain his audience, even though his music had for quite a while become increasingly esoteric. He continued to get paid more than any saxophonist, with the possible exception of Stan Getz, and his records always wound up on the *Billboard* jazz best-sellers list. He invariably wound up a winner in the *Playboy* poll. The winners of this popularity contest were supposed to make up the personnel of an all-star band, which was never actually formed, unfortunately, for sitting next to Coltrane in the saxophone session, almost invariably, was Stan Getz and the country and western "yakety" saxophonist Boots Randolph. The trumpet section usually consisted of Miles Davis, Al Hirt, and Herb Alpert. One time the vocal group was Peter, Paul, and Mary and the guitarist Jimi Hendrix. Now, there was a band the world needed to hear! The reason for Coltrane's continuing popularity is clear: his sound. Although early in his career he was attacked, rather like Lester Young was, for his sound, it was this sound that wound up haunting both listeners and musicians, even if many of them believed he was going a bit off the deep end. The spiritual power of Coltrane's music said something to his listeners that they could hear in no other modern music, or in any other area of modern expression. He presented his music much like Miles did in person, never speaking to his audience, not even to announce tunes or introduce the musicians. While Miles was often lambasted for this practice and called rude and arrogant, Coltrane was held in utter reverence and rarely criticized for the same practices, as if his audience, and even the critics, assumed that he was too spiritually advanced for such mundane activities.

As Coltrane prospered, the rest of the jazz world was in something close to a crisis. Clubs closed, records remained unsold, and jazz festivals began inviting pop musicians in order to survive. Many blamed this dissipation of the jazz audience on the New Thing musicians, with their often abrasive free jazz. But new developments in rock music were just as responsible. Groups such as the Beatles, who, like Coltrane, seemed to be experimenting with new sounds on every new album (at least starting with *Rubber Soul*), made rock intriguing to the same college crowd that previously had been such a mainstay in supporting jazz. The black audience turned to the soul music of Motown or Stax, both of which produced black pop and R&B that was both danceable and genuinely musical. Jazz seemed lodged in a cul-de-sac: turning back to more accessible styles of the past went against its grain, but where could it go after the total freedom of the New Thing?

As for Coltrane, whatever doubts he had were overcome by his musical curiosity and by his certitude that the goal of his quest lay in the outer boundaries of musical expression. He had to continue in the same direction.

As his music became freer, Coltrane increasingly took on the role of shaman, not just playing his horn but now leading a quasi-religious ritual. Until this time he had played standing in one spot, hunching forward or backward when his music really began to fly. Now he was trying all kinds of ways to connect with the sound. He would play percussion instruments when others were soloing; influenced by a Tibetan tradition, when he felt too overwhelmed by his emotions and his ability to express them with his horn, he would stop playing and pound his chest while vocally roaring at the top of his lungs. There is film, unfortunately made without a soundtrack, of a concert in Japan where he whirled around the stage as he played as if, under the influence of his idol Einstein, he were actually trying to be transformed into pure energy.

In spring of 1966 Coltrane returned to the Village Vanguard to record a live album with his new group. The only two pieces on *Coltrane Live at the Village Vanguard Again* are, surprisingly, probably the two most requested tunes in the Coltrane book, "My Favorite Things" and "Naima." Coltrane was obviously making a statement about how far he had come since both his first Vanguard album and his first recording of these two pieces. By recording such familiar tunes, he hoped perhaps to give those having difficulty with his new music some sort of familiar territory from which he could jump off to new, unexplored terrain.

His statement of melody of "Naima" here is simply stunning. He plays it relatively straight, altering it in places and adding subtle embellishments in order to give it a fresh patina, making the listener rediscover the beauties anew. His tenor sound has such weight now, so much power, that it, by itself, mesmerizes the ear. This spellbinding mood, however, is ripped asunder when Pharoah follows Coltrane's opening statement. Pharoah playes a series of sputtering phrases, building up to the inevitable screams. One is reminded of a child having a tantrum, who begins by whining and complaining and builds to out-of-control howls and shrieks. You can justify screaming and shrieking when it is musically relevant, but here Sanders is infuriatingly inappropriate. By now, this sort of solo had become a cliché. The New Thing had begun as a revolt against the tired formulas of hard bop, but now it had its own share of overworn phrases and musical devices, lacking the element of surprise and innovation that had only a few years previously made the movement so vital. What is the point of free jazz if the musicians seem caught in their own straitjackets with no more real "freedom" than members of a Fifties revivalist Dixieland band? Coltrane follows Sanders, playing a superb example of what a truly free solo could be—one is continually caught off-guard by the twists and turns of his melodic invention.

Around this time Coltrane announced that he had finally found his "universal musician"—Stravinsky! One has to be amazed at Coltrane's ability to be so catholic in his influences, both musically and intellectually. Listening to his solos during 1965–66, it is obvious that he had been paying careful attention to the polytonality of Stravinsky's music, and in solos like this one successfully adapting it to jazz improvisation.

"My Favorite Things" begins with a lengthy Jimmy Garrison bass solo. His solos had by this time often taken on some of the qualities of flamenco guitar—certainly an amazing feat simply from the technical standpoint. Coltrane enters on soprano playing a lengthy improvisation that builds toward the statement of that familiar theme. The differences between the quartet and this group came sharply into focus on this piece. Although the solo is as lyrical as anything Coltrane had ever played, its Stravinsky-inspired polytonality gives it an indigo hue, as if one is viewing the joyous tapestry of the earlier "Things" solos through a glass darkly. Again, Coltrane is followed by the twenty-six-year-old Sanders, who spends only a very short time playing those sputtering phrases that build, ineluctably, to the usual cacophony of screams, howls, and shrieks that mark Sanders's apprenticeship period. Coltrane undoubtedly saw Sanders's potential, about which he was correct. Like the early bop period, this was a difficult time to be an apprentice, with all kinds of aesthetic and social pressures and expectations. These shrieks in the Sixties—the louder and more abrasive, the better.

Coltrane's playing on *Coltrane Live at the Village Vanguard Again* touches dark emotions, ranging from foreboding to a certain weariness. He was telling intimates that he thought his best music was now long behind him. Maybe, he was saying, it was time to stop playing altogether, maybe get involved in some other aspects of the music business. He often expressed a desire to open up a place to play in Greenwich Village that would combine the best aspects of a club with those of the concert hall. The place would have the easy atmosphere of the best clubs, like the Half Note, but would be devoted solely to music and would serve no alcoholic beverages. Musicians could experiment, play several sets, the only way for a jazz group to really coalesce, and not have to put up with drunken tourists. It's difficult to see Coltrane as a businessman, although he frequently discussed the business aspects of his profession with his friend Donald Byrd. His thoughts on these matters were probably influenced, consciously or not, by the cancer that was already eating away at his liver. His doubts about the worth of his current music were passing fears of the moment, apparently, because he continued on his quest, almost to the very end.

His spirits were undoubtedly lifted by the event that was probably the greatest single triumph of his life: his tour of Japan. The Japanese love American music and are especially knowledgeable jazz fans today, with one of the world's best jazz magazines published there. Jazz musicians routinely tour Japan and often make records that are released only there. In 1966, when Coltrane toured Japan, there was not yet much awareness of the Japanese veneration of jazz. When Coltrane's plane landed in Japan, he saw a mob of people waiting at the gate and wondered who the dignitary or movie star was on his plane. It was only when he heard cheers and saw the banners as he entered the airport that he realized the huge crowd had come to see him. How moved he must have been! In America he had never been shown such mass affection; he was barely a celebrity at home, with little public acknowledgment outside the relatively small cadre of modern jazz aficionados.

Much of the music Coltrane played in Japan was recorded for radio airplay, and the bulk of it has only recently been released in America, on a four-CD set. A good deal of this music is surprisingly lyrical and accessible. Perhaps Coltrane wished to present something of a retrospective of his music to his enthusiastic Japanese fans. Perhaps he felt his own mortality slipping away and was feeling nostalgic for past triumphs. Coltrane and Sanders were each presented with an alto saxophone by the Yamaha company, and both men used their new horns during the series of Japanese concerts. Coltrane plays his new alto on an astonishing version of "My Favorite Things," and the change from his usual soprano sax aids him in rediscovering new beauties along the way of this, his signature tune.

There are signs, too, of Sanders's increasing maturity. In "Peace on Earth," a beautiful, stately Coltrane composition in the tradition of "Alabama" and "After the Rain" that Coltrane had written shortly before leaving for Japan, Pharoah takes a careful, deeply felt, and even lyrical solo. At times he sounds as if he is beginning to build toward the usual scream, but he manages to stifle the inclination and make a moving, and unexpected, musical statement. All of Sanders's solos in the Japanese concerts are inventive, even when he uses the standard screams and shrieks. Here are strong hints of the broader and more accessible style Sanders would take up when he became a leader of his own group following Coltrane's death.

Coltrane as not really stepping backward in Japan. On a new piece, "Leo," he and Sanders let loose with pure New Thing energy, at one point duetting furiously on their altos. A lengthy version of "Crescent," here expanded upon greatly, lasts for almost an hour, a little less than twice the playing time of the entire *Crescent* album! For Coltrane's current rhythmic conception, the free-flowing, meterless drumming of Rashied Ali was near perfect. Coltrane's playing had become complexly polytonal, and for that reason alone, his wife was probably the only pianist in jazz, with the possible exception of Andrew Hill or Cecil Taylor, who could possibly accompany him. Alice Coltrane solos extensively here, as she does throughout the Japanese performances. Little has been written on her piano improvisations. Her playing is fascinating, quite idiosyncratic and filled with feeling. Like her husband, she too was influenced by Stravinsky, and her rolling lines have a polytonal melodicism not unlike that of the great Russian composer.

While in Japan, Coltrane visited Buddhist temples, war memorials, and as much of this beautiful country as he could see, acting more like a visiting spiritual figure than a jazz musician. It is not a coincidence that Coltrane's last major tour was in the Far East, because his thoughts, music, and spiritual beliefs were drifting further and further away from the West.

Coltrane consented to an interview in Japan, something he had been doing less frequently. The first question he was asked was whether he had ever been influenced by classical music. For as thoughtful a man as Coltrane, this was a question with semantic difficulties. He answered, undogmatically: "I may be wrong on this, but the term 'classical music,' in my opinion, means the music of a country played by the composers and musicians of the country more or less, as opposed to the music that people dance to or sing along with, the popular music. What do you think about that? Do you agree? There are different types of classical music all over the world. I don't know if I'm correct on this, but that's the way I feel about it. As far as types of music, if you ask me what are we playing, I feel it is the music of the individual contributor. And if you want to name it anything, you can name it classical music."

After the usual questions about such colleagues as Sonny Rollins ("a wonderful instrumentalist and musician") and Ornette Coleman ("a great leader"), he was asked "What would you say to people who claim that they cannot understand your music?" This question, or ones like it, had been a staple of Coltrane interviews since the Fifties. The difference now was that perhaps Coltrane himself was wondering if his music had become too inaccessible. He answered, "You'd like an answer to this? Well, I don't feel there is an answer to this. It is either saying a person who does not understand, will understand in time from repeated listenings or some things he will never understand. You know, that's the way it is. There are many things in life that we don't understand. And we just go on with life anyway."

The next questions concerned the war in Vietnam, a subject all Americans, regardless of profession, were asked about when visiting foreign soils during the Sixties. Coltrane opposed the war and had played at antiwar rallies. The interviewer then asked, "Do black people in general have any special opinion about this war?" as if all African Americans had one homogeneous mind. Coltrane demurred.

Coltrane then was asked about his religion. He answered, "I am [Christian] by birth; my parents were and my early teachings were Christian. But as I look upon the world, I feel all men know the truth. If a man was a Christian, he could know the truth and he could not. The truth itself does not have any name on it. And each man has to find it for himself, I think." When asked about the future he said, "I believe that man is here to grow into the fullest, the best that he can be. At least this is what I want to do. As I am growing to become whatever I become, this will just come out on the horn. Whatever that's going to be, it will be. I am not so much interested in trying to say what it's going to be. I don't know. I just know that good can only bring good." At another point during this tour when he was asked what he planned to do in the next ten years he answered, "Become a saint."

These last words should give even Coltrane's most ardent adulator pause. Was he serious? This comment is evidence that Coltrane was perhaps somewhat "blissed out." Constant studying of mystical texts and intense thought given over to spiritual matters, meditation, special diets and fasting, frequent LSD trips, even his constant practicing, were possibly pushing Coltrane to live in an increasingly other-world state. He was not a saint or god after all, although in the last years he seemed to be losing his formerly down-to-earth perspective.

This statement may have had something to do, however, with his growing awareness that he was seriously ill. Many photographs from this time show him holding his hand over his abdomen, where he was probably feeling the first horrible pains of liver cancer.

Upon returning from Japan, he tried fasting, hoping that cleansing out his system would improve his health. But this was a poor move, since he was already being weakened by the cancer, and the fasting just made things worse. He stopped practicing and did not accept any offers for live appearances, including a proposed tour of Europe.

During this period Coltrane was lent an electronic Varitone

saxophone. Besides being able to create a variety of different sounds at the push of the button, the saxophone had an octave divider, enabling Coltrane to perform live what in "Living Space" he could do only through overdubbing. Coltrane was fascinated with this saxophone, but it was an experimental model and he was able to keep it for only a few days.

Coltrane's enthusiasm for the electronic instrument suggests that he would have enjoyed, and no doubt participated in, the electronic experiments that transfixed many jazz musicians just a few years after his death. That doesn't mean that he would have played jazz-rock; he didn't seem to care for rock, and all his memories of playing rhythm and blues were bad ones. But he surely would have found synthesizers and the live electronics of the Seventies useful tools in creating the music that still lay just outside his horn's reach.

Although he was too sick to make frequent appearances, Coltrane continued to develop his musical theories, according to rumor, putting together what were basically large maps that exhibited the connection between mystical, scientific, and mathematical concepts.

Coltrane's quest to find a music that was of the essence, that was the music of God's voice and the music that could transform all who heard it, his drive to "clean the mirror" and dig deeper and deeper, is reminiscent of the quests of two other twentieth-century geniuses. In the last several years of his life, Einstein worked on developing what was called the "Unified Field Theory." This theory was based on the idea that there was one underlying concept behind all of nature's most basic forces, a common logic, or, if you will, an "essence," an "absolute." He went to his grave without solving this ultimate mystery.

Similarly, one of the greatest writers of the century, James Joyce, spent the last years of his life writing his final great work, *Finnegans Wake.* The book is written in a dream language based on all the world's languages melded in mankind's sleeping unconscious. Joyce had spent his life trying to discover a universal language, one that would be understood, at least on an unconscious level, by all men. His books were not aimed at a scholarly elite, but at the mind of the average twentieth-century man or woman. When *Finnegans Wake* was published, even those most sympathetic to his work, even his own brother, protested that he had gone too far, that the work was completely inaccessible. Joyce insisted that if it were read out loud, the reader would eventually fall into its rhythms, if he just let himself go with its flow rather than fight against it. *Finnegans Wake* is not written with a linear logic. It is cyclic—Joyce believed that all history was cyclic—and the book ends at its beginning.

Coltrane probably never read Joyce, but he would have found a soulmate in the great Irish author. These similarities should not be shrugged off as just coincidence. Joyce, Einstein, and Coltrane were all plugged into the same twentieth-century *zeitgeist* and rebellion against some of the most basic Western logic and intellectual traditions. The differences between these three men were as great as their similarities, since they were in such disparate fields. But thinking about these parallels puts Coltrane into perspective in terms of the most innovative thinking of this century. If Coltrane's music is still puzzling, which is understandable, close your eyes and try to imagine, somehow: ultimate language, the essence of music, the one great force, the mind of God, all braided and inseparable, swirling endlessly in the great cycle of the universe.

Coltrane made only one appearance in 1966 after returning from Japan. In December he played the Village Theater in the East Village, which would soon be converted into the Fillmore East. As in many of his concerts of the previous couple of years, he brought with him a number of additional musicians. Besides encouraging adventurous new players, this way he could let most of the burden of playing fall on other shoulders as his strength declined.

Despite his withdrawal from public performance, Coltrane continued to record frequently. He knew the end was near. By the beginning of 1967 he was clearly quite ill and frequently in great pain. A man tremendous inner strength, Coltrane produced in these last few months some of the most innovative work of his career. In February he recorded the tracks that would make up *Interstellar Space,* an album of duets between Coltrane's tenor and the percussion of Rashied Ali. The title is perfectly fitting, for here Coltrane is free to improvise without the gravity of the bass or piano. The names of the pieces, "Mars," "Jupiter," "Venus," and "Saturn," reflect Coltrane's interest in astrology, which he valued as a complex system for relating the flow of the cosmos to human actions. The music embodies an idea he had gleaned from his study of Einstein and modern physics: that the universe was constantly expanding. Melody and rhythm, free from the constraints of harmony and meter, create a light show for the mind; one can see stars exploding, comets shooting through the vastness of space, the ceaseless, neverending expansive motion of all the stars and planets.

These saxophone-drums duets are in the tradition of such Coltrane works as "Countdown" and "Vigil." The difference is the great freedom of Rashied Ali's rhythms, which allow Coltrane liberty to explore this rhythmic landscape without being compelled forward. As John Litweiler writes in his book on post-Fifties jazz, *The Freedom Principle,* "The . . . clarity of dialogue suggests that his post-1964 ensembles had obscured his real advances. These tenor solos are longer and more reckless than anything he had previously recorded, with associations sometimes so free that only the kinetic energy he generates sustains his momentum. . . . The implications of this are enormous, for Coltrane now internalizes responsibility for structure; it's possible that future developments of his capacities of organization might have resulted in major advances in his music." Although Coltrane still uses screams at times, they are used for effect, as in such pieces as "Chasin' the Trane," and do not dominate the proceedings. One piece, "Venus," could even be called a "free" ballad; it is remarkably lovely, proof that Coltrane's lyricism had not dissipated.

Coltrane's dense, frenetic playing is at times reminiscent of the "sheets of sound" period, with the same effect on the listener of being bathed in pure sound. But the differences with the former music are far more important. Coltrane had made deep inroads into the terrain of pure musical freedom, and while maintaining important elements of his established style, he seems freed from standard Western musical theory. Moreover, he discovered in this recording that he did not have to continue screaming in order to continue his quest.

Coltrane would make one last live performance before his death. His friend the Nigerian drummer Babatunde Olatunji (for whom Coltrane had named his tune "Tunji") asked Coltrane to appear in a benefit performance for the African Arts Center he was setting up in Harlem. Coltrane played at the center with his usual quintet. Those who heard him found his playing strong, though photographs of the concert show him playing while seated, something he had never done in public.

A few weeks before this appearance he made what appears to be his final recording. (Most of the tapes he made during the last year of his life were not turned over to Impulse for release and are still being held by Mrs. Coltrane.) The album resulting from these sessions in February and March 1967, *Expression,* was surely not intended to be Coltrane's final statement. The music sounds as if he had simply turned another corner in his evolution. Pharoah Sanders does not play on most of the pieces, once again putting Coltrane at the front of a classic quartet format. The one piece Sanders does play on, "To Be," is a strange one in the Coltrane discography: on it Trane plays flute and Pharoah piccolo. Despite its lyrical moments, and the chance to hear Coltrane on such a different instrument, the track lacks cogency and seems mainly an opportunity for the two saxophonists to explore the possibilities of their new instruments.

The rest of the album is far more interesting. Coltrane is certainly more conservative here than on *Interstellar Space,* submitting to the gravity of the piano and bass, rarely resorting to screams or shrieks. This is still "outside" music making, but more careful and reflective than much of what he had been producing in the past couple of years. Simply by not using Sanders the music becomes more accessible, and perhaps that was part of Coltrane's point. *Expression* is in the tradition of his great transitional albums, *Giant Steps, Live at the Village Van-*

guard, and *Transition.* Sadly, Coltrane would not live to explore the new regions toward which his music was heading.

Those who saw Coltrane in 1967 were shocked by his appearance—he seemed bloated and weak, his eyes lacking that brilliant luminosity. In constant pain, he continued his involvement with music until he was finally too sick to play. On July 16 he collapsed and was rushed to Huntington Hospital, the hospital nearest Coltrane's Long Island home. He died the next day, just a few months shy of his forty-first birthday, of the liver cancer that he had been so valiantly struggling with for so many months.

Some have speculated that the cause of his death was related to the terrible burden he had put on his liver during his years of alcohol and drug addiction. The etiology of liver cancer is still basically unknown, and there is no reason to believe that alcohol or drugs had anything to do with Coltrane's illness.

Coltrane was gone. I remember the shock of seeing his picture in the paper and hardly believing the accompanying text. Like many Coltrane fans, I had no idea that he had been sick. No one ever seemed more vitally alive than John Coltrane—put on any of his albums and you are either almost flattened or lifted off your feet by his vibrant life force. It seemed impossible that he could have died so suddenly, at such an early age. Did he know how many lives he had shaped and changed? Did he have any real idea how his life changed the culture not just of his own country but of the world? Did he really know how much he meant to so many, and for generations to come?

Although the man is gone, his music is still with us—music that still sounds pungently contemporary and relevant more than a quarter century after his death. At the close of the twentieth century, Coltrane remains almost as controversial as when he was alive. Even in death, he continues to thrill and elevate many and infuriate others.

13 **after the trane**

Immediately following Coltrane's death came the expected outpourings of grief and appreciation of his accomplishments. As in life, however, not all critics agreed on the value of Coltrane's work. No one expressed a macabre relief that he was gone more bluntly than Philip Larkin: "Virtually the only compliment one can pay Coltrane is one of status. If he was boring, he was enormously boring. If he was ugly, he was massively ugly. To squeak and gibber for sixteen bars is nothing. Coltrane could do it for sixteen minutes. . . . I regret Coltrane's death, as I regret the death of any man, but I can't conceal the fact that it leaves in jazz a vast, blessed silence." The London *Daily Telegraph,* for which Larkin reviewed jazz, refused to publish his Coltrane obituary, which appeared three years later in his collection of jazz essays, *All What Jazz.*

Other critics, if not quite as outspoken as Larkin, continued to argue the merits of Coltrane's work just as they had when he was alive. Martin Williams and Whitney Balliett, arguably the two most prominent critics of their generation, each claimed that only one aspect of Coltrane's constantly evolving style revealed his true musical essence, and that other aspects were merely irrelevant results of his constant experimentalism.

For Balliett, Coltrane was fundamentally a "horizontal" player, a lyrical melodicist, although the critic found that getting to the core of Coltrane's musical personality was not easy, especially since Trane was so reverentially lionized. "Getting through the reverential cities of Troy that Coltrane vanished under is only the beginning of getting at Coltrane himself," wrote Balliett in his obituary. "He wasn't even easy to *listen* to. He had a blank, aggressive tone, and in his moments of frenzy, which were frequent, he repeated series of manic shrieks, wails and screams that hurt the ear and stopped the mind. . . . But every once in a while his restlessness passed and he came to a halt, stopped preaching, stopped screeching, and played a straightforward slow ballad or medium-tempo blues, and one suddenly understood what Coltrane was—the essence of good, old-fashioned lyricism. Such statements can be found in his best recording, *Crescent,* and they are magnificent, in the way of Louis Armstrong and Sidney Bechet and Charlie Parker at their lyrical best. These solos are, in the singular manner of all great jazz improvisors, more human than musical."

Martin Williams, on the other hand, wrote upon Coltrane's death, "Coltrane was a vertical player, a kind of latter-day Coleman Hawkins"—in other words, a harmonic rather than melodic improvisor. Two important critics reached two utterly divergent conclusions. The truth was, of course, that Coltrane was both a melodic and a harmonic player, both horizontal and vertical—although he had periods when he was far more devoted to one rather than the other—as well as a player of another dimension altogether, that of pure *sound.*

Both Balliett and Williams had rarely found pleasure in Coltrane's work while he was alive, and both wrote rather backhanded tributes after his death, damning him with faint praise. Balliett chose as his example of Coltrane at his peak Trane's solos on "The Drum Thing" on the *Crescent* album: a piece is taken up almost entirely with an Elvin Jones drum solo, with dark and lovely but very brief opening and closing statements that are hardly representative of Coltrane's work. That was probably Balliett's point, for he wrote: "Born poets like Coltrane sometimes misjudge the size of their gifts, and in trying to further them, to ennoble them, they fall over into sentimentality or the maniacal. Coltrane did both, and it is ironic that these lapses, which were mistakenly considered to be musical reflections of our inchoate times, drew his heaviest acclaim. People said they heard the dark night of the Negro in Coltrane's wildest music, but what they really heard was a heroic and unique lyrical voice at the mercy of its own power."

Williams seemed somewhat more positive than Balliett, despite writing that Coltrane's "musical statements . . . have brilliant moments but become static and remain unresolved"; they "are contained only by a fantastic and original saxophone technique on the one hand, or by a state of emotional exhaustion on the other." He concludes by reluctantly giving Coltrane his due: "In any case, Coltrane was bold enough to state his message so that the present knows of him, and so that the future must acknowledge that he was with us." Hardly high validation of Coltrane's musical accomplishments.

More significantly, Williams later dealt Coltrane's legacy a devastating blow, one that seemed to be a deliberate attempt to limit the degree to which the "future must acknowledge that he was with us." Williams was in charge of the Smithsonian Institution's jazz division in the Seventies when the Smithsonian released a several-record set called *The Smithsonian Collection of Classic Jazz.* Although "classic jazz" usually means that of the Twenties and Thirties, Williams broadened that definition to include the best and most essential musicians and recorded performances of the entire jazz chronology. Each of the major jazz improvisors was represented by several tracks, with one exception: John Coltrane. Trane can be heard playing on Miles Davis's "So What" from *Kind of Blue,* but the only track with him as a leader is "Alabama," a beautiful piece of music but hardly indicative of his most innovative work. Such Coltrane colleagues as Monk, Ornette Coleman, and Miles Davis are all well represented, with several pieces representing significant aspects of their careers.

This collection, having the imprimatur of the Smithsonian, is widely used by schools and colleges, where it is bound to influence how the future will evaluate the relative importance of the great jazz musicians. Whatever reservations Williams might have had about Coltrane, he definitely left him underrepresented on a collection that has helped define the jazz canon.

Williams was a great, and early, champion of Ornette Coleman. As important as Coleman was, his influence, at least his *stylistic* influence, was not nearly as pervasive as that of Coltrane. Williams's shortchanging of Coltrane in the collection is reflective not only of his own personal distaste for the man's music, but also for the radical, truly revolutionary perspective Coltrane brought to his art. Like most white writers, Williams brought a profoundly Western, European-oriented value system and critical perspective to bear in his evaluation. Coltrane's music, at least that of the last six or seven years of his career, was based more on non-Western values—social and philosophical, as well as aesthetic—than that of any other jazz musician that preceded him, including Coleman, whose main body of work is a logical extension of bop and has definite parallels with developments in twentieth-century "classical" music. Coleman has even written pieces for string quartet and a symphony, "Skies of America." Regardless of how uncomfortable some of Coltrane's music made Williams feel, no one could deny the ubiquitous nature of his influence.

In *Outcats*, an anthology of jazz essays, the critic Francis Davis writes in a piece on Williams and the Smithsonian: "Williams shares certain traits with Pauline Kael, the only film critic comparable to him in stature. Like her he has massive blind spots. Just as she has little use for John Ford or Alfred Hitchcock, Williams has never warmed to John Coltrane, whom he severely underrepresented with just two appearances on *Classic Jazz* . . . at a time when the late tenor saxophonist had jazz in a posthumous hammerlock. Still, this was one of those instances in which wrong was right. Williams correctly perceived that Coltrane impersonators were leading jazz toward a cul-de-sac, with their know-nothing mysticism, droning modality, and opportunistic black nationalism."

Follow the bouncing logic of Davis's statement: Coltrane's real legacy is nothing but "know-nothing mysticism, droning modality and opportunistic black nationalism." How can he claim that Williams has a "massive blind spot" when it comes to Trane? Either Coltrane was a great and influential musician and worthy of adequate representation in the *Smithsonian Col-*

lection, or he was merely a Sixties fad, like tie-dyed shirts and lava lamps, and not worthy of equal consideration with his colleagues. Which "impersonators" is he talking about? There were musicians like the notorious Charles Lloyd whose imitation of Trane often reminded one of a mediocre comedian doing his Humphrey Bogart impersonation: everything was there but the greatness. There were others who slavishly imitated Coltrane, just as there were those who imitated Armstrong, Lester Young, Charlie Parker, etc. Was that the fault of these innovators? Even if everything that Davis said about Coltrane's imitators was true, did this diminish Trane's own contributions? Were the accomplishments of Charlie Parker diminished by those who, on virtually every instrument, copied not only Bird's playing but also his lifestyle? It is ridiculous to deny that Coltrane, like these other great musicians, also positively affected, in a variety of ways, virtually every thinking musician who listened to him. Musicians ranging from rock guitarists Eric Clapton and Jerry Garcia to avant-gardists Anthony Braxton and Roscoe Mitchell have been influenced by Coltrane. Which of them fits Davis's description of a Coltrane acolyte? It is difficult to find a musician under the age of fifty (and quite a few over fifty), no matter how individualistic his style, who has not been influenced by Coltrane, consciously or not. The implication that Coltrane himself was a "know-nothing mystic" or an "opportunistic black nationalist" betrays absolutely no knowledge or understanding of his life.

Such revisionism about Coltrane's legacy does not end with Davis. The most dominant, or at least the most famous, jazz musician of our own time, Wynton Marsalis, proclaimed that Coltrane's "free" work of the last couple of years of his life was "Nothin'." At a recent concert co-produced by Marsalis devoted to Coltrane's work, all his accomplishments after 1964 were ignored, as if Trane had died after recording *A Love Supreme.*

Unlike these critics, however, a number of musicians were far more positive in their assessment of Coltrane's innovations and contributions. Archie Shepp, for instance, said: "That was his breakthrough—the concept that the imperatives of conception might make it necessary to improvise at great length. I don't mean he proved that a thirty or forty minute solo is necessarily better than a three minute one. He did prove, however, that it was possible to create thirty or forty minutes of uninterrupted, continually building, continually original and imaginative music. In the process, Coltrane also showed the rest of us we had to have the stamina—in terms of imagination and physical preparedness—to sustain those long flights."

David Baker, a jazz cellist, arranger, composer, and music professor at the University of Indiana, summed up Coltrane's achievements: "Using multiphonics, playing several notes or tones simultaneously; creating asymmetrical groupings not dependent on the basic pulse; developing an incredibly sophisticated system of chord substitutions and initiating a pan-modal style of playing, using several modes simultaneously. I've transcribed some of his solos for teaching my students at the University of Indiana. I think all musicians should study Coltrane solos the way we study the etudes of Bach and Brahms."

Not all of Coltrane's influence was beneficial, although this in no way diminishes the value of his own work. Davis has a point: about the "droning modality." Other than Trane himself, and Miles, few musicians could sustain interest playing modally. Due to Coltrane, lengthy solos increasingly became the rule in jazz performances. While no one soloed for an hour or more like Trane on a good night, the average soloist would often play a solo for fifteen or twenty minutes, boring the hell out of his audience. Most of the young musicians who wished to play long had not mastered improvising a coherent solo of, say, sixteen bars, or one or two choruses, as Coltrane had. In other words, they just hadn't paid their dues. Sitting in a jazz club in the late Sixties or early Seventies and listening to one long, boring solo after another could be agony. The mediocrity that reigned in those years in no way diminishes Coltrane's own ability to captivate audiences while soloing far longer than those misguided acolytes; rather, it makes that ability even more awe-inspiring.

Keith Jarrett, one of the most popular jazz musicians of the Seventies, said about the period following Coltrane's death, "Everyone felt a big gap all of a sudden. But he didn't intend to leave a gap. He intended that there be more space for every-body to do what they should do." In the quarter of a century since Trane's death, there has not emerged on the jazz scene a great innovator even vaguely his equal, or the equal of the great line of jazz innovators that preceded him, beginning with Buddy Bolden. There have been three major movements since his passing—fusion, eclecticism, and neo-classicism—though none of these movements has produced music as innovative or deep, or quite simply as wonderful as had been regularly forthcoming from jazz in its previous six or seven decades. The obvious question to be asked is: why was John Coltrane, at least apparently, the last great jazz innovator? Was this fact directly a result of the nature of his music, as well as the music of the "New Thing" movement so deeply influenced by him?

Coltrane's music in the last few years of his life—his "free" period—presented a problem for the direction of jazz. For those following in his footsteps, the complete and utter freedom of works such as *Interstellar Space* was a trap. How could any musician push the envelope even farther? Where could jazz go now?

The New Thing in jazz, for which Coltrane was greatly responsible, went a long way to turning off its audience. Just as rock was becoming increasingly popular, as well as more sophisticated and genuinely musical, jazz seemed lost in space. The public soon lost interest in free jazz once Coltrane was gone. While he was alive, he could still draw an audience to hear the young New Thing musicians he often had join his regular group. Left without a champion after Trane's passing, those musicians found it even more difficult to find outlets for their music.

Tracing the careers of musicians associated with Coltrane after his death is interesting and instructive. The three members of the original quartet all had a hard time trying to get solo careers going in the bleak atmosphere, at least for jazz, of the late Sixties. McCoy Tyner even thought of giving up music altogether. He continued to work hard at his music, forging ahead both in terms of technique and in originality, and by the mid-Seventies, even amid the dominance of jazz-rock fusion, had become the most influential pianist in jazz. His music had unmistakable ties to that of his former boss, to the extent that he seemed to be consciously trying to carry forward the pre-*Ascension* Coltrane legacy. The influence of Arab and African music, the use of modes and pedal point, the feeling of density in his groups, even the sound of the saxophonists he hired were among the elements of Tyner's music that echoed the Coltrane quartet at its height.

Elvin Jones, after his brief, disastrous employment with Duke Ellington, also had difficulty making his way as a leader. Elvin was something of a musical conservative, at least next to his former boss, and his heart remained with the hard bop of the late Fifties. Despite the radical nature of his innovative drumming, he wanted nothing to do with anyone associated with the avant-garde. He tried a variety of different ensembles, settling for a while on a trio with the bassist Wilbur Little and the saxophonist Joe Farrell, another early Coltrane devotee. Elvin played with as much fire and polyrhythmic inventiveness as he had with Coltrane, drowning out, for the most part, the other players, even when Farrell played into a microphone. Since this was often true when he played with Trane, seeing Elvin's group play live gave listeners at least some idea of the sound of the original quartet. Jones would go on to lead a variety of groups, one of the best featuring the fine tenor men George Coleman and Frank Foster, but no matter the personnel, Elvin naturally always dominated the group. On nights when he felt like it, he could still stop hearts with the power of his rhythms.

Jimmy Garrison played with a number of groups, at one point co-leading a trio with the West Coast pianist Hampton Hawes. Unfortunately, Garrison was another jazz musician to die young, passing away in the early Seventies.

The two surviving members of the Coltrane quartet, then, continued playing music along the same lines as the pre-*Ascension* quartet. Neither man made any concessions to popular taste, staying far away from rock and funk; they instead remained true to the musical principles to which they had committed themselves when working with Coltrane. That is no surprise, but what is surprising, and quite revealing, is what happened to many of the most radical New Thing musicians Coltrane had been associating with during the last two or three years of his life.

No musician, not even Albert Ayler, seemed further out than Pharoah Sanders. On his records with Coltrane he seemed devoted to being outside the outside, interested only in making the coarsest, most ear-splitting sounds in all of music. As Coltrane's most obvious musical heir—after all, wasn't Pharoah "the Son" in Coltrane's piece "The Father, the Son, and the Holy Ghost"?—Sanders appeared likely to continue to strive even further "outside" in the tradition of his great mentor.

Sanders's first album for Impulse, *Tauhuid,* was with a group that included the amazing guitarist Sonny Sharrock, who perfected a technique of strumming the strings so fast he could duplicate the effect and feeling of Pharoah's twisting saxophone screams. That record had sections that were "free" and others that were not, indicating Pharoah's flexibility and the possibility that he might not remain exclusively a New Thing avatar. *Tauhuid* became an underground hit, especially owing to Sonny Sharrock's remarkable guitar playing, but did little to broaden Sanders's audience.

On Pharoah's next album, *Karma,* over a forest of percussion and a Coltranesque ostinato bass figure (not dissimilar to that of *A Love Supreme*), Leon Thomas sang "The Creator has a Master Plan / Peace and Happiness for every man / The Creator makes but one demand / Peace and Happiness for every man," over and over, finally breaking into his famous Central African-style yodel. Pharoah's own playing is amazingly tender and lyrical; even when he finally breaks into the inevitable shriek it seems to fit, followed as it is by a return to calm lyricism. Despite the sappy lyrics, *Karma* was an immediate counterculture hit, for a few weeks the best-selling jazz album on the *Billboard* charts. Pharoah's exotically lyrical melodic ideas, the hypnotic pedal point, the piece's modalism, even the climactic shriek—all bore the Coltrane copyright in bright Day-Glo colors.

Pharoah continued to be a popular performer for a while, playing "inside" at least as much, if not more, as "outside." His improvising had a Coltranesque lyricism, particularly on ballads, but his tone was big and gruff. If he was no longer avant-garde, his experiences with Coltrane and his association with the "New Thing" had obviously deeply affected him. The bulk of Sanders's post-Coltrane work cannot be called free jazz. If anything, his playing seemed to get increasingly conservative as the years wore on, although he remained an unusually expressive improviser. In clubs and on record, he usually performed with mainstream postbop players like the pianist John Hicks and the bassist Walter Booker. When he played a basic blues with such searing power, using vocalized cries not too distant from the "outside" screams he had played with Coltrane and often reminding one of Big Jay McNeely or the other great rhythm and blues tenor men, he made it clear that his heart was with the roots of the jazz tradition and always had been.

Archie Shepp similarly became a more mainstream performer, often playing in a hard bop style with musicians such as Philly Joe Jones, Albert Daily, and on one occasion even Chet Baker, although he still performed free jazz at times. In order to make a living, he spent much of his time in Europe. Along the way he recorded one of the most moving albums of the Seventies— a duet album with the pianist Horace Parlan, also a mainstream musician, of Negro spirituals called *Goin' Home*. As with Pharoah, Shepp's trial by fire at the heart of the Sixties avant-garde had made him an unusually expressive musician, and his album of spirituals indicates that he was now finding inspiration in the entire black musical tradition. As a player and a spokesman for the New Thing, he was no longer the firebrand who had so frightened and unsettled some white critics and jazz fans.

Perhaps the strangest fate was that which befell Albert Ayler. He seemed the most dedicated to musical radicalism of all the New Thing musicians, someone so far out it didn't seem possible he would ever succumb to the same gravity that pulled so many musicians down to earth. Yet even before Miles Davis released *Bitches Brew* in 1969, Ayler turned to jazz-rock fusion. On *New Grass* (1968) he wailed against a rock background including the guitar of Henry Vestine, a member of the blues rock group Canned Heat. Against the simple blues harmonies and basic backbeat of rock, Ayler's shrieks sounded far less outrageous and cacophonous to those who had found his New Thing music intolerable. His next album, *Music Is the Healing Force of the Universe,* featured vocals, mainly by Ayler's girlfriend Mary Maria, expressing soggy versions of the peace-and-love rhetoric of the time.

As with Pharoah Sanders, Ayler's music changed soon after Coltrane's death. That was probably no accident. Things were bad enough for all jazz musicians in the late Sixties, but for those in the avant-garde they were even worse. With their champion gone, it was a very bleak picture. The audience for music itself was larger than ever, and that audience was listening now to all sorts of strange stuff under the common umbrella labeled "psychedelia." Ayler had more complicated reasons for the change in his music than merely trying to expand his popularity.

Like Coltrane, Ayler believed his music had a great spiritual purpose. After having a vision in which he saw Jesus appearing out of a flying saucer and "the new Earth built by God coming out of Heaven," he realized he had to change his music in order to communicate God's message. Sadly, Ayler did not have much time to either spread God's word or enjoy the rewards of his new, more accessible music. In November 1970 his body was dragged out of New York's East River. It remains a mystery if his was a case of murder or suicide.

Alice Coltrane continued to make music after her husband's death, though again, little of it could be called New Thing. Along with such former associates as Rashied Ali and Pharoah Sanders, who played some exquisite soprano sax on one session, she made some lovely records of deeply felt devotional music, playing both piano and harp. At times she captured the mood of such Coltrane pieces as "Dear Lord" and parts of *A Love Supreme.* Her harp playing was particularly fascinating. Her husband had loved this instrument, and when she played dense glissandos, producing a sound not unlike that of Coltrane's tenor during the "sheets of sound" period, it was easy to tell why. Still on the spiritual path she had walked with her husband, she joined the ashram of Swami Satchidananda in California. Genuinely devoted to the Vedantic philosophy, upon Satchidananda's death she became its swami. She still creates and occasionally records devotional music, some of it with orchestra and voices, much of it of unearthly beauty, and each year her ashram holds a festival in honor of her late husband.

Most of the other musicians involved in the Sixties avant-garde either faded from the scene, moved to Europe, or took a more conservative route. Marion Brown, for example, recorded an album containing Stevie Wonder tunes. Economics was the key: the clubs and record companies simply would not touch the New Thing (which was no longer new), and few of the cultural institutions gave grants, back then, to jazz musicians.

For all these reasons, the musicians most closely associated with Coltrane in the last several years of his life seemed either unable or unwilling to continue on his quest to take the music even farther along. Most of them made good music, some of it better than what they had produced when they were with Coltrane, but that age of exploring the limits of improvisation seemed to be over.

With free jazz apparently at a dead end, and jazz at about its lowest level of popularity since the Twenties, perhaps it was no surprise that the next improviser, the one who came closest to carrying the innovative musical torch after Coltrane's death, would not arise out of jazz at all.

Since the Swing Era of the Thirties and early Forties, when jazz *was* the popular music of the day, jazz would drift farther and farther from the pop musical mainstream of the day. When rock and roll's first wave of popularity swept through the country like a tidal wave in the Fifties, jazz musicians felt completely frozen out, and their attitude toward the new music was one of contempt. They had a certain belief that it was a fad that would certainly not last. They realized that rock and roll came from the same roots as their music, but they looked at it as a bastardization of those elements, a simple-minded music that would certainly die when the current crop of teenagers came of age. After Elvis went into the army, and jazz musicians found they still had a large audience among college kids and young adults, they sighed in relief: Jazz had survived yet another threat to its economic health. A few years later, of course, came the Beatles and the British Invasion. Not only were these groups as popular as Elvis, much of their music was clever and inventive. What to do? Some jazz musicians, even Count Basie and Duke Ellington, recorded Beatle songs in a lame effort to attract a young audience. Gerry Mulligan put out an album that summed up the situation: *If You Can't Beat 'em, Join 'em.* But jazz versions of rock tunes for the most part appealed neither to rock nor jazz audiences.

As the Sixties progressed, such rock groups as Cream, the Bluesbreakers, and San Francisco "acid rock" groups like the Grateful Dead, Jefferson Airplane, and Quicksilver Messenger Service began to intrude on jazz territory—not unknowingly, since most of them had spent long hours listening to jazz and particularly to Coltrane. His influence was clearly recognizable in their use of long improvisations, modes, and hypnotically repetitive phrases, combined with that Indian/Arabic style of lyricism that Trane blended so perfectly with the blues sensibility.

The British group Cream would take a blues piece and stretch it out for fifteen or twenty minutes and sometimes longer. Eric Clapton, the group's guitarist, would frequently describe the influence of Coltrane on his own playing. As he put it, although he didn't always understand what Trane was doing musically, he always responded to the saxophonist's sound, and it was that aspect of Coltrane's playing that had influenced his own sound.

In America, Coltrane's influence on the more musical rock groups of the late Sixties was even deeper. Probably the most famous example is the Byrds' song "Eight Miles High," which was directly based on Coltrane's "India." Roger McGuinn, who wrote the hit tune, even tried imitating the feeling of Coltrane's improvising in his twelve-string guitar solo.

Jerry Garcia, the guitarist with the Grateful Dead, has described Coltrane's effect on his playing: "I've been influenced by Coltrane, but I never copped his licks or sat down, listened to records and tried to play his stuff. I've been impressed with that thing of flow, and of making statements that to my ears sound like paragraphs—he'll play along stylistically with a certain kind of tone, in a certain kind of syntax, for X amount of time, then he'll like change the subject, then play along with this other personality coming out, which really impresses me. It's like other personalities stepping out or else his personality changing, his attitude's changing. But it changes in a holistic way where the tone of his axe and everything changes.

"Perceptually, an idea that's been very important to me in playing has been the whole 'odyssey' idea—journeys, voyages, you know? And adventures along the way." The Grateful Dead, with their two percussionists, occasional forays into "free" sonic territory, and four- or five-hour shows that showcase long improvisations, certainly bring Coltrane to mind.

Another rock musician who has been most vocal about the effect of Coltrane on his music is the guitarist Carlos Santana, who also got his start in the late Sixties in San Francisco. He told an interviewer, "I haven't heard anything higher than 'The Father and the Son and the Holy Ghost' from the *Meditations* album. I would often play it at four in the morning, the traditional time for meditation. I could hear God's mind in that music, influencing John Coltrane. I heard the Supreme One playing music through John Coltrane's mind."

When one considers the San Francisco groups during the late Sixties, and the counterculture itself for that matter, it is unavoidable mentioning Coltrane's spiritual/philosophical influence. The whole idea of the acid rock groups was in "expanding the consciousness" through music. That music can do more than merely provide entertainment, that it can change people in profound ways, was the theme.

Long after Hendrix had come and gone, Coltrane continued to influence new generations of rock musicians. Musicians with different agendas all could find inspiration in Coltrane. If to the acid era bands Coltrane was an exemplar of peace and love, the unleashed fury of his later music made Coltrane a spiritual ancestor of the punks of the late Seventies. One of the later punk groups, the Dream Syndicate, even wrote a tune for him, "The John Coltrane Stereo Blues." A few years ago Bono, of the Irish group U2, described his discovery of the music of Coltrane, and particularly *A Love Supreme*—not a surprise, since the group is known for its spiritual and social concerns. In one U2 video *A Love Supreme* is mentioned in the lyrics while Coltrane's face is briefly seen on the screen, undoubtedly bringing blank stares to youthful viewers of MTV.

Coltrane's musical influence even extended beyond that of popular music. Several so-called "classical" composers listened to Trane and listened hard. The composers most influenced by Coltrane were those of the "minimalist-structuralist-trance" school, which included such well-known figures as Terry Riley, Steve Reich, and the father of this movement, LaMonte Young, who often spoke quite articulately about the influence of Coltrane. The most famous of these composers, Philip Glass, has often mentioned the large amount of time he put into listening to Trane in the early and middle Sixties. The pre-*Ascension* period had the greatest influence on him.

Coltrane's static harmonies (really modes), his use of the rhythmically repetitious vamps, his snaky lyricism are all reflected in Glass's work. Glass, because of Coltrane perhaps, studied Indian music. Glass worked with Shankar on the soundtrack of a film and, like Coltrane, aspects of Indian music were eventually subtly melded into his own music. As John Rockwell writes in his book *All American Music,* "Although Glass's music then and now sounds nothing like Indian music, the very fact that it was Shankar and Indian music that triggered his mature musical thinking is yet another indication of the impact of Oriental ideas on vanguard American composers." Glass's study of Coltrane must have made him very aware of this important aspect of the saxophonist's music, which had been part of Coltrane's musical conception long before Glass worked with Shankar. Unlike Glass but like Indian music, Coltrane's music was largely improvised, making it by nature closer in feeling to that of Shankar and other great Indian musicians. The point is that Coltrane's musical legacy cut a wide swath.

Not very long after Coltrane's death there was an event that had a tremendous impact on American music. The occasion was the Monterey Pop Festival. Held on the same grounds as the annual jazz festival, the pop festival was the first such event to treat rock and pop with the same seriousness as jazz. Acts included in the festival ranged from Janis Joplin with her original band, Big Brother and the Holding Company, to the Grateful Dead, the Mamas and the Papas, and even Coltrane's friend, Ravi Shankar was included. The festival demonstrated the new levels of sophistication of post-Beatles rock, with groups employing improvisation and other forms of musical experimentation. Most of the improvisation of the rock groups, particularly those of the San Francisco "acid rock" scene, was modally based. No coincidence, because most of these musicians had listened long and hard to Coltrane, particularly *A Love Supreme*, with its fusion of religious revelation and Eastern-inspired modal improvisation. This new rock was winning an audience not just of teenagers but also of college students and other sophisticated young people who a few years earlier would have listened *only* to jazz and folk.

No single musician exemplified more the possibilities inherent in rock than the great left-handed guitarist Jimi Hendrix, whose band The Jimi Hendrix Experience had its American debut at the Monterey Pop Festival. After his performance, American music would never be the same. Much of the Hendrix show was jive. He played his guitar behind his back, over his head, with his teeth; he humped his guitar as if in sexual heat, and he closed things out by setting his axe on fire and then smashing it onstage. All of this wowed the tripped-out audience, but beneath these psychedelic burlesque turns there was some serious music playing. Hendrix didn't just play his guitar—he played the electronics of his instrument, using feedback and distortion to create, like the free jazz players who had preceded him, sounds and aural vistas that were truly new. Like a great jazz musician, like John Coltrane, no matter how far out his music might go, it still remained tethered to the blues, it still had "that thing," as Miles Davis called it.

If there is one musician who helped fill "that gap," in Keith Jarrett's words, left by Coltrane's death, it was Jimi Hendrix. Not that Hendrix at that time was in stature anything near to Coltrane. It is possible he might have been if he had lived, like Trane, to be forty or older. But he died at twenty-seven, sug-

234 ascension

gesting to musicians all sorts of tantalizing musical possibilities which he was unable to live long enough to explore himself.

In the British journalist Charles Schaar Murray's book on Hendrix, *Crosstown Traffic,* is a chapter called "Hear My Trane A'Comin' " ("Hear My *Train* A'Comin'," a blues, was a staple in the Hendrix repertoire). The chapter focuses on the influence of jazz on Hendrix and, in turn, his own influence on jazz. As Murray points out, since Hendrix was part of the Greenwich Village music scene before he went to England and formed his band the Jimi Hendrix Experience, he could not have avoided the revolutionary jazz sounds that, as Murray put it, literally spilled out onto the streets: "Whether Hendrix studied and applied the methods and techniques of the New Thing or the earlier jazz mode or whether he was simply plugging into the *Zeitgeist* and developed them independently, the fact remains that they're there." Murray accurately points out how similar Hendrix pieces such as "Third Stone from the Sun" (on his first album) are to jazz, in terms of improvisational development.

The difference is Hendrix's stunning use of electronic effects, creating a brilliant tableau of aural images. Simply think of his wonderful "Star-Spangled Banner," at Woodstock, in which he used feedback and distortion to create explosions and chilling humanlike screams to turn the national anthem into a powerful antiwar statement.

This sort of thing was unheard of in jazz. Although jazz musicians, particularly Charlie Christian, pioneered the use of the electric guitar, there had been little innovative work done on jazz guitar. In fact, most jazz guitarists were among the most conservative players on any instrument. In jazz, electric instruments were usually played so as to sound as nonelectric, as "natural" as possible. For instance, Milt Jackson, the great vibraharpist with the Modern Jazz Quartet, was lauded for his extremely conservative use of the machine's motor, creating a sound as close to "acoustic" as possible. If Hendrix had tried to play his style in the jazz world, he would have been quickly ostracized for his "tasteless" use of electronic distortion and feedback. Twentieth-century music and technical innovation are tightly intertwined. Jazz could not have existed and thrived if it had not been for the invention of the phonograph. In the world of "classical music," electronic music was old hat by the time Hendrix became famous. No one until Hendrix had really explored all the nuances of electronic, blues-based improvisation. At times he produced a wall of furious sound reminiscent of the "energy music" of the New Thing players. When Hendrix was improvising full force with "his Elvin Jones"—as he described his drummer, Mitch Mitchell—the parallels to Coltrane were inescapable.

The problem with Hendrix is that for most of his short career he lacked the discipline to explore thoroughly the new aural avenues he was opening up. His albums are a frustrating blend of moments of earth-shaking brilliance and true sonic inventiveness mixed in with hit tunes and psychedelic high jinks. Toward the end of his life Hendrix began to reevaluate his career and the direction of his talent. He had a rather paranoid friendship with Miles Davis (he would have an affair with Miles's wife, Betty), and he began talking with the great arranger Gil Evans about collaborating on an album. You can get at least a small notion of what that would have sounded like by listening to the album *Gil Evans Plays Jimi Hendrix,* recorded a few years after the guitarist's death. From the standpoint of a young jazz musician in the late Sixties, worried about the state of his own music, Hendrix at his best seemed to have it all: he played innovative and adventurous music and he commanded a huge audience.

No one was more aware of these circumstances than the ever-youthful Miles Davis. At the same time Hendrix was braving the mud at the Woodstock Festival, Miles was recording *Bitches Brew* in New York. There is a silly story that Miles was forced to record *Bitches Brew* because the head of Columbia Records put pressure on him to make more commercial music. Whoever spread that story never listened to *Bitches Brew.* Although it is usually described as the album that launched the jazz-rock fusion movement, it bears little resemblance to any rock and roll. The album reflects an awareness of the most progressive rock of the late Sixties. Which is only saying that, like all great jazz, it is of and for its time. Basically, *Bitches Brew* is Miles's musical reaction to both the work of Hendrix and that of Coltrane's last few years.

Each track has what might be called a "rock beat" and is combined with two or three other percussionists, producing dense polyrhythms not unlike those Trane experimented with in the last few years of his career. The use of group improvisation, with two or three electric pianos playing lines, guitar, and bass clarinet—an instrument that instantly reminds one of Coltrane's collaborations with Dolphy—is clearly a reflection of "New Thing" innovations. At one point near the end of "Pharaoh's Dance," there is a group explosion of free energy, including wails and cries, that is unmistakably resonant of Coltrane's *Ascension* period. The key difference between Trane's and Miles's use of this technique is that Miles plays the main theme over the group's wailing, riding it until it settles down as if it were a madly bucking bronco, thus keeping things under his tight control.

The frequent use of pedal point around which the soloists improvise, and the utilization of two basses (albeit here one electric—playing a rock/funk bass line repetitiously—and one "acoustic," played very freely by Dave Holland), gives the music that effect of "elastic time" so prevalent in much of Coltrane's later work. The most basic similarity here is that exhilarating and courageous sense of the "shock of the new," so clearly indicative of the deep shade of Coltrane imbued throughout *Bitches Brew*.

While it is true that Miles expressed disdain for much of Coltrane's later work, he undoubtedly found many of his former sideman's innovations intriguing. He was aware of Coltrane's dominance of the jazz scene in the Sixties. Coltrane's influence in terms of overall feeling, the mystical mood of the music, even its social overtones—that feeling of the coming of Apocalypse—are unmistakable in *Bitches Brew*. The use of electronic effects (Miles's psychedelic echo on the title tune), the funky electric bass lines (especially on the piece with the very Hendrix-esque title "Miles Runs the Voodoo Down"), and John McLaughlin's electric guitar all betray the influence of Hendrix on Miles.

Jazz-rock was nothing new when Miles released *Bitches Brew*. Tunes like Lee Morgan's hit "The Sidewinder" or Herbie Hancock's "Watermelon Man" were for all intents and purposes jazz/rock or jazz/funk. A number of young musicians of the "baby boom" generation like Gary Burton, Larry Coryell, and Jeremy Steig had been experimenting with fusing elements of rock with jazz improvisation for two or three years by the time *Bitches Brew* was recorded in 1969. Even some members of the avant-garde, such as Ornette Coleman and Archie Shepp, had experimented with elements of rhythm and blues. This fused combination of elements from Coltrane with Hendrix's and Sly Stone's and James Brown's electronic funk lit the fire that created the fusion movement.

Miles made a statement around this time that jazz had wandered too far from its folk roots. This was true of much of the "New Thing." The folk music of the time was rock and funk and Afro-Cuban—the music and rhythms that governed people's lives, which they danced to, which they listened to on the street and in the cars, and to which they made love. Jazz had to incorporate these rhythms if it was to remain vital and relevant. The promise of *Bitches Brew* was that the new wave of jazz would be a movement evolving out of the free jazz of the Sixties as well as the new sonic avenues being explored by progressive rock and funk musicians and the rhythms of the street. It seemed, to many in the jazz scene in the late Sixties, to be the next place that jazz had to go. Coltrane, who had already experimented with electronic effects, would have been at least intrigued with the innovations suggested by *Bitches Brew*. It should have been a brilliant new chapter in the history of jazz. But fusion turned into a disaster. What went wrong?

Part of the problem was, paradoxically, the enormous skill of the jazz musicians who moved into fusion. Miles Davis once said that he could "put together the greatest rock band in the world." Since jazz musicians were far more musically sophisticated as well as having, for the most part, incomparably greater technique, it seemed logical that they could outplay rock musicians, particularly those who improvised. Coltrane's techniques, at least a slick, simplified version of some of his techniques—the use of modes, and improvising around pedal point—were perfect devices for the fusioneers. Playing fast licks is too difficult with

chord changes, and pedal point provided a function for the repetitious bass line, so basic to rock and funk. Fusion thus became
a music of fast and furious licks, expertly played and often
dazzling from the standpoint of technique, but with little real
feeling or soul.

The other factor that destroyed fusion was another paradox:
its popularity. Suddenly jazz musicians found themselves playing
the rock palaces of the day, and selling far more records than
most jazz musicians could even dream about. With this pressure
to compete with the big rock groups, fusion became even more
commercial, often adding vocals and using electronic gimmicks
simply to give their audience a further jolt on the soulless aural
roller coaster that this music had become.

Besides his Eastern lyricism, modal improvising, and pedal
point, there was another aspect of Coltrane that seemed to
greatly influence the fusioneers. This was his deeply felt spiritual
perspective. As with Charlie Parker, who influenced countless
musicians to become drug addicts (unwittingly—he always discouraged young musicians from using dope) in the hope of being
able to play on the level of their hero, this new generation of
musicians hoped to gain the spiritual intensity for their music
that was so movingly prevalent in Coltrane's. Instead of Coltrane's fascination with all forms of religion, and his belief that
many paths lead to the ultimate truth, the fusioneers, at least
many of them, seemed to latch on to one of the faddish sects so
prevalent in the late Sixties and Seventies, and then to proclaim
the profound influence of this newfound faith on their music.
The fusioneers' music became increasingly commercial and pop-
oriented the deeper they immersed themselves in their religion,
unlike Trane, whose spiritual seeking caused his music, as we
have seen, to enter dark areas of the human soul, turning off a
good deal of his audience. It would seem logical that the greater
one's faith in an Ultimate Being or Truth, the less one would
need material goods, and the more one would pursue music, like
Coltrane, for its spiritual gains. The opposite seemed true for
the fusioneers. As soon as they latched on to one or another
form of religion, the more blatant was their pandering to an
audience, usually stoned kids who discovered that fusion, with

its electronic gimmickry and speedy chops, was great "head" music.

Such phenomena was reflective of the social and cultural milieu of the Seventies, the era dubbed by Tom Wolfe the "Me Generation." With the Vietnam War winding down and the great social movements of the Sixties stymied by the growing apathy and the infiltration of the government, the counterculture in a state of disarray partly because of the growing use of hard drugs like cocaine and speed instead of grass and psychedelics, with the Beatles breaking up and pop music changing from the experimentalism of acid rock to the brittle musical corset of heavy metal, and Richard Nixon—who many of us in the Sixties believed and hoped had been long banished from the national scene—in the White House; that shining moment of hope that seemed so real in the Sixties appeared to be gone. If that golden dream of community seemed lost forever, perhaps it was time, many thought, to tend one's own garden and to go for yourself. It's hard to imagine how Coltrane would have functioned in this environment; he may have had a hand in changing it for the better. Looking back at that era, the concept of his quest, and his intentions to "uplift" all people, seem like a round peg for the very square hole of the Seventies. Once again, the music would reflect its time, too often in quite dispiriting ways.

The first real fusion group, called Lifetime, was fronted by Miles's former drummer, Tony Williams. Although Williams had not played on *Bitches Brew*, he had been helping Miles develop his new "fusion" music, as one can hear on the preceding albums, *Filles de Kilamanjaro* and *In a Silent Way*. The original Lifetime consisted of Williams, whose drumming was almost as complex as that of Elvin Jones, the Scottish guitarist John McLaughlin, and organist Larry Young. Both Young and McLaughlin were profoundly influenced by Coltrane, and that could be plainly heard in their Trane-lyricism, febrile intensity, the chromatic lines at the heart of their improvisation. Most of the music of Lifetime was modal, and each piece was kaleidoscopic, changing in tempo and meter and feeling as the three men improvised freely together. That feeling of group improvisation, so central to Coltrane's music in his last two years or so, as well as that of Ornette and many others in the avant-garde, was always at the heart of Lifetime's music. McLaughlin and Young utilized electronics to give the music sonic depth and shifting textures, albeit far more subtly than Hendrix ever did.

Other than Miles's bands, Lifetime was not only the first, it was the best of all the fusion groups. Listening to it in 1968–69, jazz seemed to have a bright future, one based on the immediate past, particularly the freedom and intensity of Coltrane's best work, as well as awareness of what was transpiring in the contemporary music scene with "progressive" rock, and looking forward to an exciting future. The group could simply not stay together. They hired bassist Jack Bruce, who had been part of the hugely successful group Cream, but Bruce's bass interfered with Lifetime's unfettered flights. The group was never quite the same. Shortly thereafter, they broke up. Williams and McLaughlin (Young died shortly after the breakup of Lifetime) both went on to lead fusion groups. Perhaps the original Lifetime was too free and fluid for the Seventies. Williams eventually lead other fusion bands under the Lifetime name, but all of them were far more brittle and strait-jacketed and similar to so many other fusion bands of the time, more improvised rock than the jazz with rock influences.

McLaughlin found religion by joining Indian guru Sri Chinmoy's sect, along with fellow fusioneer Larry Coryell and Carlos Santana. He formed the Mahavishnu Orchestra (Mahavishnu was McLaughlin's Hindu name, bestowed by Sri Chinmoy). The group became quite popular for a while, playing the large rock venues like the Fillmore East/West. Despite McLaughlin's occasionally brilliant Coltrane-esque playing, the Mahavishnu Orchestra quickly became a loud bore. There was a sameness about the solos—his sidemen, including an electric violinist and keyboardist, seemed intent on imitating McLaughlin's guitar sound as closely as possible. Like most keyboardists in the fusion movement, Mahavishnu's Jan Hammer didn't explore the rich possibilities of a synthesizer, rarely producing sounds, like Hendrix, that belonged only in the world of electronics. The instrument was programmed rather to sound as much like an electric guitar as possible. The Mahavishnu Orchestra, like all of the groups that imitated it, had a great flaw that alone probably would have sunk the movement—simply, it is difficult for most musicians to play *jazz-style improvisation* at such high volume with the subtlety and nuance of straight ahead "acoustic" jazz playing. Playing electric instruments requires a completely different conception in order to improvise with a personal sound and with nuance and subtlety. Rock musicians like Hendrix and Clapton had a much better understanding of the dynamics of electronic instruments, as well as of simply playing loud, while jazz musicians playing fusion often wound up neither playing good jazz nor good rock.

Following Mahavishnu, McLaughlin formed a far more satisfying group called Shanti, whose members played "acoustic" instruments and a fusion of rock, Indian music, and jazz—no need to point out where the inspiration for that came from. If you have any doubt about Coltrane's influence on the guitarist, I refer you to *Love, Devotion, Surrender,* a 1973 album McLaughlin recorded with Carlos Santana of Coltrane-influenced spiritual Afro-Cuban jazz-rock. The first and longest track is a reworking of the first section of *A Love Supreme.* As in the original version, the pedal point bass line is the anchor around which Santana and McLaughlin play their modal improvisations, although here that line is played like a heavy metal riff. This cut perfectly demonstrates how Coltrane influenced the fusion movement, for better or (I'm afraid mainly) for worse.

At least as popular as the original Mahavishnu Orchestra was the group Return to Forever, founded by former Miles keyboard player Chick Corea, who also played on *Bitches Brew.* Before joining Miles, Corea had been a genuinely brilliant and original pianist in the mid-Sixties, a musician with apparently great promise. When Miles first had Corea play electric piano in his group, Corea instinctively hated the instrument, mainly because it forfeited such properties of fine piano-playing, elements that Corea had spent his life developing, as individual touch and pedal in exchange for volume and such occasional effects as wah-wah and ring modulator. With Miles, he pounded and tore at the instrument like a plugged-in Cecil Taylor, so frustrated was he at not being able to create the personal sound he had spent years developing. He wound up actually producing some intensely provocative sounds reminiscent of Sun Ra at his most manic. After leaving Miles, he formed with the iconoclastic and cerebral multi-reedman Anthony Braxton and his bassist in Miles's group, Dave Holland, a fascinating group called Circle, in which elements of the New Thing were explored with both discipline and adventure. The group played terrific music, and was acclaimed by critics and fans in Europe, but was a financial disaster in America. Corea then found Scientology. Sure enough he reevaluated the electric piano, and jazz-rock itself, and decided he really liked it after all! After a brief period playing Brazilian-oriented music with singer Flora Purim and her husband (and fellow Miles alumni), percussionist Airto Moreira, which did not bring in the big bucks, he put together a group modeled after the then-popular Mahavishnu Orchestra. Corea, like most of the fusioneers, realized that he had ten times the chops of his rock counterparts. Since most of the fusion crowd was undiscriminating, fast, facile licks were all that was demanded, something the fusioneers, after years of playing jazz, found as easy as cashing a check.

For whatever reasons, guilty conscience, public relations, whatever, Corea was always vociferous in defending his turn to fusion, even writing articles in *Down Beat*. He was, so he explained, "communicating," reaching out to his audience by playing these loud, fast, empty licks. The rejoinder immediately comes to mind: Didn't Coltrane or Miles or Bird, or Mozart for that matter, "communicate"? If he really wanted to communicate, why didn't he emulate, say, Guy Lombardo, who had been "communicating" for decades? Needless to say, the influence of Scientology—which wanted nothing more than to "communicate" with large numbers of people—could be heard whispering in this once brilliant musician's ear. Corea was often used by Scientologists as something of a poster boy for new recruits, and the themes of his tunes often referred to ideas gleaned from Scientology.

Another musician under the Coltrane spell was Herbie Hancock. After playing with Miles since 1963, he formed a sextet when he finally left the trumpeter's band in 1969. This new group was often superb, employing not only many of the advances of the Miles group but also many elements associated with Coltrane. The group would play lengthy—sometimes far too lengthy—solos in modal compositions, as well as long interludes of sometimes quite intense group improvisation. Hancock told an interviewer that he invariably listened to a late Coltrane album, usually *Meditations* or *Ascension*, before going onstage with his group. Hancock was also interested in exploring new areas suggested by the experiments with electronics so pervasive in the music of that time. He used an electric piano, not for solos but to accompany the soloists, using the electronic elements to blend with the horns and producing a rich group sound. Late in the group's existence, he hired a synthesizer player, who used the instrument to create unique electronic textures, rather than just an elaborate electric piano, against which the group improvised.

Hancock was frequently barraged with requests for his early-Sixties hits, particularly "Watermelon Man" and "Maiden Voyage," but he stoutly refused to play anything but his new music. He often lectured his audience before beginning a set, chastising them for living in the past, announcing that he would never again play any of his older music, and pleading with them to roll with the new. That was the past, he told his audience, and like Miles or Coltrane, that was of no interest to him now. Hancock saw himself in the great tradition of jazz torchbearers, particularly Coltrane, in his commitment to often difficult music, his refusal to kowtow to his audience's demands by repeating past successes, and his awareness of the social resonance of his musical direction.

Then Hancock, too, found religion—in his case the Nichiren Shoshu Buddhist sect that chanted "ham-myoho-renge-kyo" (made famous in the Jack Nicholson film *The Last Detail*) for world peace, an end to hunger, but mostly for material gain. Undoubtedly influenced by spiritual revelations, he folded his sextet, which had been an artistic but not a financial success, formed a smaller Sly Stone–influenced group called the Headhunters that featured his electric piano and funk rhythms, and even began playing "Watermelon Man" again, during virtually every set. He began to put out very commercial, pop-oriented albums and even had a hit tune ironically called "Chameleon."

Hancock's fusion music began more and more to resemble disco. In 1983 "Rockit" would prove to be an even bigger hit than "Chameleon." From time to time he would return to jazz, but never again with the promise suggested by his post-Miles sextet, of being in line with the great jazz innovators. He even briefly put back together Miles's great Sixties quintet, including Wayne Shorter, Tony Williams, and Ron Carter, with Freddie Hubbard substituting for Miles. Although the group played well—how could it not with such extraordinary musicians?— the spark that had made Miles's original group so adventurous was missing. As Miles, the last of the great jazz existentialists (along with Sonny Rollins), pointed out, music, or any work of art, cannot be separated from its particular moment in time, and the moment for this group was long gone. Hancock would become a celebrity, hosting variety shows on cable TV, writing scores for movies and television, making pop albums and even videos.

The fusion group with the greatest potential was Weather Report, founded by Joe Zawinul and Wayne Shorter, both of whom had played on *Bitches Brew*. The idea, as they originally described it, was to combine group improvisation with electronic textures played over jazz/rock and Latin American (especially Brazilian) rhythms. Shorter had been friends with Coltrane, and the two often practiced together. In the mid-Sixties, Shorter recorded a series of albums for Blue Note. The first few were with Coltrane's rhythm section and had a modal lyricism that, while personal and individual, nevertheless clearly exhibited the impress of Trane. Zawinul had been with Cannonball Adderley for several years, in whose group he had played the electric piano, a first for a straightahead jazz group (actually, he was second— Sun Ra was first—that is, if you consider his Solar Arkestra a "straightahead jazz group").

Their first album, the eponymously titled *Weather Report,* was a disappointment. Described accurately by one critic as "musical wallpaper," it lacked tension and shifting dynamics. The improvisation was tepid, as if both Shorter, one of the best post Rollins/Coltrane saxophonists, and Zawinul were afraid to shake the album out of its somnolent mood.

Despite such bleak beginnings, the group became extremely popular. Some of their ideas were truly innovative—for instance, they virtually never relied on that standard jazz arrangement: theme . . . solos . . . restatement of theme. At their best, they attempted to fuse improvisation with composition, often in imaginative ways, but gradually improvisation became so minimal as to amount to only minute detail. As the group progressed, Zawinul's compositions began to dominate the group, and most of them rarely allowed full-blown improvised solos (Shorter, one of the best jazz composers of the Sixties, contributed to the group's book with increasing infrequency). The emphasis became that of texture and atmosphere, with room only for Shorter, who almost exclusively played soprano, rarely tenor, with the group, or Zawinul's noodling little phrases here and there as far as improvisation was allowed. Despite moments of true brilliance—these were, after all, extremely talented men—rarely did Weather Report's music rise to anything more than rather atmospheric "furniture music," in Erik Satie's elegant phrase.

If their music ultimately fell well short of expectations, financially Weather Report, like most of the other fusion groups with the exception of Emergency, was a great success, at least for a jazz group. Soon, fusion of various sorts began to totally dominate the jazz scene. There were a number of groups, so bland they made *Weather Report* sound like *Ascension*, with names like Spiro Gyra and Yellowjackets. That was to be expected. The really sad part was the number of veteran musicians who latched on to fusion hoping to make a quick comeback: Donald Byrd, Stanley Turrentine, Freddie Hubbard, Benny Golson, even Sonny Rollins! Big-toned tenor man Gene Ammons was interviewed on the radio during this time, discussing his new album of Neil Diamond tunes. He, like other jazz musicians recording rock hits, didn't seem to realize that Diamond fans had no interest in his versions of these tunes and jazz fans had no interest in any versions of these warmed-over ditties.

Some fusioneers who did make it big suddenly sold enormous

amounts of records and filled large venues, the same places where the big rock groups of the day played. It must have seemed a totally separate reality from the time in which they came up in jazz, when they were happy to fill a small club like the Village Vanguard. Now the pressure was on—their managers, their accountants, their record company, maybe their own families were counting on them to continue their successes. For a reflective, creative musician, which is what most of the fusioneers at least used to be, this atmosphere had nothing to do with innovative music, and everything to do with the bottom line. Before the Beatles changed the record industry and some acts routinely began to sell a million or so albums, there was a place for the creative jazz musician. In the Seventies, however, at the height of the "Me Generation," a personal artistic and spiritual quest like that of John Coltrane would have been laughed at, if not ignored, unless there could be a way to cash in on it.

It's really hard to blame Corea or Hancock or Zawinul—why shouldn't they make a decent living commensurate with musicians with far less skill, experience, and imagination? Who had the right to demand that they starve for the cause of great music? They could not be faulted, of course, for feeling this way. When commercial considerations led to the creation of music so archly manipulative, predictable, and emotionally thin, and when this music dominated the jazz scene as it did in the first few years of the Seventies, the light of that torch handed from Buddy Bolson to John Coltrane seemed to get very dim.

One of the most basic reasons why fusion was doomed was the profoundly different natures of jazz and pop. Jazz had a close relationship, before rock, to pop music when it was able to borrow its tunes for its own uses, usually as a basis for improvisation. After rock came to dominate pop music, the two musics rarely touched each other, until the late Sixties. At its heart, pop music is basically conservative, reactionary even. Since it is, by definition, music that aims at great popularity, trying to hit the lowest common denominator, it cannot help but be, in terms of form and complexity, a conservative music. Most pop music is also vocal, which in itself tends to make it more conservative. Those creating it aim to grab an audience, or make it want to dance, or sing along, which means that experimentalism and musical curiosity are curtailed. In the Sixties, the Beatles, Bob Dylan, and others did try to experiment with pop and rock, but the basic shape of pop music was not transformed. It remained a music of catchy melodies and basic harmonies and rhythms. It is not a coincidence that those in the record business refer to the music of pop/rock musicians as *product*. This product is not meant to be of great lasting value, it has built-in obsolescence—whatever is number one on the hit parade this week will be replaced next week and forgotten the week after, and the following year will be designated as a "golden oldie."

I am not condemning pop/rock music, the truth is I love a great deal of it and God knows the world would be a whole lot grayer without it. Its nature is at odds with that of jazz, which has always been, at least until recently, a radical art form, always in creative ferment, and constantly changing. How can you really control, after all, improvisation? Jazz musicians have ripe musical curiosities and some, like John Coltrane, change their music constantly and never play a tune the same way twice. This is also true, of course, of the great jazz singers like Billie Holiday and Sarah Vaughan. Pop audiences and jazz audiences have completely different expectations when hearing their music live: the pop audience basically wants to hear the records of the pop stars reproduced note for note, the jazz audience expects (almost demands) the "sound of surprise." There are some rock bands, like the Grateful Dead and the Allman Brothers, that do improvise, and there are some jazz musicians who really don't improvise—but these are exceptions. Mick Jagger at one point said, a couple of decades ago, that he couldn't imagine himself still on stage singing "Satisfaction" at the age of forty-five—yet he is past that age and still singing basically the same music, including "Satisfaction," that he was performing almost thirty years previously. Miles Davis, on the other hand, could not even remember the tunes he played thirty years previously, and for this he was proud—his forgetting was a powerful factor forcing him to continue to innovate. For this simple reason it seems impossible for a true melding of these two musical states of mind.

* * *

There are two major exceptions to the bleak parade of Seventies jazz fusioneers. They were Miles Davis and Ornette Coleman, who by this time had already done more than their share of earth-shattering innovative music. Following *Bitches Brew*, Miles continued to explore and create the electric, polyrhythmic, group improvisational, and multi-ethnic musical ideas on which *Brew* had been based, and Coltrane continued to be a shadowy influence. At one point, the Indian influence Coltrane brought to jazz was made palpable when Miles employed an electric sitarist and a tabla player. Miles believed that for jazz to return to its "folk roots," it needed the rhythmic vitality of James Brown for it to reach people as viscerally as it once had, and from that funky base it could go on in any direction it pleased. With the new sonic colors made possible by electronics (he was even using a wa-wa pedal on his trumpet), it could speak directly to the young generation who had, until the advent of the rock era, traditionally supported jazz.

Usually Miles's band had one or two guitarists (at one point including John McLaughlin), sometimes an electric keyboard player, a drummer, and various percussionists, and a Coltrane-influenced saxophonist. Miles's work of the Seventies, through his "retirement" in 1975, with its emphasis on texture, its consistent use of a droning bass line at its center, its feeling of free (but not "free") collective interaction and African rhythms, and its multidimensional challenge to its listeners' ears and nervous systems, certainly gave it an overall feeling closer to Coltrane's work of the mid-Sixties than to anything in his own musical past. Its use of a funky bass ostinato, a rock backbeat, and Latin percussion was a sharp contrast to the free, spread rhythms used by Coltrane in his later work.

By the mid-Seventies, Miles would often play one piece per set, and that could last anywhere from forty-five minutes to an hour and a half, depending on how far out on a limb Miles and his musicians went—again, remindful of Coltrane at the height of his powers. The music was often cacophonous, and so rhythmically dense that any comparisons to rock and funk really missed the point. Unlike most of the fusion created in the Seventies,

Miles's complex new music challenged, and often confused, its audience rather than pandered to it. One could certainly feel Coltrane's brave spirit when this music hit its height of intensity. Very often Miles's Seventies music simply didn't work—it was so multidimensional, it required such tight interaction between the musicians, and took such daring by a soloist to work his way over this tenuous musical tightrope. Certainly one could not count on that miracle of serendipity when all the parts of this whole did work. Miles's willingness to take the existential riskiness of this music in attempting to reinvigorate so many aspects of his music was certainly Coltranesque in its defiant bravery. Unfortunately, some of the best of this music on record, especially albums with Trane-influenced discordant power such as *Panagea* and *Dark Magus,* have only been released in Japan. The memory of Coltrane, more than any of the other great musicians he had played with, was always close to Miles's heart and mind. In the house on Seventy-seventh Street, where he lived for decades before moving to the West Coast, he had a picture of only one musician, other than himself (Miles's vanity was even closer to his heart and mind). That picture was of a reflective Coltrane, his luminous eyes looking off into the distance, filled with distracted wonder.

Miles's Seventies work deserves much more discussion than I have given it here; Jack Chambers's *Milestones II* has the greatest detail. Unlike so many of his former sidemen, Miles remained adamantly nonreligious. He had given up religion as a boy when he discovered that the local churches in East Saint Louis were segregated—if there was one thing Miles hated more than a tired musical cliché, it was blatant hypocrisy.

It should be no surprise that Ornette Coleman would once again, along with Miles, create music so perfectly relevant to our time. While others were still trying to catch up with his work of the late Fifties and Sixties, Coleman formed Prime Time, an electric band of various combinations of electric guitarists, usually two electric bassists, and usually two drummers, one of them being his own son Denardo, who played complex versions of funk rhythms. Ornette had begun his career in a rhythm and blues band, and had used such a group in his famous Town Hall concert in the Sixties. Prime Time was far more than standard jazz/funk. The band provided a shifting, droning kaleidoscope of electronic pantonal colors against which Ornette improvised. So dense were the sonic hues, he was able to play works originally written for a symphony orchestra, like parts of his "Skies of America."

As with Miles, Ornette deserves deeper discussion. Coleman began to discuss his "harmolodic" theory, which I think was greatly influenced by George Russell's Lydian Theory of Tonal Organization, around the time of the formation of Prime Time. Basically, Ornette's "harmolodic" theory is a method of permitting the jazz player to improvise vertically, that is to improvise his harmonic structure at the same time he is improvising horizontally—playing melodically—an approach that George Russell calls "supravertical." Both theories greatly expand the very concept of the tonic, providing freedom, but not freedom completely without laws ("Which is not really freedom at all," according to Russell), for the improvisor and composer. If nothing else, Ornette's "harmolodic" theory, a theory which I have never heard adequately explained, even by Ornette, at least answered those critics who claimed that Coleman's music was simply the work of an anarchic eccentric, with no intellectual structure to support it. A few one-time Coleman associates began to use the "harmolodic" rubric for their music, including drummer Ronald Shannon Jackson and guitarist James "Blood" Ulmer, who also played a very advanced and sophisticated version of fusion.

Ornette's and Miles's music worked because it wasn't really fusion, although it used elements of rock and funk. They were not trying to build a bridge between rock and jazz, they were simply playing the logical jazz style for its time. They refused to make concessions in order to pander to the huge rock audience—their music remained as personal as ever, a logically evolved progression in their innovative careers. Electronics also provided a solution to a basic problem jazz musicians had been trying to solve since the Twenties: how to use the massed sounds and colors afforded by the arrangements of a big band or large group while remaining truly improvisational. Ellington and Basie both took on this challenge in the Thirties and Forties, Ellington by integrating specific improvisors within his compositions, Basie by giving the soloists in his band great leeway, backing them only with the most basic sort of riffs. Later on Mingus, too, worked on this dilemma; his solution was closely patterned on Ellington, from a post-bop perspective. Coltrane attempted his own New Thing resolution of this difficulty in *Ascension*. The new electronic technology offered perhaps the best solution. With electronic instruments, a few musicians are able to create the large sound and varied tonal colors of a large band, while still able to improvise freely like a small group. The loud volume itself, as Frank Zappa once pointed out, gave a small group of musicians, even three or four, the aural heft and weight of a large orchestra.

So Miles and Ornette, once again leading the way, perfectly demonstrated how jazz could incorporate the new sonic textures made possible by electronic improvising, the use of rock/funk rhythms, often in combination with the new rhythmic challenge of polyrhythmic Afro/Cuban/Brazilian/music and many of the ideas explored by Coltrane and the New Thing musicians of the previous decade. This last part of the equation was critical; jazz had always evolved out of the innovations of the previous generation or jazz movement. That is what tradition is all about, and this new music of Ornette and Miles, despite the predictable carping of reactionary critics, those same critics who had plagued Coltrane in the Sixties, was very much part of the jazz tradition, music which spoke of and to its time.

Except for one thing—Ornette and Miles *were* the previous generation. The musicians playing this innovative music should have been their musical progeny, the new, young torchbearers who came up in the Sixties. That generation of musicians who should have been leading the way had somehow gotten lost, doing something the great jazz musicians, including Miles and Ornette, of the past never did, pandering to their audience. Despite the fact that their music was often quite complex and at times rather opaque, both Ornette and Miles drew large audiences fascinated by the chances these great innovators, and the young, eager musicians in their bands, continued to take. How did Miles and Ornette triumph over the oppressive social and cultural atmosphere of the Seventies? Quite simply: like Coltrane, both men were visionaries whose perspective extended far beyond the landscape of their own time, while at the same time, like all good art, reflecting that time.

Other than the work of these two geniuses, at least for the most part, the fusion that dominated the Seventies resulted in producing the least amount of important music of any decade, at least up until that time, in the history of jazz.

There was other jazz being produced in the Seventies, although most of it remained relatively obscure.

The most important of the new generation of young musicians to be influenced by Coltrane and the New Thing had their roots in Chicago. A co-op organization of musicians called the Association for the Advancement of Creative Musicians (AACM), formed in 1965, produced a number of important young players eager to explore and expand upon the concepts of the Sixties free jazz musicians. Among them were the reed men Roscoe Mitchell, Anthony Braxton, and Joseph Jarman; the trumpeter Leo Smith; the bassist Malachi Favors; and the drummer Steve McCall. All three of the reed men's musical approach was shaped to a large extent by listening to Ornette and Coltrane, particularly Trane's post-*Ascension* playing.

Braxton was probably the most famous and influential of these musicians, and his musical output in the Seventies was prodigious. He composed pieces, usually with titles consisting of obscure mathematical symbols, for performing forces ranging from solo alto saxophone to three orchestras. Braxton's brilliance was undeniable, but many found his work cerebral, cold, and forbidding. Perhaps responding to such complaints, he made a series of albums called *In the Tradition,* playing standards and tunes from the jazz repertoire, attempting, and often succeeding, in displaying the heart in his music. Still, he remained more a critic's favorite than a popular member of the jazz mainstream.

Of all the groups to emerge from the AACM scene, the most famous was the Art Ensemble of Chicago. This eclectic group, which included trumpeter Lester Bosie, Roscoe Mitchell, Malachi Favors, Joseph Jarman, and drummer Don Moye, was capable of playing everything from pseudo-Dixieland to hard bop to the free jazz that was at the heart of their music. The Art Ensemble enjoyed a greater success than most of these second-generation New Thing musicians. Another important post-Coltrane reedman/composer is the eclectic Henry Threadgill, whose interest in experimentation is very much "in the tradition." He is one of the few potential sources for genuine innovation on today's jazz scene.

Most of the new generation of free jazz players eventually moved to New York, where there was something of a thriving New Thing scene taking place in the same out-of-the-way places where the original movement had been born, such as loft concerts and coffeeshops in SoHo and the Lower East Side. Gary Giddins once pointed out that the avant-garde cannot expect, by the very nature of its musical endeavor, to be at the heart of the jazz mainstream or to find a large audience. This new generation didn't get one, though it did find at least some enthusiasm among those seeking greater musical intelligence and depth than that provided by fusion.

One more musician must be mentioned due to his popularity and, to some degree, his influence—pianist Keith Jarrett. More than any other musician, Jarrett stood out as a symbol of the "Me Generation," a man who played his ego as much as he played piano. Jarrett was basically an eclectic (although John Litweiler in his book on post-1960 jazz classifies him as a fusion player), not a new generation free jazz musician, although he played at times in a group with musicians associated with Ornette. Jarrett, a technically brilliant player, became most famous for his solo concerts, one or two of which became best-selling records. These concerts were completely improvised and more just a mishmash of several styles than real eclecticism. He would begin with some Bill Evans–style impressionism, switch to pseudo-Liszt romanticism, change to rollicking bucolic funk, segue to Cecil Taylor–type atonal thunder, and then switch again to pedal-point, Coltranesque Eastern modality, all in the confines of one improvised piece. He refused to play electric keyboards, although he had done so for the short period when he was with Miles Davis (who told me that Jarrett was the best pianist he had ever played with), making pretentious pronouncements like

"The electricity has to come directly from me, not the key-board." His remarks were so annoying to some on the jazz scene that they found themselves defending electric instruments. As remarkable as Jarrett's actual playing was his overly wrought body English. While playing even the simplest melodic idea, he would half stand on the keyboard, grimacing as if he were being electrocuted, moaning, groaning, and writhing as if he were giving birth to the piano rather than playing it. On some level, I'm certain he believed that he was following Ornette's and Coltrane's lead in unfettered expressionism, but watching him play after the second or third time was rather like seeing a magician perform once you know the secret of his tricks. Once one saw through Jarrett's act, it was virtually impossible to take him very seriously. Jarrett's pretentiousness was undoubtedly a direct product of Coltrane's quest in his adaptation of the idea of musician as shaman rather than entertainer, and that improvising at such length was as much a spiritual experience as an aesthetic one, both for player and listener. However, although Coltrane's style, as we have seen, evolved constantly throughout his career, he was never an eclectic. By committing himself to a particular conception during each step along that road of change, he demonstrated the tenaciousness necessary to be a true musical explorer, as well as a man who was, in Sartre's term *engagé,* deeply involved and committed to social—in that he believed that his music "uplifted people"—and spiritual involvement.

Jarrett's anti-electric crusade was largely a one-man crusade since, for the most part, and despite Jarrett's own great popularity, the jazz mainstream was dominated by electric fusion. Every pianist found himself ineluctably playing an electric piano, even such subtle stylists as Bill Evans. The best thing that could be said about the electric piano was that there was something democratic about it: virtually everybody who played it sounded the same. The years of work someone like Bill Evans put into developing his individual touch went down the tubes when he was forced to play electric. Now any mediocre pianist could sound pretty much, at least in terms of tone, like a great one. Listening to Sonny Rollins release album after album of useless jazz/funk, material to which he responded with the least inspired playing of his career, was a depressing experience. Yet what could be done? Fusion had, after all, re-established interest in jazz and was reaching the large young audience it needed to survive. It seemed once again that jazz had been backed into an alley, although this time the problem it had had with free jazz had been turned inside out: jazz now commanded a large audience but had sacrificed its artistic integrity. It was almost as if it were in some kind of Faustian pact with the devil.

Arriving like a knight on his charger, the great tenor saxophonist and major Coltrane influence Dexter Gordon returned to America after years of living in Europe and turned everything around. Playing with a so-called "acoustic" group—just the standard piano, bass, and drums—his big, warm tenor and straightahead swing sounded like heaven. After years of frustration for many jazz fans, the deep feeling and lyricism of Gordon's music, and the joy of once again hearing straightahead swinging, seemed to puncture the pretensions of the New Thing and the empty flash of fusion like the boy who discovered that the emperor simply had no clothes. Fusion and free jazz were not as nakedly worthless as the emperor's new clothes, but rather Gordon simply reminded many of us why we were drawn to jazz in the first place. Dexter himself had been listening and growing: one could clearly hear the influence of Sonny Rollins and Coltrane in his playing now, both of whom, of course, owed a big debt in turn to Gordon for *his* influence in the development of their own styles. Gordon was anything but an eclectic—he had a gloriously original voice. Although his music was warmly accessible, he never pandered to his audience. He made us feel as if we all had returned home together.

The success of Gordon's triumphant return resulted in a shift of the jazz mainstream toward what some called "neoclassicism"—in other words, a return to pre-Sixties straightahead jazz. It augured the return of other veteran jazz voices who had been silent during the "free" period and the fusion period which followed. Some, like Gordon, had become European emigrés, others had opted for the economic security of the studios, or teaching, either here or on the West Coast, still others had just disappeared from the scene. Soon, musicians such as tenor man Johnny Griffin (who had been known as the fastest sax in jazz pre-Coltrane), Art Farmer, Art Taylor, Benny Golson, Jackie McLean, and numerous others returned to performing in the American jazz scene at least part time. Even one of the earliest jazz emigrés, Kenny Clarke, made some brief Stateside appearances shortly before his death, playing with astonishing swing.

But this neoclassicism was mainly spurred on not by these jazz veterans, but rather by a number of critics and one very insistent, and talented, new voice. That new voice was trumpet prodigy Wynton Marsalis. Marsalis first made his mark playing with Art Blakey's Messengers, a route that had become something of a tradition in jazz for bringing young musicians into the focus of the jazz scene. Marsalis was obviously talented, although there was, at least at first, little original in his playing, a by then common blend of Clifford Brown and Miles Davis. His ace card was his ability to play classical music, and to play it quite well, which instantly earned him a place in the cultural landscape. His main dedication was to jazz, and to straightahead jazz, not fusion or free jazz. He considered fusion a gross commercialization of jazz, and he expressed scorn for those who played it, even his former idol Miles Davis.

Many of Marsalis's ideas about the nature of jazz he had gleaned from the writer and critic Stanley Crouch. This in itself was a first: usually it was the critics who learned from musicians the tenets, philosophy, and direction of the music, not the other way around. Crouch basically had little use for any aspect or achievement touched by fusion and not much more respect for the avant-garde of the Sixties. Like most critics, he was emotionally tied to the music he grew up with, the hard bop of the Fifties and early Sixties. Critics usually affect only their readers, and only in limited ways. Crouch wound up influencing not only Marsalis, but a new generation of musicians who emerged in the Eighties and took Marsalis as their model and mentor. Having the perspective of a critic usually means, and here definitely did mean, a backward perspective, a thorough understanding of the past but little comprehension of the forces, especially in jazz, that drive artists ceaselessly forward.

When Marsalis went on his own, he continued to play music that would have been considered conservative before he was even born. He played this music well, as did many of his acolytes, and has even become an increasingly moving player, something that he was not in the first several years of his career. He has recently begun to look even further back, incorporating elements of New Orleans jazz and writing music quite reminiscent of Duke Ellinigton. That passion, that feeling of visionary brilliance and almost scary feeling of walking the tightrope into an uncertain future—those things that make jazz so special, really, and on which John Coltrane staked his life, those things are missing in the music of Marsalis and his generation of jazzmen. It is no surprise that such an attitude would appear in the Age of Reagan and Bush; jazz has usually reflected its times, although it was often created as inherently music of rebellion *against* a reactionary and inhumane status quo. Because of the very nature of this music, such conservatism would not flourish in jazz. The oppressiveness of these times was even more all-consuming than we feared it would be, and for the first time jazz became a reactionary art form rather than a radical one.

With the advent of the Marsalis generation, the influence of Coltrane's great quest seemed to end, although Coltrane's music itself, at least his pre-*Ascension* music, continued as a major influence on these young musicians. In the Eighties, Sixties revisionism, in which the Sixties were attacked as if they were a single movement or social philosophy, permeated every aspect of our culture, partly as a way of justifying the Reagan/Bush era of selfishness and greed. By the end of the Eighties, with the financial success of Marsalis and a number of his colleagues, the image of the jazz musician had changed from the Coltrane/Coleman era's musical and spiritual seeker to that of smooth businessman.

Because of this situation, some have declared that "jazz is dead." Jazz has been pronounced dead so many times that its supposed demise has become almost as much a part of its tradition as blue notes and drum solos. Obviously, jazz is not dead. There seems to be some new young trumpeter or saxophonist arriving on the scene every other month. The fact that few of these new players has anything resembling a genuinely fresh idea or original conception is another matter. They *are* playing real, honest to goodness jazz, unless you feel that jazz without the forward momentum of innovation is too empty a vessel to be truly considered "in the tradition." Milt Jackson, John Lewis, Doc Cheatham, Sonny Rollins, Benny Carter, Max Roach, Ornette Coleman, Gerry Mulligan, Art Farmer, and numerous other genuinely great jazz musicians, are alive and playing.

The difference beween the current cries that "jazz is dead" and previous proclamations of its demise is that those earlier declarations were reactions to the latest important innovations and changes the music was going through. For every great change, there were reactionaries who were convinced that the latest innovations meant the death knell for jazz. Even back in the Twenties, there were those who felt that the innovations of Louis Armstrong, which made the solo improvisor rather than the ensemble the heart of jazz performance, surely meant the end of the music. If you doubt this, read the clarinetist/marijuana peddler Mezz Mezzrow's bizarre and fascinating memoirs, *Really the Blues*. Of course, similar cries were heard during virtually every major change in the music, including the advent of bebop, the free jazz movement, and fusion.

The difference this time was that the cries of "jazz is dead" were the result of the *lack* of innovation. It's true that one can't expect the likes of great geniuses like Armstrong or Parker or Coltrane to conveniently pop up when the music needs new energy. Those of us who have followed the music are a bit spoiled, there having been so many truly brilliant musicians springing forth from the jazz soil in such a comparatively short period of time. The current mood in jazz, despite the influx of young players, is a reverie for the past, not a Coltrane-like quest into the future. Most of what is called "innovative" these days is really eclecticism, musicians surveying the past and playing music based on innovations from various periods in jazz's history. If a young musician had arrived on the jazz scene in, say, 1964 playing licks from jazz of the Twenties or Thirties, he might have been a curiosity, but nothing more; there were too many exciting things happening for such revivalism. These days, a young musician who plays like Clifford Brown or the Jackie McLean of the Fifties is hailed as an important new voice. Is it any wonder that some say that this music is dead?

Not surprisingly, the cultural establishment has enthusiastically embraced this new generation of jazz musicians, now that the music is so safe and conservative. One example is the new Department of Jazz established at Lincoln Center, which has been presenting a series of concerts featuring music from various periods in jazz's past, usually designed as tributes to various musicians from jazz's past. These concerts are produced primarily by Marsalis and Crouch, and usually feature young musicians of the neoclassicist generation, often including members of the Marsalis group. No one ever thought of doing this thirty years ago, when so many of the people they are saluting now were still alive. Back then, the music was so vibrant with creative turmoil, and individualism was still the measure by which greatness in jazz was evaluated, that such a series would never have even been attempted, and of course it wasn't. When anyone did try to put together a regular series of concerts back then, it was always a presentation of new and often excitingly innovative music. Now jazz has been made safe for the museums that our large cultural facilities like Lincoln Center have become.

Although many of the Marsalis generation of jazz musicians have been heavily influenced by Coltrane, the pre-*Ascension* Coltrane, he is no longer the dominant influence that he had been— a number of other post-boppers are almost as important now. That is probably a healthy thing. The neoclassicists seem to have no understanding of Coltrane's creative spirit, or that of Miles Davis for that matter, whom they also emulate—that is, the pre–*Bitches Brew* Miles. Admittedly, there are other, more positive, reasons for this movement than just cultural conservatism. One example: Coltrane lessened the influence of European music on jazz considerably, substituting techniques and aesthetic values from non-Western music. This had social as well as musical relevance. To an extent, the neoclassicists have been acting as a corrective to this change, bringing back the balance between African, and other non-Western sources, and European twains that has always existed at the core of jazz. Perhaps that is quite necessary. They have not done this through evolutionary change but rather through a reactionary return to pre-Sixties styles, and the result is an often brittle and heartless music.

Partly because of Coltrane, there was a changed attitude toward the lifestyle of the jazz musician. Now it is no longer "hip" to be addicted to drugs or to be an alcoholic—certainly the examples of Miles and Coltrane made it obvious that sobriety was far more conducive to aspirations to greatness—although such behavior still exists in jazz, as it does in every other segment of society. Most of this generation live clean, dress fashionably, and are more knowledgeable about the entire history of jazz than most musicians of previous eras. Many of them have studied jazz in college, in courses that have been available only recently, which accounts for their knowledge of the music's past. The effects of academia can be heard throughout the music of this generation—in its precision, its basis in knowledge of the past, its arch-conservatism.

This new jazz is perfect for the age of the CD, relatively hip background music that is now safe for a neighborhood fern bar or just a pleasant game of Trivial Pursuit. Perhaps jazz has been overly mystified, maybe even by writers like myself. Yet the deeply felt passion of those who love this music, even if that passion is too often evoked in purple and mawkish prose, must indicate how meaningful jazz is to those who are dedicated to it. A music that has changed so many lives has to be far more profound than just a pleasant background for exchanging tips on the stock market.

The notes that John Coltrane played, the chords or scales that he used, the brand of reeds in his mouthpiece—none of these things, or at least *knowing* these things, has much to do with the power of his music. This new generation "knows" the music, but that is irrelevant if it hasn't *lived* the music. As Charlie Parker once said, "Music is your own experience, your thoughts, your wisdom. If you don't live it, it won't come out of the horn."

Just as no modern composer would think of composing Baroque music, so a jazz musician must reflect his own time. While some critics have said that maybe jazz is just another style of playing music (although few jazz musicians would say that), if one considers a jazz player as being as much of a composer as a performer, the reason for the emotional failure of the music of the neoclassicists, who are playing music that was both played *and* *lived* by musicians thirty or so years ago, should be obvious.

Trying to fit the round peg of jazz into the square hole of the European musical tradition has been probably the main misunderstanding that has resulted in such modern phenomena as neoclassicism and jazz repertory. Here is an excerpt from a recent review of a neoclassicist group: "It was young people creating nostalgia from a time they were too young to have experienced, much as classical musicians play repertoire hundreds of years old to honor it and to become grounded in its roots." The difference between these two musics, the fact that, unlike classical music, jazz is being created at the same time it is being performed, is a profound one. Jazz has to be understood on its own terms.

After reviewing and reliving John Coltrane's incredibly brave career and his burning musical curiosity, which was tied to a desire to know God and the very rhythms of the cosmos, it is especially hard not to be put off by such reactionary music and aesthetics. Wynton Marsalis is becoming a better player every time I hear him, and now there is beginning to be heard some real emotional resonance in his playing. Yet there is something missing, and it is missing in just about all of those neoclassicists that I have heard. Miles would call it "that thing," and it has much to do with the chances we must take in life in order for our souls to survive. I think of Marsalis's music, and those of his acolytes, as post-modern, more a comment on the history of jazz than the creation of someone passionately involved with the musical adventure of this century. It is music the way a jazz critic would create it, rather than that of the musical explorers who have been at the heart of jazz since its beginning. In the past those, like Marsalis, who announced that the only true jazz was that of decades past were usually branded with such unpleasant terms as "moldy figs."

* * *

All of the above is part of the Coltrane legacy, directly or indirectly. One can argue that much of what happened to jazz was a negative reaction to Coltrane's music: fusion was a reaction to the New Thing, an attempt to make jazz more accessible than it was even in the Fifties. The music of Wynton Marsalis and his generation is a reaction both to fusion and to the New Thing itself, an attempt to define jazz completely in terms of its past, like Reagan's "Morning in America," rather than make music relevant and topical to the present and continue to surge into a perhaps scary and dangerous future.

I am far from being alone in my feelings about the state of jazz now. I have heard many musicians, and a number of critics, express similar despair, despite the proclamation of Stanley Crouch that this is a new "Golden Age" of jazz. Even Keith Jarrett has spoken out. I say "even" because Jarrett is still one of the most popular jazz figures on the scene, someone who would seem to have no axe to grind. Yet in an article in *The New York Times* he wrote, "More recordings are being made than ever before . . . but there is less meaningful music. . . . Music seems to have slipped out of the hands of the true makers and into the hands of the producers and promoters. . . . Let's not allow self-appointed experts to tell us what jazz is when we can hear in their music that they have no voice." (This last bit is almost certainly a blast at Wynton Marsalis.) Jarrett sees hovering above this empty scene the legacies of Coltrane and Miles: "John Coltrane could not have led a television band. . . . Think of Miles (not Miles's image, his music) and then think of the rest of the music world—where is the music?"

That reference to the "television band" is an allusion to Wynton's saxophonist brother, Branford Marsalis, who is now leading "The Tonight Show" band, following in the hallowed footsteps of Doc Severinsen. In an article in *The New York Times Magazine,* Branford, despite his reputation among the neoclassicists as the leading saxophonist of his generation (his style reflecting the usual Coltrane-Shorter-Rollins influences of most neoclassical saxophonists), revealed that he intended to give up jazz sometime in the future and move on to a real career, like acting, or maybe hosting "The Tonight Show" himself if Jay Leno retires. Along with Jarrett, I find that the contrast between Branford Marsalis and the great musicians of a previous generation, who saw in jazz possibilities—aesthetic, cultural, spiritual—as high as an "open sky," to paraphrase Sonny Rollins, speaks loudly about the difference between this present generation of jazz musicians and that which preceded it. For Branford, playing jazz is just another job, the type of thing to get him into the limelight so he can move on to the more gaudy branches of show biz.

He then made a most revealing statement: "A few years ago I had one of the worst nights of my life. I heard a Miles Davis bootleg featuring John Coltrane, from Stockholm [probably *Miles Davis and John Coltrane in Stockholm,* on Dragon Records]. Trane was massive, intense. I wanted to quit. It wasn't like I could say, 'Well, if I start to do this or that I might get there.' Forget it. How do you explain that to people who say 'You're on "The Tonight Show," ' isn't that the ultimate achievement?' I think to myself, 'Obviously you've never heard Trane live in Stockholm.' " They've probably never heard Coltrane at all, if they consider leading "The Tonight Show" band some ultimate achievement.

Coltrane shares with his predecessor Charlie Parker a legacy that extends beyond the specifically musical. After his death, "Bird Lives" became the hip graffiti so ubiquitous around all hip, or would be hip, enclaves. Parker became a symbol of the hipster rebellion famously articulated by Norman Mailer in his essay "The White Negro." Bird was the ultimate bohemian hero, and was constantly portrayed, in poems, stories, novels, and even a Clint Eastwood film, as the ultimate martyr to his art and a genuine American rebel, the risk-taking sensualist who lived for the moment. Jack Kerouac attempted to write the way Parker played, and more than one hipster tried to emulate Bird in one way or another. Parker's drug addiction was partly responsible for the heroin epidemic that took so many lives and wrecked the careers and lives of so many musicians and scene-makers in the jazz world of the late Forties and Fifties. The positive aspects of the Parker legend—his musical bravery, his love of beauty, and his existential attitude toward life and art—continue to exert an influence on anyone touched by his life and music.

Coltrane's admonition to "live right," and the example he set with his own life, had a great effect on the new generation of jazz musicians. That is no small thing: to be a great artist, according to Coltrane, one must live an ethical and productive life. In addition, he remains a symbol of black pride; his use of Third World music—the *blackness* of his music—has empowered a generation of African Americans. Colleges and universities have named musical programs after him, and various inner city groups have conducted Coltrane festivals. One sign of the continuing influence of his legacy is all the tributes, ranging from a special section in *Down Beat* to concerts in various parts of the country commemorating the twenty-fifty anniversary of his death.

Coltrane's quest was primarily a spiritual one, and in this realm, too, his legacy creates a sometimes rather bizarre shadow. Alice Coltrane has bestowed on him the Hindu name Ohnadaruth. Her Vedantic ashram holds an annual festival honoring him as much for his spiritual status as for his musical accomplishments.

Far more bizarre is St. John's African Orthodox Church in San Francisco, the "St. John" being John William Coltrane, or St. John "Will-I-Am" Coltrane, as he is called by the church leaders. The church gives free hot meals to the hungry, free clothing to the needy, counseling to the troubled, and even free music classes, since the church believes that "the universal language of music [is] a healing force, bringing mind, body, and soul into harmony with God." They also have a weekly three-hour radio program, presenting the word and sound of their St. John. It's easy to snicker at a church with a jazz musician as its patron saint (can you imagine the Church of Saint Bix Beiderbecke or Saint Charlie Parker?) but I can't help feeling that Coltrane would have approved of this church's humane and compassionate services, although he was far too genuinely humble—and shy—to feel comfortable having a church named after him.

Coltrane's shadow continues to haunt young musicians, uplifting and providing encouragement to some, inspiring thoughts of alternate venues for employment in others. His music has influenced and transformed countless lives, and will continue to do so. Yet the question remains: was his quest ultimately successful? Did Coltrane accomplish that goal that he could feel and hear but never adequately describe? Or was his quest ultimately down a dark and dangerous alley with no light waiting at its end?

epilogue

To come to some final conclusions about Coltrane's great quest puts me in the position of a fourth blind man trying to figure out what that elephant really looked like. I have the dubious benefit of looking back over the conclusions of a vast field of blind men, some critics, some musicians, and, lastly, Coltrane's audience. Most arguments about Coltrane are concerned with the direction he would have taken if he had not died at such a young age. The positions taken reflect various perspectives on just who John Coltrane was and what he was trying to do: Coltrane's last period was an aberration; he intended to turn back to his music of the late Fifties and Sixties. No, he was heading even further outside, if such a thing could be imagined, playing pure abstracted sound. His music would have become more accessible, though much different from his earlier music. And according to an oft-repeated rumor, he intended to give up music altogether, to become an A & R man or record company executive.

For Coltrane, his musical growth was inextricably intertwined with his spiritual search; his quest was to find the "essence" of music and the mind of God, roads that he believed led to the same place.

Did he reach that destination before he died? If so, his final album would be a likely indicator. Yet *Expression* is a transitional

266

album, a new turning point rather than an ultimate revelation. The preceding album, *Interstellar Space,* sums up his work in the area of pure sound, which he had been exploring in the last couple of years of his life. *Expression,* by comparison, is almost low key (for late Coltrane), its introspective mood reminiscent, strangely enough, of one of Coltrane's earliest important recording sessions, *Mating Call,* the album he made with Tadd Dameron in 1956.

If *Expression* is a genuine clue to the direction Coltrane was heading—which is far from certain, given the fact that he was dying at the time and knew it—it seems clear that his music was on the verge of becoming less abrasively free and more mainstream and accessible. If so, that would follow a pattern in his career that can be traced all the way back to his "sheets of sound" period. Those "sheets of sound" were often as abstract as much of the "pure sound" period, and he had found it necessary to back off from extreme abstraction into something more accessible in order to move ahead. That is not to say that Coltrane would have returned to music of previous periods—say, his style when he was with Miles's band of the late Fifties, a period that he had been telling friends and associates was still a high point in his career. He had come too far by now; he had learned that making his music more accessible was not the same thing as retreat.

Expression might be read as an indication that Coltrane's notions about himself and his life were becoming a bit more earthy, less blissed-out; maybe he was returning to the less abstract feelings he usually expressed in the blues. Blues had always kept his feet on earth, both musically and personally, no matter how far his head floated into the clouds.

No matter in what direction Coltrane may have been heading, one thing is clear from the *Expression* album—this was one more step along a continuing quest, not the final statement of a dying man or of someone thinking of retiring from playing. "My goal is to live the truly religious life and express it in my music," he once said, and that is exactly how he lived. The implausible notion of his becoming a record company executive is probably an endearing one to cynics who find it easier to doubt the sincerity of Coltrane's quest than to accept the implication of his pursuit.

Did Coltrane die in frustration, feeling the completion of his quest still far out of reach? The best way to answer that is to read his own words: "There is never any end. There are always new sounds to imagine, new feelings to get at. And always, there is the need to keep purifying these feelings and sounds so that we can really see what we discovered in its pure state. So we can see more clearly what we are. In that way we can give to those who listen the essence, the best of what we are. But to do that at each stage, we have to keep cleaning the mirror."

Coltrane knew that there would never be any point where he would finally arrive at his destination, that the quest had no real end. The endless trek itself was the ultimate discovery, the only way of living what Coltrane termed the "religious life." This does not mean that he was a sax-playing Sisyphus who found meaning in the very meaningfulness of his endless task. Coltrane would have peak moments, as in the creation of *A Love Supreme* and *Meditations,* moments of transcendent connection with what Einstein called "the mind of God," but he never thought of these as final destinations in his quest. His constant striving is what makes his music so alive, so consistently filled with energy and momentum. The idea of living in this neverending quest gave his life meaning and his music such profound resonance that even, say, an Irish rock musician twenty years after his death can be deeply moved by the ecstatic compassion of Coltrane's music.

I began this book by stating that perhaps those of us who love jazz, and play, write about, or just listen to it, have been lacking somehow in communicating the reason this often difficult music means so much to us. I do not know if I have made that at all clear myself, so let me end by stating why the music of John Coltrane has meant so much to so many, and specifically to me. That is not the same thing as extolling his innovations or his influence, or any of the things that critics usually write about.

I know that for people of color all over the world Coltrane has become a symbol of black pride. More than any other jazz musician, he made clear the power of non-European music, both in terms of music itself as well as the place of music in the society. Coltrane's use of African, Indian, and Arabic musics made it clear that they were not "primitive" forms as opposed to European music's "sophistication." If he had done nothing else but that, his importance to black culture and black self-image would be of the highest sort.

Jazz is deeply American music in its equal emphasis on the individual voice and place of that voice in the larger group. In many ways, jazz reflects not the America that exists today in reality, but the America as it was imagined by those who invented the idea, men like Thomas Jefferson and Tom Paine. America was the place where the individual could redefine himself according to his own terms, not those of the state or Church. This is exactly what jazz musicians have done throughout the history of their music. The idea of improvisation means that every night a musician plays he can redefine himself, and has one more chance to discover the beauty within. It is perhaps not as ironic as it may outwardly seem that the people, African Americans, who have been the least free in our society have had the greatest understanding of what freedom is. Just as Jefferson said, there should be a revolution in this country every fifty years, the constant evolution of jazz reminds us of the power of change and growth. There is no musician who has been more committed to change and growth than John Coltrane.

Jazz in its synthesis of African and European musical elements is a cultural phenomenon that could only have taken place in the "melting pot" of America. Unfortunately, that melting pot has been too often an ideal rather than a reality in American life, but in jazz, at least, one can hear the musical fruit of that wonderful idea. Although European and African/non-Western musical and aesthetic concepts seem to contradict each other, jazz embraces the yin/yang at the center of this apparent contradiction. Either way, as both Coltrane and his idol Einstein would point out, these concepts are all relative, from the cosmic point of view, anyway. Jazz does give us hope as to the inherent possibilities if America were to become a true "melting pot." These are some of the reasons those of us who love this music feel so strongly about it. In it we hear nothing less than a musical realization of the true American dream.

I might have sounded somewhat severe in my judgment of the current generation of reactionary neoclassicist jazz musicians. I feel that the trumpeter Lester Bowie was correct when he said that innovation is as much a part of the jazz tradition as improvisation or the blues. The career of Coltrane, and the spirit of jazz itself since its beginnings, has always been attuned to the present, and is always restlessly, often perilously, plunging ahead into the future. That is another central reason why jazz, and Coltrane in particular, have had such a powerful influence on, and been so central to the lives of, those of us who have loved him and his music. For blacks it was the one creative outlet in which they could express their deepest feelings, and for the white musicians who entered the jazz life, it was a new way of thinking, feeling, and playing that made them feel awake and free, a way of breaking from what they perceived as a moribund European culture. It might have meant continually tottering forward on that existential tightrope, but it also made one always vitally aware of being alive. It is not easy music and it does not make life easy. It does make us braver, stronger, and, unlike so much of our mass culture, never accepting of a life of "quiet desperation."

I have greatly exaggerated perhaps, and the critic is right who said that all this "existentialist" stuff was pretentious claptrap and jazz, after all, was just "another style of playing music." I really don't think so.

Coltrane was punished by many critics for what they saw as the pretension of his ideas, that he dared search for God and life's meaning through jazz, a music that used to be played in bawdy houses. Yet thousands of people, even those who knew little about his life, have found the deepest feelings and meaning in his music. Coltrane believed that "life certainly has meaning," and he attempted to perceive that meaning and express its joy through the act of creation.

There is much I could write about the way Trane's music has affected my own life. I know that in the Sixties, following his career was a wonderful adventure for us listeners. Each of his records guided us deeper into that crowded, melodramatic decade, sometimes dark and dangerous, at other times ecstatic. Most of Coltrane's albums provided needed light; others added to the growing confusion, but we found truth there, too. His intentions were to bring us to that light, to uplift us, and that is why he was so profoundly committed to his musical quest.

There is one thing about John Coltrane that I know for absolute certain. When I have been at my lowest ebb, when I have searched for the direction forward, like all of us do at times, his music has given me the hope that I needed to go on. That is saying a lot. Whether we know it or not, we are all pursuing a quest right alongside John Coltrane.

selected discography

A while back, I mentioned to someone I had just met that I was writing a book about John Coltrane. He told me that he was interested in learning more about jazz, had heard a few records. Miles and Monk were okay, he said, but there was something about Coltrane that really intrigued him. He asked me which Coltrane album I suggested he buy first. This is the type of question us jazzbos are often asked by those just getting initiated into this mysterious music. I thought about it for a while, because how does one choose a "typical" Coltrane album? With the myriad changes in his style, it is virtually impossible to select one album that is truly indicative of his entire career.

One jazz writer, answering a similar question in his column, suggested *Blue Train,* which I consider a poor choice. Yes, *Blue Train* is a great record, but, recorded in 1957, it hardly gives a listener any idea of the kind of music for which Coltrane became most famous. Obviously, the choice would have to be pre-*Ascension*, unless I was in a nasty or prankish mood. Probably, *My Favorite Things* or *Plays the Blues* from the Atlantic years or *Crescent* or *A Love Supreme* are the best choices—all are certainly accessible and give a new listener some idea of Coltrane's mature sound.

But the best way, really, to understand Coltrane is to listen to him whole and consecutively, from his earliest solo with Dizzy Gillespie through the Miles years, the great quartet, and the free

272

jazz period of his final years right up to and including his final album, *Expression*. Because Coltrane recorded so prolifically, it is possible to follow the evolution of his musical thinking in great detail from 1955 on. This is the only way to appreciate every increment of change, each small advance and giant step, he took his music through. Of course, that kind of encyclopedic listening is far beyond the financial resources of most listeners. So here I present a selected discography that both reflects Coltrane's evolution and offers his greatest moments on record. For the most part, I include only officially recorded albums, not bootlegs, of which there are a great number, many of them fascinating. I exclude bootlegs not only for ethical reasons but because they are not readily available in most parts of the country. All the albums included are available on CD, and probably cassette too, although I used availability on CD as my rule.

1. Early Coltrane— or relatively early Coltrane, since there is only one available CD with any of his pre-Miles work. That CD is a Dizzy Gillespie collection, *Dee Gee Days* (Savoy). This contains only one track with Coltrane, "We Love to Boogie" (1951), which was apparently his earliest tenor solo on record. The rest of this album (originally a two-LP set) consists mainly of minor Gillespie tracks, including several vocal novelties (of which "We Love to Boogie" is one).

The first Miles Davis quintet album, *Miles* (Prestige/Fantasy), came out in 1955. That album, *Workin',* and *Steamin'* are recommended. The other quintet albums, *Cookin'* and *Relaxin',* are almost as good. Prestige/Fantasy offers a boxed CD set containing every note Miles ever recorded for Prestige in the Fifties, including all of these classic quintet sessions with Coltrane. Also recorded around this same time was Miles's first album for Columbia, which also was with this classic group, *Round About Midnight*. It is probably the best but that is a close call. It does contain Coltrane's first truly great solo, on Thelonious Monk's "Round Midnight."

Prestige/Fantasy has also released a 16-CD set containing every cut that Coltrane recorded for Prestige, both as a sideman and leader (except for the Miles quintet sides). All of Coltrane's important work on Prestige is also available on separate CDs. Some of the sessions where Coltrane was a sideman are loose and casual jams where long strings of solos by often far less involving musicians precede a Coltrane solo. These sessions, for the most part, are for aficionados and Fifties jazz nostalgists only.

The albums under Coltrane's leadership from this period that I recommend are:

Coltrane, his first album as leader. He plays superbly, especially for this period (1957, but pre-Monk), and the album contains some intriguing compositions.

Traneing In, recorded in August 1957 while he was playing with Monk at the Five Spot, clearly presents the gains he had been making with the pianist.

Soultrane, recorded in January 1958, when Coltrane had just left Monk and rejoined Miles Davis, is not only fascinating for Coltrane's increasing involvement in his "sheets of sound" but also, in comparison to *Traneing In,* definitive evidence that he was becoming one of the most powerful musicians in jazz.

Black Pearls is Coltrane headlong into the "sheets of sound," playing almost pure harmony, and some of the oddest, and most fascinating, music of his career.

Settin' the Pace has a highly charged version of Jackie McLean's angular composition "Little Melonae" that contains a Coltrane solo that looks toward some of his New Thing–influenced work of the mid-Sixties.

Also recorded during the Prestige period is *Blue Train,* recorded in September 1957 while he was still with Monk. Coltrane cited it in the early Sixties as his best record with other horns. His solo on the title cut is one of the great blues solos of the Fifties and should not be missed.

Three albums on which Coltrane is a sideman are also recommended. The first, from 1956, is the Tadd Dameron session *Mating Call* (Prestige; also included on the complete Coltrane/Prestige boxed set), in which Coltrane exhibits the lyricism for which he would later become famous. The other albums are the only artifacts of Coltrane's momentous five months playing with Thelonious Monk at the Five Spot. For a long time, the only extant recordings of this important group were the three cuts on *Thelonious Monk/John Coltrane* (Jazzland/Riverside—now issued by Fantasy). At the time when he was playing with Monk, Coltrane was under contract to Prestige, while Monk was recording for Riverside, and for whatever reasons, it was impossible to arrange recording a full album of the group. But Riverside's owner, Orrin Keepnews, recognizing the importance of this quartet, arranged for the group to record in the studio the three selections heard on this album (he is not sure exactly when they were recorded—it is possible that they were made even after the group broke up), and they are among the great treasures of jazz.

However, recently Blue Note has released tapes privately made by Coltrane's wife Naima on the album *Thelonious Monk Quartet Live at the Five Spot*. Although the sound quality is extremely poor, it gives us a fascinating glimpse of Coltrane at work during perhaps his most momentous period of transition—a time when he was metamorphosizing from a good bop player to one of the greatest saxophonists in jazz history.

2. Middle Coltrane. At the end of 1957 Coltrane rejoined Miles Davis's group, with which he recorded three classic albums. Two of them, *Milestones* (1958) and especially *Kind of Blue* (1959), both on Columbia/Sony, are landmarks in twentieth-century music making. Miles's modal concepts on these albums would dominate Coltrane's own perspective for the next few years. These albums announced Coltrane's mature style.

The third is a live recording of the Miles group, without Cannonball Adderley, in 1960: *Miles Davis and John Coltrane in Stockholm* (Dragon), the only bootleg album on my list. Recorded on the last major tour Coltrane would make as a member of Miles's group, it demonstrates why he felt he had to move on—his playing had become simply too innovative and individualistic for him to be playing in somebody else's band. This two-CD set also has some brilliant playing by Miles, who is at his own peak, as well as Wynton Kelly's wonderfully funky piano.

Coltrane signed with Atlantic Records in 1959, and the first record he recorded under his sole leadership was a masterpiece, *Giant Steps,* an important transitional album between his harmonically centered "sheets of sound" period and his modal explorations of the Sixties. Of the other Atlantics, *My Favorite Things* is essential for being one of the first albums recorded with the great Coltrane quartet, as well as the title tune, which still stands as one of the most lyrical moments in jazz. *Coltrane Plays the Blues* should not be missed for the varied moods Coltrane could create within this traditional form, and especially the medium slow "Blues to Elvin," as roots-basic and riveting a blues performance as ever was recorded by a modern jazz musician. I also recommend from the Atlantic period *The Avant-Garde,* in which Coltrane attempts playing his style in Ornette Coleman's *mise en scene.* If not entirely successful, it is always interesting, particularly in regard to Coltrane's future direction.

After Atlantic, Coltrane moved to the ABC Records affiliate Impulse, where he remained and for which he recorded exclusively until his death. The reissuing of the Impulse catalog, including the crucial Coltrane works, has had a rocky road. First MCA, which owned the ABC catalog, started issuing them on CD but, as with many other important digital reissue programs, did a horrendous job—bad sound, no additional material from the vaults, poor remastering. Fortunately, David Grusin's GRP Records (yes, ironically enough, Dave Grusin of jazz Muzak fame) took over the catalog and has done outstanding work. It is unfortunate that they couldn't have overseen the Impulse reissuing program from the start.

Among the early Impulses I recommend the two albums containing material recorded at the Village Vanguard in 1961, *Live at the Village Vanguard* and *Impressions,* with Eric Dolphy on some selections. Also important is *Coltrane,* often called "the Blue Album" because of the cover photograph or "Out of this World" because of the longest and most powerful cut on the album. Right after the furiously intense "Out of this World" comes Coltrane's version of Mal Waldron's luscious ballad "Soul Eyes," one of the most exquisite moments of Trane's Impulse period.

I also recommend the *Ballads* album (1962) just as a demonstration of how moving a player Coltrane could be even when playing as minimally as he does here. And I cannot understand how anyone with even the smallest interest in jazz could ignore the *Duke Ellington and John Coltrane* album. Even if it does not quite live up to expectations, it is still a fascinating artifact.

Coltrane Live at Birdland is dominated by Trane's soprano work, including "Afro-Blue," one of those soaring $\frac{6}{8}$ items in the "My Favorite Things" tradition. It is the two tenor tracks, however, that stand out. The hauntingly moving "Alabama" is on this album, and Coltrane plays a coda to a fairly straight reading of the ballad "I Want to Talk About You" (originally from the Prestige *Soultrane* album) that will make your hair stand on end.

Finally, from 1964 are *Crescent* and *A Love Supreme*, Coltrane's last albums before committing himself to the New Thing. I don't know what more to say about these two magnificent works of art, except that they are on that list of things that make life worth living.

3. Late Coltrane. First of all, don't go near the albums from this period until you have digested Coltrane's work through *A Love Supreme*. It will probably also help if you have done some serious listening to Ornette Coleman, say, *Change of Century* (Atlantic), and late Eric Dolphy—I recommend *Out to Lunch* (Blue Note). As for Coltrane, best start with *The John Coltrane Quartet Plays,* which resembles earlier Coltrane work except it ventures further outside. "Chim Chim Cheree" and Nat "King" Cole's old chestnut (although I doubt if he would recognize it) "Nature Boy" are particularly fascinating when compared with Trane's earlier work. Also important as a transitional album is the aptly titled *Transition.* As of this writing, it is out of print, but I am certain that this fine album will soon be reissued on CD. Now we get to *Ascension.* If you are curious about this important New Thing milestone, go to it, but you are forgiven if you give up on it after the first five or six minutes. More important, I feel, is *Meditations,* in which Coltrane takes ideas garnered from Albert Ayler and bandmate Pharoah Sanders and produces a powerful and unforgettable work of art. Also recommended from the late era is *Coltrane Live in Japan,* with his last group, including his second wife, Alice, on piano. A superb package put together by Michael Cuscuna for GRP, it contains some surprisingly lyrical Coltrane, and even more surprisingly, lyrical Pharoah Sanders.

Lastly, there is *Interstellar Space,* Coltrane's fascinating duets with Rashied Ali and the genuinely freest work of his career. And his final album, *Expression,* is recommended for the implications of Coltrane's possible musical direction right before he died.

I have skipped some fine records in the above list, but I believe that these are the essential items in Coltrane's musical legacy. It is also true, however, that on virtually every record John Coltrane ever made, even some of those loose jam sessions he played on for Prestige, there are always at least a few moments of pure brilliance.

Other titles of interest

IN THE MOMENT
Jazz in the 1980s
Francis Davis
272 pp.
80708-4 $13.95

FACES IN THE CROWD
Musicians, Writers, Actors &
Filmmakers
Gary Giddins
288 pp.
80705-X $13.95

BIRD: The Legend
of Charlie Parker
Edited by Robert Reisner
256 pp., 50 photos
80069-1 $13.95

BIRD LIVES!
The High Life and Hard Times
of Charlie (Yardbird) Parker
Ross Russell
431 pp., 32 photos
80679-7 $15.95

BLACK BEAUTY, WHITE HEAT
A Pictorial History of
Classic Jazz, 1920–1950
Frank Driggs and Harris Lewine
Foreword by John Hammond
360 pp., 1,516 illus.
80672-X $29.95

BLACK TALK
Ben Sidran
New foreword by Archie Shepp
228 pp., 16 photos
80184-1 $10.95

CELEBRATING THE DUKE
and Louis, Bessie, Billie,
Bird, Carmen, Miles, Dizzy
& Other Heroes
Ralph J. Gleason
Foreword by Studs Terkel
New introduction by Ira Gitler
302 pp., 9 photos
80645-2 $13.95

CHASIN' THE TRANE
The Music and Mystique
of John Coltrane
J. C. Thomas
256 pp., 16 pp. of photos
80043-8 $12.95

DEXTER GORDON
A Musical Biography
Stan Britt
192 pp., 32 photos
80361-5 $13.95

FREE JAZZ
Ekkehard Jost
214 pp., 70 musical examples
80556-1 $13.95

THE FREEDOM PRINCIPLE
Jazz After 1958
John Litweiler
324 pp., 11 photos
80377-1 $13.95

IMPROVISATION
Its Nature and Practice in Music
Derek Bailey
172 pp., 12 photos
80528-6 $13.95

JAZZ PEOPLE
Photographs by Ole Brask
Text by Dan Morgenstern
Foreword by Dizzy Gillespie
Introduction by James Jones
300 pp., 180 photos
80527-8 $24.50

JAZZ SPOKEN HERE
Conversations with 22 Musicians
Wayne Enstice and Paul Rubin
330 pp., 22 photos
80545-6 $14.95

JOHN COLTRANE
Bill Cole
278 pp., 25 photos
80530-8 $14.95

JAZZ
The 1980s Resurgence
Stuart Nicholson
352 pp., 88 photos
80612-6 $14.95

MILES DAVIS
The Early Years
Bill Cole
256 pp.
80554-5 $13.95

MINGUS
A Critical Biography
Brian Priestley
320 pp., 25 photos
80217-1 $13.95

NOTES AND TONES
Musician-to-Musician Interviews
Expanded Edition
Arthur Taylor
318 pp., 20 photos
80526-X $13.95

ORNETTE COLEMAN
A Harmolodic Life
John Litweiler
266 pp., 9 photos
80580-4 $14.95

'ROUND ABOUT MIDNIGHT
A Portrait of Miles Davis
Updated Edition
Eric Nisenson
336 pp., 27 photos
80684-3 $14.95

STRAIGHT LIFE
The Story of Art Pepper
Updated Edition
Art and Laurie Pepper
Introduction by Gary Giddins
616 pp., 48 photos
80558-8 $17.95

TALKING JAZZ
An Oral History
Expanded Edition
Ben Sidran
535 pp., 20 photos
80613-4 $16.95

DANCE OF THE INFIDELS
A Portrait of Bud Powell
Francis Paudras
Foreword by Bill Evans
432 pp., 191 photos
80816-1 $18.95

SATCHMO
Gary Giddins
240 pp., 255 illus.
80813-7 $19.95

BLACK MUSIC
LeRoi Jones (Amiri Imamu Baraka)
288 pp., 4 photos
80814-5 $14.95

A CENTURY OF JAZZ
From Blues to Bop, Swing to
Hip-Hop: A Hundred Years
of Music, Musicians,
Singers and Styles
Roy Carr
256 pp., $9^5/_8 \times 11^1/_2$
350 illus., 200 in color
80778-5 $28.95

ERIC DOLPHY
A Musical Biography and
Discography
Revised Edition
Vladimir Simosko and
Barry Tepperman
156 pp., 17 photos
80524-3 $11.95

FORCES IN MOTION
The Music and Thoughts
of Anthony Braxton
Graham Lock
412 pp., 16 photos, numerous illus.
80342-9 $15.95

FROM SATCHMO TO MILES
Leonard Feather
258 pp., 13 photos
80302-X $12.95

KEITH JARRETT
The Man and His Music
Ian Carr
264 pp., 20 illus.
80478-6 $14.95

Available at your bookstore

OR ORDER DIRECTLY FROM

DA CAPO PRESS, INC.

1-800-321-0050